MIDDLE ENGLISH LITERATURE

MIDDLE ENGLISH LITERATURE

A Critical Study of
the Romances, the Religious Lyrics,
Piers Plowman

by

GEORGE KANE

BARNES & NOBLE, Inc.
New York
METHUEN & CO. Ltd
London

First published, 1951

This edition reprinted, 1970
by Barnes & Noble, Inc.
and Methuen & Co. Ltd.

Barnes & Noble ISBN 389 04051 7

Methuen ISBN 416 07700 5

Printed in the United States of America

I. M.
G. G. S.

PREFACE

THIS book is an attempt to apply methods of literary evaluation to certain Middle English works that have long suffered neglect as literature because the scholarly world has been largely preoccupied with commentary upon their historical, social, philological and religious content. The results of such preoccupation have been invaluable either as a preparation for literary studies or in their own right as scientific or historical findings. They have, however, by their direction of emphasis encouraged the opinion that, with a few notable exceptions, Middle English literature is without particular artistic value or interest, and of no great significance to the understanding of more recent writings. This opinion is especially strong in the case of the three main topics of this book—the Metrical Romances, the Religious Lyrics and *Piers Plowman*.

An evaluation of the kind attempted here is inevitably too subjective to meet with complete acceptance, but this should not invalidate it. Literary criticism is a kind of wisdom after the event, and should be a continuous process. If the expression of my opinion provokes anyone to disagree with me there is the possibility that he will benefit by my mistakes to form a better judgement ; thus the cause of literature as well as my immediate purpose will be served. At any rate he and I will for the moment have considered the subjects under discussion as something more than quarries for the production of historical topicalities, sources and analogues, foreign influences, ancient mythological figures in disguise, folk-lore motives, history of doctrine, social customs or phonological forms. We shall have acknowledged that these works, however naïve and unpolished they may seem by comparison with more recent literature, preserve experiences of life similar to those recorded, for instance, in *The Winter's Tale* and *Christabel* and *The Windhover* and *The Journey of the Magi* and *The Divine Comedy*, and that their authors were men of flesh and blood, whose names may indeed have been lost, but whose emotions and aspirations were as real and as important in every sense as our own.

In the discussion of the three main topics of this book it has proved both convenient and profitable to employ distinct methods of classification and analysis. In the case of the romances I have studied most of the surviving material with the intention of discovering how far qualities of permanent interest and appeal occur there, and have classified this material according to my results. I have been able by this means not only to confirm that there are genuinely good specimens but also to show that the whole class of romances, in so far as it has a common nature, is much closer to modern experience than is generally allowed, and that some elements in the romances now regarded as separating them from us are less symptomatic of differences between the Middle Ages and the present time than indicative of inferior individual work-manship and lack of taste or literary experience. In such a treatment it was essential to refer to at least the majority of the ' bad ' specimens, those of which the artistic inferiority was readily apparent from comparison with the others of their own *genre*. Such a survey of indifferent material is inevitably tedious, but it has the advantage not only of setting the quality of the better specimens in its proper relation but also of challenging the opinions published from time to time in the past by editors of these bad romances who, absorbed in their subjects and very naturally confusing their own interest in them with a good literary effect, expressed themselves more favourably about their texts than these actually warranted.

The case with the religious lyrics is quite different. My intention there was to establish a classification which might illustrate the relationship between poetry and the religious subject, and might also, more particularly, help to fix the point at which the distinction occurs between an imaginatively unformed statement made in verse concerning religion, and a divine poem produced by the exercise of artistic selection and arrangement. The extremes were evident at the outset : those lyrics in which verse is simply used for a religious communication, with no more effect on the imaginative apprehension of the subject than if the medium is the customary prose of homily, and those which are the result of occasions

when an emotional apprehension of the subject, combining
with an operation of the creative faculty, has produced divine
poetry. The classification adopted reveals not only that there
are many intermediary stages between these two extremes, but
also that there is a general, approximate correspondence
between the type of religious activity reflected in a lyric, and
the poetic success of that lyric, and that exceptions to this
approximation are comparatively rare. It distinguishes two
simple intentions that directed the efforts of the authors, one
to communicate the sense in the manner most effective from
a purely religious point of view, the other, moved either by a
feeling of craftsmanship or by inspiration, to perform an act
of creative expression in terms of a religious subject ; and it
establishes that the absence, subordination or equality of the
second intention is the principal factor in determining the
artistic nature of a religious lyric. At the same time my
classification seems to demonstrate a general effect of the
religious subject upon the nature of the lyrics in which it is
expressed, and to show that there was no necessary relation
between the religious ' theme ' of a lyric, or (with the exception
of the carols) between the form of a lyric and its poetic quality.
Indeed the general problems of the Middle English religious
lyrics appear very similar to those posed by the religious
poetry of other periods, notably that of the seventeenth
century, and the study of the mediæval occurrence of these
problems in circumstances of relative literary simplicity could
be profitable to the student whose main concern is more recent
literature.

The fundamental question of the relationship between a
religious motion and the imaginative or creative excitement
applies also to *Piers Plowman*, where, however, the circumstances in which it is to be studied necessitate the adoption of
another method. Here the problem is confined, as I believe,
to the work of a single man, in the form of three versions of the
same poem, but on the other hand the bulk of these three
versions is probably greater than that of the whole body of
religious lyrics surviving from the English Middle Ages. In
these circumstances I have subjected the three versions of
Piers Plowman to an analysis designed to isolate the principal
actively formative elements in the author's personality in
I*

order, by a synthesis of these, to account for and illustrate the nature of the poem. The results produced in regard to the perennially troublesome questions of the plan and symbolism of *Piers Plowman* seem to me valuable enough to certify the legitimacy of the method, if that be needed.

It would not be possible to name here all those scholars to whom I have incurred obligations in the course of my reading. Directly I owe debts of gratitude which I publish with pleasure : to Miss Beatrice White for reading the book in typescript and suggesting numerous corrections ; to Professor A. G. Mitchell for the benefit of his highly qualified opinion on the *Piers Plowman* section ; to Professor F. Norman for his interest and suggestions ; to Dr. Harold Jenkins for most generously devoting a considerable time to minutely careful criticism of the whole book ; to Mr. Arthur Brown for his friendly help with proof-reading and checking ; and to Professor A. H. Smith for his unfailing encouragement, inexhaustible patience, and for many other kindnesses.

December 1949
UNIVERSITY COLLEGE
LONDON

G. KANE

PREFACE TO THE 1970 REPRINT

WHEN I wrote this book in 1948 most of those persons likely to read it nowadays had not yet learned to read; like them I have changed in the mean while. I could not now revise, let alone rewrite it; what has persuaded me to consent to its reproduction is the consideration that it has become a period piece, such as librarians might wish to include in their documentation of the history of medieval studies.

CONTENTS

PART   PAGE

I. THE MIDDLE ENGLISH METRICAL ROMANCES — 1

II. THE MIDDLE ENGLISH RELIGIOUS LYRICS — 104

III. 'THE VISION OF PIERS PLOWMAN' — 182

INDEX — 249

NOTE

In Part II the following abbreviations are commonly used :

C.B. *XIII*	.	Carleton Brown, *English Lyrics of the Thirteenth Century* (Oxford 1932)
C.B. *XIV*	.	Carleton Brown, *Religious Lyrics of the Fourteenth Century* (Oxford 1924)
C.B. *XV* .	.	Carleton Brown, *Religious Lyrics of the Fifteenth Century* (Oxford 1939)
EEL	. .	E. K. Chambers and F. Sidgwick, *Early English Lyrics* (London 1937)
Greene	. .	R. L. Greene, *The Early English Carols* (Oxford 1935)

PART I

THE MIDDLE ENGLISH METRICAL ROMANCES

WHILE it is self-evident that the study of the Middle English verse romances must begin with relating them to the historical and social circumstances in which they originated, it is less obvious but equally true that preoccupation with their backgrounds interferes with an evaluation of the romances themselves ; for if we make sufficient allowances of a historical and social kind we explain away and excuse every one of their shortcomings and find them all equally interesting as illustrations of the past while we remain little the wiser about their relative literary value. As my purpose in this study is to renew literary interest in them I propose to consider them, in the second instance, not so much out of their historical context as without primary reference to it. By this means I hope to show that there are in many of the romances permanent qualities of the kind to be found in good narrative art of any age which can reduce to their proper relative unimportance those external conventions of the romance kind by which the surviving specimens can most readily be classed together and separated from other *genres*. I believe that this consideration will result in a more just appreciation of their significance in the history of English literature than can be reached by considering them principally as documents from which to define the word ' mediæval ', a method inclined to form in the critic the habit of excusing rather than evaluating.

It seems to me most important to distinguish the external qualities by which the romances are classified from possible essential characteristics. In so far as the surviving romances can be said to have a common definable nature,[1] this seems

[1] The best discussion of this point was published twenty years ago by Dorothy Everett : ' A Characterization of the English Medieval Romances ', *Essays and Studies by Members of the English Association* xv (1929), 98 ff. I do not think that she has closed the subject ; that the discussion has not been resumed indicates a lack of interest in

to consist first, in a very general purpose of entertainment by narrative, second, in this narrative being concerned with some one of a very wide range of subjects,[1] and third, in the frequent occurrence of certain characteristics of treatment, some of which are fundamental, and others more properly classified as *accidents* rather than *essentials* of the *genre*. The essential characteristics are that the story should be treated in terms of chivalry, and that it should not be naturalistic, but that instead its setting, characters and action should be heightened to enable the escape from the limitations of actuality which the romances were designed to afford.[2] I detect four principal accidents of treatment. First, whatever the subject of a romance, this was translated into a contemporary setting by a process almost inevitable in the Middle Ages and, therefore, not so much characteristic of the romances as of the times in which they were written. Second, the boundaries of probability in the romances extend much more widely than they would in modern fiction ; the marvellous in all its forms is common fare in them. This again is a feature not of the romances but of their age. What Jeanroy described as a characteristic of mediæval taste is more deep-seated than he allowed ; it is not merely the literary appetite of a public *avide de sensations rares et fortes* [3] but a capability of belief unhampered by modern scientific notions of physical probability, and a concept of a world in which supernatural agencies could readily, and for the smallest reasons, interfere in the course of

what she properly fixed on as a most important point rather than that there is nothing more to be said. N. E. Griffin, in ' The Definition of Romance ', *Publications of the Modern Language Association of America*, xxxviii (1923), 50–70, is concerned with a distinction between ' epic ' and ' romance ' which hardly bears upon the Middle English specimens.

[1] These comprise not only the Matters of France, Britain and Rome the Great but also the additional material discussed by Laura Hibbard in *Mediæval Romance in England* (New York 1924), especially iii–v. The point made here by Miss Hibbard is not sufficiently emphasized in A. C. Baugh's *A Literary History of England* (New York 1948), 174–5 and ff.

[2] This heightening should actually render them unsatisfactory as evidence of mediæval *mores*.

[3] A. Jeanroy, *Les Origines de la Poésie Lyrique en France au Moyen Age* (Paris 1904), 11. ' Au moyen âge il y a . . . un abîme entre le monde réel et celui de la poésie ', etc.

Nature.[1] The third accidental characteristic, a specifically literary form of the second, occurs when, in the hands of inferior artists, the essential quality of heightening is replaced by exaggeration beyond the point of artistic usefulness. Finally, most romances have a happy ending, but a number of exceptions, notably the *Morte Arthurs* and *The Knight of Courtesy*, show that this feature is not essential to the kind.

In terms of this distinction between essential and accidental characteristics the question arises whether, having once accounted for the accidental qualities of the romances by historical and social means, and having made ' excuses ', less for those qualities than for the forms they took in the hands of inferior users, we should not regard them as a common factor which, once recognized, may be cancelled out, and whether such a simplification would not facilitate the examination of the romances in terms of their common, essential purpose of entertainment. May we accept the historical approach as indeed indispensable to a full understanding of the romances, but having made it, may we take it for granted and get on with the task of evaluation ?

Such a step is proper if it is safe to assume first, that the discriminating contemporary reader or hearer of the romances would have had anything like the same preferences, or would have made anything like the same criticisms as we do ; second, that the importance of the accidental characteristics of the romances to their contemporary success has been overstated ; and third, that the public of the romances was not so simple in its tastes as is generally assumed. The first assumption is supported by our knowledge that certain artistic qualities make a permanent appeal to the mind and the imagination, and that certain inartistic features could give offence to persons with highly developed taste in the days of the romances.[2] The second and the third find support in the romances themselves. There the existence of two extremes of taste is at once

---

[1] The importance of the growth of scientific knowledge in the decay of the romance *genre* was recognized as long ago as 1810 by Weber in his *Metrical Romances of the Thirteenth, Fourteenth and Fifteenth Centuries*, I (Edinburgh 1810), xiii.

[2] See below, 54–6.

evident : the one with which it was practically impossible to
fail as long as a story contained enough dragons, giants,
marvels, quests, tournaments, reversals, discoveries and such
like ; the other discriminating and exacting, with a highly
developed faculty for distinguishing the bad and appreciating
the good. To the first extreme of taste the accidental qualities,
especially that of exaggeration, might be important ; the
opinion of the other is implied in *Sir Thopas*. But in addition
to the two extremes there must in the nature of things have
been a great middle group the existence of which can be
confirmed by *a posteriori* argument from the quality of many
of the romances. It seems altogether probable that the volume
of relatively educated taste, and the correspondingly discriminating public, were larger than is generally recognized.
Every romance in which there is any evidence of sensitivity
of treatment, of an awareness of significant form, of a desire
to make the marvellous credible, or of any striving after
ideas of structure and expression, rules out the notion
that it was composed by someone simple in the literary
sense.

A hearer or reader for his part would have preferred the
better romances by so much as he had intelligence and literary
experience. The good romances contained the same elements
as the bad ; they conformed generally to the same social and
literary conventions, were founded on the same principles of
chivalry, indulged in the same lavish description and the same
heightening of effects, cultivated the same modernity and
were made fantastic by the same marvels. At the same time
they possessed other qualities by which, we may assume, the
common material would have been enhanced. They were
better presented, better constructed, with due emphasis
applied to those features and qualities which would increase
the effect of the traditional subjects, or else they had special
merits likely to capture and hold the imagination ; above all
they appealed to more universal impulses of the mind and
spirit. To me it seems probable for these reasons that, while
there would certainly be a section of the public to whom the
extremes of exaggeration and improbability, however baldly
presented, would appeal for their sensational quality as
gratifying ' the multitude in its wandering and irregular

thoughts ', nevertheless those romances distinguished by signs of genuine creative activity reflect and correspond to a variety of combinations of understanding and literary education all distinctly above the lowest level of taste in author and public. The better romances would be beyond the understanding of this lowest level ; a member of the more intelligent public might not, unless he had exceptional literary experience, actually find fault with the worst specimens, but he would certainly prefer something better, and be conscious of differences in quality even though he might not use our terms to identify and describe them.

It seems necessary, then, even after having allowed for the greater readiness with which the public of the thirteenth to fifteenth centuries would surrender to the kind of fictional experience afforded by the romances, and for a great many stylistic features connected with the manner of publication and transmission,[1] to infer that the same difference between contemporary popularity and literary quality which exists, for instance, at the present day, applied in the case of the romances. What was eagerly received then was no more necessarily good at the moment of its popularity than it is now that the historical circumstances have changed ; the good qualities of the romances were and are the permanent ones which, if we take the trouble to find them out, require to be justified by no historical allowance.

For these reasons it seems to me a profitable method, and one not too radical, to make an evaluation in which the *accidents* by which the romances are commonly identified play only a secondary part, and in which one sets less store than usual by the explanation that a particular feature ' appealed to contemporary taste ', and the implication that this appeal conferred upon a romance excellences which it has since lost. There was evidently no greater uniformity of taste at the time of composition of the romances in England than there is now, and the discrimination between good and bad art was as

---

[1] These are fully discussed in Dr. H. J. Chaytor's *From Script to Print* (Cambridge 1945), a book which makes a great contribution to the understanding of mediæval literature. See especially 3, 48 ff., 53, 55, 59, 82, 117 ff., 142–8. See also Ruth Crosby, ' Oral Delivery in the Middle Ages ', *Speculum* xi (1936), 88 ff.

sharp, if not as widely or consciously made, as it is today. The historical point of view must indeed be preserved in such an evaluation, but it must not be allowed to interfere with the process by obscuring the importance of permanent qualities in the works concerned.

In such an evaluation, if we regard the romances as a type of narrative fiction defined by its essential qualities, the ' excellences proper to the kind ' seem to be first those which one might expect of any μῦθος, namely an arrangement of contents logically according with the author's own limits of his subject and his point of view ; then, if not verisimilitude, at least the power of inducing the ' willing suspension of disbelief ' [1] ; and in addition such other qualities of conception of subject, selection, arrangement and presentation of material as were not only ' persuasive ' in the sense of making a story credible, but possibly also moving.   And if, as I believe, the assumption is a correct one that the *accidents* of treatment, especially that which takes the form of exaggeration, did not necessarily guarantee success to the romances in their own time, then it seems reasonable to look in this *genre* for other excellences not historically limited but of a kind likely to appeal to the human imagination in any age.

In such a search there is little correspondence to be found between the various classifications of the romances according to their chronology, form or content, and their literary quality.   They seem to reflect almost every stage of development and every shade of literary cultivation or crudity discernible in the French originals upon which their authors and adaptors or translators drew.   The English borrowings were made over several centuries, after the great models had been created by the French poets, and while the nature of the romances in France was being repeatedly changed.   After

---

[1] It is not a fantastic or marvellous subject-matter to which one objects in the romances, but the failure to make this credible.   The better authors were aware of a duty in this direction ; see e.g. below 62–3, 74–6 for two striking instances.   The writers who filled their romances with bald treatments of the marvellous were not so much characteristic, as bad artists, or simple.   Cf. Dorothy Everett, ' A Characterization of the English Medieval Romances ', 107–13.   The limits to the credulousness of an intelligent man of the fourteenth century were more widely set than our own, but they did exist.

Jean Bodel's day their subject-matter was being extended beyond the Three Matters ; the exquisite courtliness of Chrétien de Troyes was giving way before bourgeois elements which included both common sense and an increased appetite for sensationalism. Meanwhile, until the end of the thirteenth century, the number of French romances available to choose from was multiplying enormously. From this bewildering variety the English romance writers selected and refashioned, or simply translated with no apparent system, as their own inclinations or those of their patrons or public moved them. All kinds of stories, French, Norman-French, native, oriental or classical, were apparently equally acceptable. Combinations of subject, kind of treatment and quality occur in no generally predictable relationship. Extremes of good and bad occur even within the several versions of a single story. In the Auchinleck version of *Guy of Warwick,* for instance, the author's appetite for the marvellous has got him into a strange predicament. Guy, preparing to fight a giant, is armed with a shield that can be damaged by no sword. To enhance the hero's prestige the giant whom he will kill must also be equipped to perfection, and so he is made to attack Guy with a sword that once belonged to Hercules, and has been tempered in the River of Hell until no armour can withstand it. When this sword that cannot be turned meets the impenetrable shield and penetrates it the author's comment is, ' This never happened before '.[1] In the Cambridge University Library version of the same story, however, there is by contrast a description of Guy, with twenty squires, receiving the accolade, which for significance as well as economy of effect cannot be bettered in the romances.[2] No classification by subject could be made to account for such diverse effects arising out of the same original.

Few of the romances can be dated with assurance, and in addition the surviving versions are not necessarily the latest or the most authoritative forms of their stories or the best that were current. Even so it is possible to observe that there was no general, steady development of quality in the English

[1] EETS (ES) 42, 49, 59, ed. J. Zupitza (London 1883, 1887, 1891), stanzas 93 ff.

[2] EETS (ES) 25, 26, ed. J. Zupitza (London, 1875, 1876), ll. 387–422.

romances, that the exceptional romances, for instance those of Chaucer, had little influence on the *genre* as a whole ; and that the date of a romance, if we are able to fix it, need have no relation to its quality. The division between popular and courtly romances is of little more value as an index of quality. The fault which we would most confidently expect to find in the romances composed for uncultivated audiences, namely the reduction of stories to their simplest elements until they become bare accounts of incidents, occurs also in treatments evidently designed for a courtly public. In absurdities of exaggeration the courtly romances can offend as badly as the popular. For instance, many of the cultivated specimens fall in with the tradition set by the early *remaniements* of the *chansons de geste* that a Saracen must always behave with an excess of Mahoundy ; only one, *Partonope*, is conspicuous for its emancipation from this convention. In *Partonope* the Saracens behave like rational human beings ; they are not inevitably routed by smaller numbers of Christians, and they do not change character automatically upon conversion to the True Faith. In this respect *Partonope* resembles most the popular *Floris and Blauncheflur*. The same is true of the treatment of warfare. Here only *William of Palerne*, and again to a lesser degree *Partonope*, in the story of the great tournament, show any sign of a sense of verisimilitude in their authors. The worst offender for tedious exaggeration among a strong field is *The Laud Troy Book*, a learned romance, and other cultivated and courtly pieces are nearly as bad. Almost the only courtly romances in which our expectations of an artistically superior handling are consistently fulfilled are those of Chaucer, which are in any case generally a law unto themselves.

To classify the romances by their prosody is of little advantage in a literary evaluation. The tail rhyme stanza in which many of them were composed seems a measure uniquely unsuited for narrative use ; its unrobust and mincing pace constantly breaks the flow of the narrative, and it is quite without dignity or importance. Yet two of the best romances are written in this medium, and some of the others attain a certain degree of excellence despite it. The octosyllabic couplet, probably the measure most suited to the purpose and material of the romances, light and rapid in its motion, with wide ranges of pace and mood, by no means guaranteed success to its users. It could become irritatingly breathless or, conversely, have its back broken by being made to carry heavy or involved ideas. Its very virtue of ease of use sometimes led poets to give it insufficient attention, and in consequence to write loose and slipshod verse. Not even the alliterative long line, although so distinctive in its nature, allows one to predict the effects or the quality of the romances in which it was used. One might imagine that an instrument employed only by specialists trained in an ancient tradition, with an archaic prosody and obscure vocabulary, would not be used without a certain competence and some uniformity of effect. Instead, in addition to the poetically successful uses of the alliterative long line in the romances, there occurs a variety of faults of monotony, of obscurity, of unnatural and artificial English, or of cultivation of style for its own sake sometimes carried so far that the result is like a *trobar clus*. Two only of the romances in this medium have a relatively plain style, namely, *William of Palerne* and *The Alliterative Alexander Fragments*. One, *Cheuelere Assigne*, is artistically incompetent; another, *The Siege of Jerusalem*, ornate and precious. Even in the best alliterative romance, *Sir Gawain and the Green Knight*, there is marked stylistic idiosyncracy, evident not so much in the matching of initial sounds as in the cultivation of certain tricks of syntax.

Wherever we turn, the usefulness of classifications of the romances according to their subject, kind, form or manner is diminished for our purpose of evaluation by their refusal to run true to form. The impression of similarity conveyed by their common end of entertainment, their repeated uses of the same subject matter, and their common faults does not extend to their literary quality. However we may try to arrange and classify the romances we throw into prominence differences which lead us again and again to the point that, once the common materials and media are allowed, the important factor in their production was the man primarily responsible for each surviving specimen. If we need assurance that the ' convention ' and the ' tradition ' and all the other formulae which we have developed to simplify the study of literature are in the last analysis less important than the individual qualities of the single author, adaptor or translator, we can obtain such assurance by comparing the versions of *Guy of Warwick*, or the two Alexander romances, or the two *Morte Arthurs*, or *The Laud Troy Book* with *The Gest Hystoriale of the Destruction of Troy*, or *The Siege of Jerusalem* with *Titus and Vespasian*, or *Emare* with *The Man of Law's Tale*. Or we can note the remarkable originality of treatment in *Sir Degrevant*, where a human situation is handled on the natural, human level with no intrusion of marvel or magic, or how the unsupported judgement of the author of *The Erle of Tolous* suggested to him that a simple account of the love of two decent people and of the obstacle that kept them apart might be worth telling. We can observe how a sense of the dramatic, rare in the Middle Ages, taught the author of *Partonope* to use magic not as part of the furniture of his story but as an element in the development of character, or how the invention of the author of *Golagros and Gawane* enabled him to develop a dilemma such as later delighted the classical French theatre. Equally striking are the insensitivity of Henry Louelich which left him unresponsive to the most magical material, the calculated attempt in *The Jeaste of Syr Gawayne* to show the darling of English Arthurian story in a bad light,[1] the burlesque of *Syre Gawen and the Carle of Carelyle*, the deliberate exercise in the horrific of *Athelston*. In the moments of brilliance of otherwise unexceptional romances, like the accolade passage in *Guy of Warwick*,[2] or the description of the heroine in *Beues of Hamptoun*,

> Iosiane þat maide het ;
> Hire schon wer gold vpon hire fet.
> So faire ȝhe was & briȝt of mod
> Ase snow vpon þe rede blod.
> Whar to scholde þat may discriue ?
> Men wiste no fairer þing alive,
>   (Auchinleck vers. ll. 519–24.)

the principle is confirmed again, for the brilliance is the result of the individual having come upon material which perfectly

[1] In the version printed by F. Madden, *Syr Gawayne* (London 1839).
[2] See above, 7.

suits his particular gifts, and the product is often better than similar treatments by men of greater general competence.[1]

The wide variety of treatments and effects in the romances, and the dependence of the success of these upon individual discrimination, taste and talent, prevent the use of any of the customary classifications of the romances for the purpose of evaluation, which must therefore be carried out without primary reference to the other analyses. The arrangement of the romances according to their literary and artistic qualities cuts across all the other classifications. It does not pretend to supplant them or to question their great value for other purposes, but it does account for circumstances of success and failure which by their nature these other classifications cannot explain.[2] That it is an arbitrary method cannot be denied : it depends on a fallible judgement and it is restricted to consideration of the ' excellences proper to the kind ' and to the permanent qualities relatively independent of changes in time and society. The subjective nature of the process is unavoidable ; there is no other instrument than the intuition of the critic, backed by his powers of rationalization, with which to make such an evaluation. The arbitrariness of the restriction is, however, more apparent than real, for the same allowances must be made for the best romances as for the worst ; it departs from traditional methods only by distinguishing between genuine historical and social differences, which it takes for granted while employing them on occasion to explain particular features, and those recurrent forms of inartistic treatment which have given the romances their bad name, but which seem to originate less in the historical and social context than in the bad art of individuals.

[1] The poetic suggestion in this description of Iosiane, with the symbolism of the second verse and the startling image of the fourth to confirm the sense and deny the pretended ingenuousness of the two final verses may be instinctive, but the result is better in almost every way than a learned and laboured description like that of Helen of Troy in *The Gest Hystoriale* (ll. 3019 ff.)

[2] It can, indeed, be regarded as only the beginning of the literary study of the romances, for there remains the huge task of demonstrating, wherever an individual author is identifiable or ' separable ', and the sources of his work are known, whether he has shown himself to be a good or bad artist in relation to those sources.

This evaluation is applied to some sixty English verse romances,[1] which include the farthest extremes of good and bad work. About a dozen of them are outstanding, the majority are middling good, and the worst are painfully bad. These last are disfigured by faults of treatment which would condemn them in the eyes of the discriminating in any age and which are either not found in the romances of better quality, or are somehow compensated for. With them the evaluation must begin, for the study of their shortcomings usefully emphasizes the excellences of better works whose quality we might otherwise take for granted, while at the same time it completes the picture of the range of quality in this *genre*.

More than twenty of the surviving romances must be called artistic failures ; these twenty are individual even in their lack of excellence, for at least five general types of failure occur among them. There are romances which might have been the subject of the parody in *Sir Thopas* ; these are distinguished by the faults for which the romances as a class are often condemned. Stock incidents, fantastic marvels baldly and unconvincingly represented, prolixity, tags and padding, defects of form and construction, and incompetent use of the tail rhyme stanza are some of the commonest and most objectionable of their generic faults. Then there are the uncouth romances, vulgarizations by authors both insensitive and without skill. A third kind of failure comes from affectation and pretentiousness. Some of the romances, technically often not as objectionable as those which come under the preceding heads, are bad for a fourth reason, the failure of their authors to appreciate the possibilities of development in their stories. Finally, there are those in which the treatment required by the material of the story seems to have been misconceived, or even, in one case, deliberately misapplied.

[1] All the surviving specimens are described in J. E. Wells, *A Manual of the Writings in Middle English, 1050–1400* and supplements (New Haven 1916 ff.), with the information available, in the present state of the subject, about editions, dating, sources and location of the romances. The MSS. of the romances are listed in Carleton Brown and Rossell Hope Robbins, *The Index of Middle English Verse* (New York, 1943).

The best-known failures are those of the kind which Chaucer satirized in *Sir Thopas* by a compilation of their characteristic faults. It may safely be inferred that they appear as ludicrous to him as they do to us. The difference between *Sir Thopas* and *Sir Isumbras* or *Sir Eglamour of Artois* or *Lybeaus Disconus* or *Sir Degare* or *Torrent of Portyngale* is only one of relative concentration of such faults, if we leave out of account the practical certainty that in the first case the effect was intended, whereas in the others it was the apparently inevitable result of those circumstances which combine to determine the quality of a literary production. The popularity of some of these romances in their own time must not be made into a plea for letting differences of time and taste conceal their badness which, in any event, was evident to at least one contemporary.

Sir Isumbras [1] is bad because, although it tells its story with an honest didactic intention, the fantastic subject matter is made credible by no competence of construction or presentation. An improbable story in itself would not necessarily condemn a romance ; in *Sir Isumbras*, however, the improbabilities are made to seem the more monstrously improbable because they are communicated in a tone of flat mediocrity. There is not a single sign of any kind of inspiration or imaginative excitement in this romance. Piece by piece, like Job, Isumbras loses first his possessions and then his family, but no impression is conveyed of his increasing suffering as the process continues. As his fortunes recover there is again no evidence of growing excitement ; the tone is still equally flat. Good and bad fortune, separation, reversal and recognition are all described in the same predictably conventional language. The natural inference is that the author took a simple-minded pleasure in narrative at its most elementary, and was incapable or ignorant of anything artistically more advanced. This was not the case with the author of *Sir Eglamour of Artois*,[2] who displays some ingenuity in contriving to give new turns to old proven plots and situations. There is nothing so serious as a moral in this romance, which sets out to entertain by

[1] Ed. J. O. Halliwell, *Thornton Romances*, Camden Soc. 30 (London 1844).
[2] Ed. J. O. Halliwell, *op. cit.*

including all the sensational features of the fantastic romances :
giants, bears, fiery serpents, royal children carried off by
monstrous beasts, mistaken identities, recognitions, reunions
and great tournaments.   Artistically, however, the compendium of all romances to which this romance amounts is
impossible ; its inclusiveness rules out any question of unity
of either structure or effect.   *Torrent of Portyngale* [1] is a similar
case, but a worse one for being the work not merely of a botcher
and a hack but an incompetent one at that.   This romance has
none of the merits of ingenious construction sometimes
apparent in *Eglamour*.   Its story meanders without definition
along a trail of those absurdities of conception and crudities of
execution which have given the romances their bad name.
The themes are elementary and almost never rise above the
level of giant-slaughter and recognitions.   There is no attempt
to make the motivation of character plausible : for instance,
the king's hatred of Torrent, a necessary property of the story
to keep Torrent busy at his giant-killing, is unreasonable and
unfounded.   In this romance again it is not the events, indeed
far enough removed from the world of reality, that offend,
but the bald, episodic account of them.   Nothing compels
belief, for the author is not brave enough to cast off all pretence
of actuality, but clings unhappily to the shreds of the circumstantial which survive in his story ; he therefore neither wins
our imaginative surrender to a world of his fantasy nor leaves
us at ease in the real one.   *Sir Degare* [2] and *Lybeaus Disconus* [3]
are romances unremarkable even in their failures.   *Sir Degare*,
ordinary in conception, construction and expression in the
worst sense of the word, reflects the personality of a man both
uncritical and uninspired.   *Lybeaus* opens promisingly with a
situation that is a mixture of *Sir Perceval* and *La Cote Mal
Taile*, but goes on badly, for its author evidently had too
little power of invention and ends by having recounted in a
dull, expressionless manner a string of stock marvels at best
mechanically joined.   His dullness prevents any sympathy
for the youth and romantic origin of Lybeaus, and the boy's

    [1] EETS(ES) 51, ed. E. Adam (London 1887).
    [2] J. W. Hales and F. J. Furnivall, *The Percy Folio MS.* III (London
1867–8).
    [3] J. Ritson, *Ancient English Metrical Romances* II (London 1802).

gratuitous *affaire* with La Dame d'Amore is quite tastelessly introduced and handled. The effect of the whole romance is insipid.

Each of these five romances is written in the tail rhyme stanza, and all, with the possible exception of *Sir Isumbras*, are ' composite '. But artistic failure in all of them comes not from the choice of medium or subject but from the inadequacy of the author. The same principle holds for the ' rough ' romances, *Thomas of Erceldoune,*[1] *The Grene Knight,*[2] *Horn Childe and Maiden Rimnild,*[3] the Bodley *Sir Ferumbras,*[4] *The Sege of Melayne*[5] and *Roland and Otuel,*[6] in which the insensitivity or coarse fibre of the author, manifested in both the conception of the story and the manner of its expression, is the reason for failure. The first two examples are extreme cases even in this company, for they combine flatness of treatment with an apparent pointlessness which actually at times makes it hard to discern what effect their authors intended. They may indeed be debased versions of material which deserved or had elsewhere received a finer treatment, but as they stand these romances are conspicuously bad in form and expression. The remaining four invite similar comparisons. Thus, set beside the charming simplicity of *King Horn,* the treatment of subject in *Horn Childe* is tasteless. In the latter, situations have been introduced from other romances, possibly versions of *Sir Tristrem* and *Amis and Amiloun,* which distort and cheapen the story, and the medium, superior to that of *King Horn* in making the story go with considerable impetus, is nevertheless quite insensitively used. The result is tasteless and crude. *Horn Childe* differs from most of the inferior romances in that its matter has been rather brutalized than popularized ; for instance, the beating of Rimnild by her father is described with quite evident relish. The English Charlemagne romances here named are much inferior to their French equivalents in their lack of any kind of inspiration and

---

[1] EETS 61, ed. J. A. H. Murray (London 1875).
[2] Ed. F. Madden, *Syr Gawayne* (London 1839).
[3] Ed. J. Hall, *King Horn, A Middle English Romance* (Oxford 1901),
[4] EETS(ES) 34, ed. S. J. Herrtage (London 1879).
[5] EETS(ES) 35, ed. S. J. Herrtage (London 1880).
[6] EETS 198, ed. M. I. O'Sullivan (London 1935).

in their mechanical handling. In both the French and the English versions one incident seems to follow another for no apparent reason beyond the author's wish to keep the narrative going by a new complication, but at least in the former there is the enthusiastic partisanship inherited from the early *chansons de geste* to enliven the material. In the English stories there is little relief from the succession of cut-and-thrust:

> Þe forthirmaste come a saraȝene wyghte,
> Sir Arabaunt of Perse he highte,
>   Of Gyon was he kinge ;

> He said þer was na cristyn knyghte
> Ware he neuer so stronge ne wyghte
>   To dede he [ne] solde hym dynge.

> And one Sir Ataymnere of Beme
> Þat was Sir Olyueres Eme
>   Byfore þe stowre þay thrynge,

> And euen at þe first countire right
> The Saraȝen slewe oure cristyn knyghte ;
>   It was dyscomforthynge—
>   (*Sege of Melayne* ll. 229–40.)

If the authors had any feeling for their subjects, their craftsmanship was too little for them to convey it. The Roland and the Oliver of the *Chanson* have fallen into the hands of versifiers in the merest sense of that word, with no talent beyond the bare gift of forcing words into patterns, overwhelmed by the difficulty of moving their characters from here to there. Their most commendable quality is the doggedness with which they see their stories out to the end.

A similar doggedness and insensitivity must have been the principal qualities of the Henry Louelich who signs *Merlin* [1] and *The Holy Grail*.[2] The personality that he reveals in these

---

[1] EETS(ES) 93, 112 : EETS 185, ed. E. A. Koch (London 1904, 1913, 1932).

[2] EETS (ES), 20, 24, 28, 30, ed. F. J. Furnivall (London, 1874, 1875, 1877, 1878) : EETS (ES), 95, ed. D. Kempe (London 1905).

monuments of dullness is oppressive by its excessively un-humorous application and diligence ; there is not one relieving feature in the thousands upon thousands of lines that he wrote, not one moment of brightness, or any change of any kind from level mediocrity. Louelich seems to have had no notion of developing the possibilities latent in the material under his hand. In his *Holy Grail*, for instance, which surely deserved better than to be made into such a vast, inert bulk of a book, there is no evidence that he felt any of the many kinds of response to the subject which might have existed between the extremes of von Eschenbach's unrestrained and eager spirituality and Malory's uncomfortable, almost shame-faced piety. Louelich was an unimaginative and insensitive clod, capable only of further inflating his already huge originals.

The failure of *Lancelot of the Laik* [1] and *The Romance of Partenay* [2] is stylistic in origin. *Lancelot of the Laik*, a romance of which the subject should have predisposed to success, is perhaps the least appropriate imitation of the Chaucerian manner that has been preserved. The style quite destroys the power of the associations of this familiar material ; the preamble,

> Quhen that tytan withe his lusty heit
> Twenty dais In to the aryeit
> Haith maid his cours and all with diuers hewis
> Aparalit haith the feldis and the bewis   (ll. 335–8),

illustrates one of its mannerisms. The alternative, when the story compels the author to leave rhetoric for narrative, is a prosiness as profuse as his grand manner. A language swinging from one to the other of these extremes, with occasional excursions into the aureate style, conventional laments, talking birds, the god of love, quotations from Ovid, all between them prevent the adventure of the willing imagination which this old and famous story might so easily have afforded. *The Romance of Partenay* is not simply bad stylistically ; it is impossible to read, for it is, properly

[1] EETS 6, ed. W. W. Skeat (London 1865).
[2] EETS 22, ed. W. W. Skeat (London 1866).

speaking, not written in English. The author's account of his method of translation explains some of its curiosities of expression :

> As ny as metre can conclude sentence
> Cereatly by rew in it haue I go.
> Nerehande stafe by staf, by gret diligence
> Sauyng þat I most metre apply to ;
> The wourdes meue, and sett here & ther so,
> Like As of latin hoso will fourge uers ;
> Wourdes most he change sondry & diuerse,
>
> Whilom þat before put, And sette behynd,
> And oft that at end gretth best before . . .
> Be it latyn, frensh, or our tonge tobore.
> Ho it metre will, so do moste euermore,
> Be it in balede, uers, Rime or prose,
> He most torn and wend, metrely to close
> And so haue I done after my simplesse.   (ll.6553–67)

There are other singularities to which he does not admit here, such as the omission of personal pronoun subjects, and sometimes even the direct translation of French idiom, as in the line *Full moch good hath within thys dongon*, which must in the context mean ' There is much treasure—'. This mode of expression is evidently the product of taking great pains ; its originator was clearly not an unlettered or incompetent man, but simply remarkably mistaken. His romance is bad not only because of the ' forging ' itself, but also because his intentness upon this process prevented him from refining under his hammer metal which was itself far from pure or precious. Both *Lancelot* and *Partenay* demonstrate how, with all the literary resources of the late fourteenth century at his disposal, a man could still produce a result artistically inferior to those of the relatively uncultivated but unpretentious and competent workmen responsible for the majority of the romances.

The fault of *The Romance of Partenay* is one of judgement, of a kind so extreme that it obscures the other deficiencies of the romance. Mistaken judgement accounts, as well, for a much more ordinary set of failures, the romances which are sometimes called moral tales. These are *Amadas*,[1] *Sir Cleges*,[2] *Roberd of Cysylle*,[3] *The King of Tars*[4] and *Titus and Vespasian*.[5] From their number and their common element of moral teaching one might infer that didacticism is fundamentally unsuited to the romances, if their failure were not to be explained more immediately in terms of the artistic incompetence of the authors. In *Amadas* the principal fault is a dispersal of emphasis which destroys the unity of effect. With great generosity Amadas expends the last of his fortune in redeeming a dead man's debts ; but the ' grateful dead ', who returns to reward him, first subjects him to an agonizing emotional ordeal both gratuitous and improper in view of his obligation to Amadas. *Sir Cleges*, an undistinguished treatment of traditional motives, is told in a manner quite unsuited to the romance *genre*, of bourgeois primness and affected gentility distinct from the usual fondness of the romance writers for high life. *Roberd of Cysylle* in all the versions I have seen,[6] is a crude, sprawling and morally unimpressive story which, by the correct use of emphasis and heightening, could have been made into something both artistically better and successfully didactic. *The King of Tars* is a thoroughly pedestrian romance remarkable only in containing one of the most exaggerated paynim rages in all the surviving literature of this kind ; this was no doubt intended to emphasize the extent of the transformation both internal and external effected by baptism that is the pietistic theme of the romance.

It is probably correct to assume that the use of the material of these romances for didactic ends was an error of artistic judgement, not so much because the didacticism was foreign to the *genre* as because to fulfil successfully both a teaching intention and one of entertainment would overtax the abilities of all but the most gifted. A successful pietistic romance

---

[1] Ed. H. Weber, *Metrical Romances* III (Edinburgh 1810).
[2] *Ib.* I.
[3] Ed. E. V. Utterson (London 1839).
[4] Ed. J. Ritson, *Ancient English Metrical Romances* II (London 1802).
[5] Ed. J. A. Herbert (London 1905).
[6] That contained in B. M. Additional MS. 22283, fol. 90 b, col. 3 ff., is praised by Laura Hibbard, *Mediæval Romance in England*, 60–1, but I was unable to discover its merit, and found it a tasteless and ill-conducted *exemplum*.

indeed exists in *The Man of Law's Tale*, but its success as such is no accident of combination of intentions but a triumph of discernment, for Chaucer evidently perceived that the material of this story would not allow of a successful handling in any other way.[1] Many of the romances suffer because their authors lack a corresponding discernment ; seven of them at least fail most particularly in this respect.

Three of these, the Percy Folio *Merlin*,[2] the Marquess of Bath's *Arthur*[3] and *Cheuelere Assigne*[4] are elementary and unremarkable instances of such lack of perception. The author of this *Merlin* has indeed produced a less monstrous work than Louelich's version, which stands condemned for other faults, but his response to his material is, if possible, even less, and his manner much rougher and simpler than that of Louelich. The totally uninspired *Arthur* is distinguished only by being in all respects the least successful of the surviving English treatments of the Matter of Britain. *Cheuelere Assigne* is a curiosity for the style in which it is written, but otherwise it is quite unimaginative. There is no sign in any of these three undeveloped romances that its author even guessed what could be made of his story.

The Sege or Batayle of Troye,[5] *Emare*,[6] *The Knight of Courtesy and the Fair Lady of Faguell*[7] and *Sir Tristrem*[8] reflect similar insensitivity and unresponsiveness which, however, take the form not so much of failing to develop the material in hand as of mistaking it and developing it wrongly. The authors of these romances were not quite incompetent, and in some respects their works have merit, but because they wrongly conceived the direction which their treatments ought to take, the effect of what they wrote is largely negative.

A mediæval writer on the subject of Troy should have had everything in his favour, for its long story was invested with

---

[1] See below, 62–5.
[2] Ed. Hales and Furnivall, *Percy Folio MS*. I (London 1867–8).
[3] EETS 2, ed. F. J. Furnivall (London 1864).
[4] EETS(ES) 6, ed. Lord Aldenham (London 1868).
[5] EETS 172, ed. M. E. Barnicle (London 1927).
[6] EETS(ES) 99, ed. E. Rickert (London 1906).
[7] Ed. J. Ritson, *Ancient English Metrical Romances* III (London 1802).
[8] Scottish Text Society 8, ed. G. P. McNeill (London 1886).

many kinds of glamour ; it was remote, heroic, splendid and tragic in the mediæval sense. Any treatment which even suggested these effects might be sure of at least some success, but to suggest them required the presence of two qualities : a Troy romance must be developed in a fashion both reasonably learned and courtly. In both these respects the author of *The Sege or Batayle of Troye* failed his material, for he vulgarized it out of recognition. He developed it not as an account of the downfall of a cause whose partisan he was, to be given in the most sympathetic manner he could command, nor as an adventure in *olde stories of stithe þat astate helde*, with an emphasis upon its heroic antiquity, but as a fund of curiosities and marvels to be described in a cheaply sensational manner. We get glimpses of the knowing leer that typifies the quality of his mind :

> So long was Achilles in bour
> With þe maidons of grete honour
> Þat þe kinges douȝter with childe was.
>> (Egerton MS. ll. 1248–50)

To this unpleasant personality he adds ignorance of his subject rather beyond the limit of what can be excused even in his times. Paris begins well when he tells his father of the encounter with the goddesses and their judgement :

> Dere fader, herken me—
> In þat forest þat tyme was goand
> Foure ladyes of Elfen land—
>> (Egerton MS. ll. 506–8)

such a translation needs no excuse, but the four ladies turn out to be Saturnus, Jubiter, Mercurius, and Venus. It is the same ignorance which makes this author quite to ignore the lavish possibilities of description in the subject. His one merit is to tell the story quickly, with plenty of control and energy ; his rapidity and strength of narration makes his work superior in this one respect to the other English Troy romances. But this energy cannot compensate for the faults ; no treatment of this subject can have a good effect which debases it as does *The Sege or Batayle.* The man was not adequate to his

2

subject, and, in consequence, the combination of ancient matter
and mediæval manner here effected is crude. It is typical of
this romance that its best moment is the description of the
brawl when Achilles is ambushed and killed in the temple.

Emare is less offensively but just as unmistakably a failure.
The Constance story which it tells is inherently difficult matter
for a romance. Told by Chaucer as a kind of *exemplum* of
divine providence, with supreme technical skill and a fine
show of piety, it only just passes muster ; here, retailed purely
for entertainment by an author evidently quite unaware of its
exacting nature, it is bad both as a romance and as a moral
tale. Not even its considerable pathetic possibilities are
developed beyond an occasional unconvincing apostrophe.
In addition, the manner of narration in *Emare* is neither
simple nor skilful enough to impress by its honesty or competence. Under these circumstances its pretences to elegance
and ornaments of style are generally objectionable, and the
whole falls disappointingly flat. Even in *Sir Eglamour of
Artois*, where another unfortunate mother is cast adrift with
her child, there is one single moment of poetry as her boat
makes a landfall at a wild sea isle:

> Nothyng ellys fonde sche thare
> But fowlys mony that wylde ware
> Faght faste on euery honde.
> (*Eglamour* ll. 838–40)

The moment is brief, of course ; the maladroitness of the
rhymer breaks the spell at once. But *Emare* has not even one
corresponding line ; it lacks both the magic of marvels and
the wonder of religion to redeem its author's original lack of
perception or to enliven the unimaginative competence of his
narration.

The author of *The Knight of Courtesy* was similarly uninspired. He had in hand a story potentially full of tragic
irony, and he failed it in almost every respect, probably because
he was without imaginative strength in any direction. His
work is bare of even the commonest evocative methods of the
romances, such as the elaborate embroidery of detail, or lavish
description to appeal to the love of splendour for its own sake,

or depictions of the familiar gracious attitudes of chivalry held just a little longer and more graciously than they would be in real life for the pleasure of contemplating them. This is a drab and colourless work, with many incredibly prosy lines. The knight makes a *compleynte*:

> ' From mournynge can i nat refrayne,
> This ladyes love dothe me so wounde,
> I feare she hath of me disdayne ' :
> With that he fell downe to the grounde. (ll. 61–4)

He fights a dragon :

> The dragon gave this knight a wounde
> Wyth his tayle upon the heed
> That he fell downe unto the grounde
> In a sowne as he had ben deed. (ll. 249–52)

The lady, described as ' Replete with feminine shamefast-nesse ', is given her lover's heart to eat and then told of it.

> Up she rose, wyth hert full wo
> And streight up into her chambre wente,
> She confessed her devoutly tho,
> And shortely receyved the sacrament. (ll. 449–52)

This gift for the unintended anticlimax marks the author as egregious even among the bad romance writers, and spoils any magic that there might be in the story of *The Knight of Courtesy*. He simply does not see the potential tragedy in the situation of the two chaste lovers hated by a husband maddened by suspicion ; he leaves story and characters both in an elementary, undeveloped state ; his own requirements seem to be satisfied by protestations of feeling as unconvincing in effect as they are conventional in expression.

Sir Tristrem, which also fails because its material is mis-applied, has a certain excuse for its poor quality. The love story of this romance is not easy to tell successfully ; it must be given a lyrical and passionate turn, and its emotional and dramatic elements must be given the strongest emphasis, while the treatment of events is subdued. Otherwise the story is likely to become an ugly little account of adulterous trickery in which the successive complications serve only to heighten the effect of the element of deceit. We must be made to feel a deep sympathy with the two lovers if we are to be able to forgive or ignore their repeated and callously dishonest subterfuges. Even in the best versions of this story, mediæval or modern, the casuistry of Isolde's justification by oath can be distasteful. In all these respects our author fails because he is neither competent nor sensitive enough to perceive what is required of him. His first mistake is his choice of an awkward stanza, hardly suited to narrative use,[1] as a result of which his energy seems to be largely dissipated in fitting words to his medium, with little left for the primary task of telling the actual story well. In addition he quite mistakes the value of his material, for he exaggerates the importance of the events at the cost of neglecting their emotional value. In consequence he never seems to get beyond them, and his romance is neither passionate, nor tragic, nor poetic, as it ought to be, but a rough bare piece of jingling versemaking which leaves in unhappy prominence the least pleasant features of its story.

The failure of each of these romances was mitigated by signs of some degree of competence in it. It would hardly be correct to extend this observation to *The Wife of Bath's Tale*[2] which, considered as a romance only, is technically a failure, but which artistically is beyond comparison better than most of the romances. In both structure and expression it is superbly finished, and as a part of the plan of effects of the whole *Canterbury Tales* it is an entire success. As a romance, however, it is a deliberate failure, a calculated perversion of a literary kind, designed for external reasons to prevent, not to induce, the willing suspension of disbelief, and by repeated suggestion that the material with which it is concerned is incredible, to direct attention to the character of the narrator from whom such suggestion originates. If we assume, as I believe we must, that the purpose behind the tale was the further illustration of the character of the Wife, we may still properly examine it as a romance, just as in a large canvas we

---

[1] *abababab(c)bc* where (c) is a bob. Except for (c) the lines commonly have three stresses.

[2] All Chaucer references are to *The Complete Works of Geoffrey Chaucer*, ed. F. N. Robinson (Cambridge, Mass., 1933).

examine the detail to see how it contributes to the effect of the whole. Indeed, by scrutinizing the *Tale* as a romance, we both confirm the suspicion that its grotesque effect was quite intentional, and at the same time improve our understanding of the nature of the romance *genre*.

The failure of *The Wife of Bath's Tale* as a romance is the result of its connexion with the Wife, in the course of which this abnormal woman with her undisguised self-interest, her callous refusal of belief in anything but the physical, and her shameless distortion of values, imposes her personality and her point of view upon old magical material in order to make her preposterous case. The first result of the association is the creation of a sense of disbelief, and the second an impression of cynicism from which the tale thenceforward takes its character. To both these qualities the romance *genre* is antipathetic. Despite the Wife's overpowering personality the suggestion of another, sympathetic treatment clings to the romance material she employs, which increases the discordancy and thus continues to serve the author's purpose by further illustrating the narrator's character. The romance of the knight and the loathly lady then becomes a romance as the Wife of Bath would tell it, and therefore anomalous in relation to its *genre*, for she rejects the escape which was the underlying purpose of this, belittles instead of heightening her material, and slights the masculine knightly ideal essential to the kind. Its success belongs to the *Canterbury Tales* as a whole and consists in the enlargement of our insight into her remarkable personality. By Chaucer's art, the Wife has assumed responsibility for the conception of the story and for its tone, he for the creation of the Wife, for the transference of her personality to the tale she tells, and for the technical perfection of that tale. He has seen fit, for a larger purpose, to make her do violence to a *genre* and a convention and turn a story with potentialities of both romance and romanticism into a piece of barefaced sophistry saltily told.

With *The Wife of Bath's Tale* ends the list of failures among the romances, a depressing recital indeed, but not so long as to justify an outright condemnation of this literary kind. I have not hesitated to include in it even those romances about whose utter failure there might be some doubt, for fear of prejudicing the credit, small or large, that I claim for the remainder. In each of the remaining specimens there is enough good to compensate in some degree for its artistic shortcomings. It will, of course, be appreciated that the degree of excellence varies considerably, and that it is necessary to read the romances at least with understanding, if not with sympathy, in order to perceive it. There is, however, in all the romances, except those I have described as failures, some reward for the effort, and in the few successes the experience of the fullest development of which the *genre* admitted.

As might be expected, the majority of the romances are neither outright failures nor completely successful, but belong to a middle group in which there is a wide range of quality, from works on a level of general competence, high enough to make them readable, to brilliant *tours de force* which nevertheless contain some grievous fault or flaw. Most of this middle group possess in some degree the qualities that have brought the romances into disrepute, yet even those which offend most have redeeming excellences ; a kind of principle of compensation seems to operate there, by which the accidental characteristics of the *genre* become unimportant by so much as there are merits to set against them. The operation of this principle conforms to the general purpose of entertainment which underlies the romances. The imaginative surrender is induced by the compensating qualities, and the more successfully it is induced, the less the faults seem to matter.

First among the works of intermediate quality come *Joseph of Arimathie*[1] and *The Laud Troy Book*,[2] in which an intelligent, restrained and relatively competent presentation allows the subject-matter to have its full effect. *Joseph of Arimathie* is a translation of an early section of the Grail history in alliterative verse. The matter is so loosely and episodically assembled that the romance has little formal unity ; it is rather a chapter of the vast history of which Louelich retailed the whole than a self-contained entity. There is, however, compensation for this fault of structure in the author's successful communication of his imaginative apprehension of his subject. His use of the alliterative long line, without particular affectation, sensitive

[1] EETS 44, ed. W. W. Skeat (London 1871).
[2] EETS 121, 122, ed. J. E. Wuelfing (London 1902–3).

and varied, is enhanced by a fine gift of visualizing ; this combination of qualities of feeling, vision and expression makes *Joseph of Arimathie* good reading despite its formlessness.

The Laud Troy Book is not a typical romance except in its author's uncritical attachment to the repetitive, intolerably long accounts of battles and single combats. It lacks emotional effect ; author and readers must move too far and too quickly to take more than a passing interest in each figure or situation as this becomes important for the moment. The charming intimacy of romances like *Beues of Hamptoun* or *Havelok*, where we attach our sympathies to the fortunes of a single character, is wanting here. The author's interests, if not always his gifts, are intellectual and learned, and provide the perfect contrast to those of the author of *The Sege or Batayle of Troye*. *The Laud Troy Book* reflects something of the imagination of the antiquary and historian ; its author seems to take pleasure in the size of his subject and the manner in which his account ranges in time and place. His treatment also pretends to be more factual than other handlings of the same theme. Despite his lack of partisanship he does, however, transmit a pleasure which he experienced in his association with the old and splendid story ; the relative finesse of his dispassionate treatment compares favourably with the crude sensationalism of *The Sege or Batayle*, and his antiquarian relish must be allowed to stand beside the more emotional conception of the subject itself in *The Gest Hystoriale of the Destruction of Troy*.[1]

The Weddynge of Sir Gawen and Dame Ragnel[2] and *The Sowdone of Babylone*[3] make a good contrast with the quiet learning of *The Laud Troy Book*, for, while neither is a cultured work, the authors of both take the strongest emotional interest in their subject. The first of these is an analogue of *The Wife of Bath's Tale* which shows Gawain in a good light. In technique and construction, although reasonably competent, it is decidedly cruder than Chaucer's version, but it is better as a romance in the strict sense of that term because it tells the story more honestly than does the Wife of Bath,

---

[1] See below, 56–9.
[2] Ed. F. Madden, *Syr Gawayne* (London 1839).
[3] EETS(ES) 38, ed. E. Hausknecht (London 1881).

with a simple but infectious enthusiasm more likely to persuade its hearer or reader into imaginative participation in the
actual events.

A comparable emotional energy enlivens *The Sowdone of
Babylone*. This romance is full of faults, which begin with its
subject-matter, an episodic succession of those expeditions,
captures, rescues, battles and conversions which originated in
the ingenuity of the French *remanieurs*, and attracted by their
sensationalism English audiences to whom the austere treatment and tense nationalism of the *Chanson de Roland* might
have appealed but little. In this story the inner details of
motivation are poorly developed and seem to have been
determined rather by the traditional conduct of the familiar
characters in a given situation than by relation to actual life.
Little is made here of the love affair of Guy and Floripas
which adds so much to the pleasant quality of the Fillingham
Sir Firumbras.[1] Tone and style are imperfectly set and
maintained ; once the author introduces a Chaucerian
apostrophe,

> O Thow rede Marʒ Armypotente
> That in the trende baye hase made þy trone,
> That god arte of bataile and regent,   (ll. 939–41)

another time a parade of courtly love, both of which are
incongruous with the essential effect posited by the subject-
matter. Nevertheless this is a strong, almost a heroic work.
In compensation for its want of finesse of conception, structure
or presentation, it tells with compelling energy a story of
fantastic violence, crusading indignation, noble devotion,
courage, and knightly performance in arms, with a gusto that
compensates for its lack of polish.

The serious faults of *The Life of Ipomydon*,[2] the Cotton
Octauian,[3] *Amis and Amiloun*,[4] and *Sir Tryamour* [5] are
relieved by other less simple excellences. *Ipomydon* is an

[1] See below, 40–1.
[2] Ed. H. Weber, *Metrical Romances* II (Edinburgh 1810).
[3] *Op. cit.* III.
[4] EETS 203, ed. E. Leach (London 1937).
[5] Ed. E. V. Utterson, *Select Pieces of Early Popular Poetry* (London
1817).

insufficiently unified story, badly constructed and motivated, pieced together out of borrowings from various, principally Arthurian, sources. But its deficiencies of structure cannot outweigh the virtue of this romance, which consists in creating, through a heightening not of material circumstances but of the manners and chivalry which underlie them, a company of agreeable people distinguished by their courtly good breeding. It is significant that there is no real villain in *Ipomydon* ; the intention of the author was to afford his audience the chance of escape into a world of gallantry, beauty and gracious conduct. He took his names from the *Roman de Thèbes*, many of his situations from Arthurian legend, freed the mixture as much as was possible from associations with known story, and gave it novelty by conferring upon it a general air of distinction which, whatever his shortcomings in other, artistic respects, he conveyed with complete mastery. His intention was thus fulfilled by the creation of yet another province in the world of fancy of the romance writers.

The effect of a comparable infusion of personality is shown in the Cotton version of *Octauian*,[1] The other, inferior, Cambridge version is a bumbling and inconsequent collection of marvels, buffoonery and giant-killing, quite without appeal, and reflects a colourless and unattractive personality. The Cotton version is quite another matter. Its opening is conventionally fantastic. An innocent queen is exposed with her two infant sons. One is promptly seized by a she-ape, rescued by a knight, taken from the knight by brigands and sold to a butcher on his way home to Paris from a pilgrimage. The other child is carried off by a lioness which, with the child in her mouth, is in turn taken by a stooping griffon and carried to a desert island where she kills the griffon. Meanwhile the child's mother is brought by chance to the island ; she takes back her son from the lioness, which naturally respects their royal blood and thenceforward follows them devotedly. But from this beginning the author of the Cotton version develops a tolerably well-related series of mistaken identities, heroic deeds, restorations of kingdoms and recognitions, which he

[1] The version printed by Weber is from MS. Cotton Caligula A II, that printed by J. O. Halliwell in *Publications of the Percy Society* xiv (London 1844) is from MS. Cambridge University Library Ff.2.38.

2*

interprets with warm humanity. To evident enthusiasm for his subject he adds a fair technical competence. But principally he shows a sensitive understanding of character, notably displayed in his descriptions of the king's son trying to be a butcher's apprentice and a money-changer, and of the butcher, Clement Vilene himself, with his kindly wife, puzzling over the vagaries of royal blood as it reveals itself in the behaviour of a foundling. By this understanding, and by his exploitation of incident to illustrate personality, he endows his romance with permanent qualities.

Amis and Amiloun has as many absurdities of subject and faults of construction as *Octauian*, some of which are perhaps to be explained by the fact that it was first designed with a didactic intention which was wanting in later versions but still continued to affect action and motivation at cardinal points. Although this story is told swiftly and energetically, its style is commonplace, marred by the usual tags and padding. The romance has, however, distinct virtues of characterization, which compensate for its faults of structure and expression. Its principal characters are all pleasant people, the most attractive the boy Amoraunt who cares for Amiloun in his misery, the finest the heroine Belisaunt, a frank, forthright and loyal woman who is splendidly typical of the active type of romance heroine. Her rebuke to Amis, when he hesitates to accept her love, illustrates one side of her character :

> Sire kniȝt, þou nast no croun . . .
> Wheþer artow prest oþer persoun
> Oþer þouart monk oþer canoun
> Þat prechest me þus here ?
> Þou no schust haue ben no kniȝt
> To gon among maidens briȝt ;
> Þou schust haue ben a frere ! (ll. 614 ff.)

In this sentiment she is own sister to Floripas and Melidor and Meliors ; like them she wins our good opinion for having the courage of her affections. The other side of her personality, which makes the first the more admirable by proving that its source is courage, is her fierce loyalty to the unhappy Amiloun who sacrificed himself that she and Amis might escape the consequences of their rashness.

Sir Tryamour is relieved by a quite different quality of its author's temperament, a sense of order most unusual among romance writers. The weakness of this romance consists in its commonplace expression, in failure to make its conventionally fantastic subject matter credible by any of the available means, and in at least one grievous neglect of the motivation of action, when a principal character shows himself too ready to believe evil of those who wish him well. Within these restrictions, however, the author of *Sir Tryamour* shows himself to be a master of design and construction, capable of planning effects and laying the foundations of situations far in advance, with the consequence that his improbable story is so much more closely and skilfully knit than most of the romances as to be quite remarkable in this respect.

These four romances, which are at best only relieved from artistic failure, invite comparison and contrast with a group of seven in which the question begins to become less one of redeeming qualities than of a good effect diminished by artistic shortcomings. These romances, *Eger and Grime*,[1] *Sir Gowther*,[2] *Sir Launfal*,[3] *Golagros and Gawane*,[4] *Generydes*,[5] *The Erle of Tolous*,[6] and *Le Bone Florence of Rome* [6] all have moments of brilliance.

Eger and Grime is marred by a serious misdirection of sympathy for which the author is responsible by his uncritical acceptance of an unsatisfactory plot. Eger is the hero of the story, but his sworn brother Grime, in the course of an expedition to win the Lady Winglaine for Eger, earns not only our admiration but also all the sympathy that we should have had for the hero. The author may have been aware of this deficiency, for he attempts to excuse Eger's precedence on the grounds of his higher rank. In fact, however, this justification not only fails but is completely set at naught by the direction which the development of sympathy for the char acters takes ; the persuasive power of this romance consists in

---

[1] Ed. D. Laing, *Early Metrical Tales* (Edinburgh 1826).

[2] Ed. E. V. Utterson, *Select Pieces of Early Popular Poetry* (London 1817).

[3] Ed. J. Ritson, *Ancient English Metrical Romances* I (London 1802).

[4] Ed. F. Madden, *Syr Gawayne* (London 1839).

[5] EETS 55, 70, ed. W. A. Wright (London 1873, 1878).

[6] Ed. J. Ritson, *op. cit.* III.

the effect of the personalities of Grime and the mistress whom he acquires in the course of his expedition. The author has with firm snobbery assigned them and their love affair to the second place, but they come so far first in our affections that we have none left for Eger or his tediously exacting Winglaine. Not many of the romances can muster two characters as highly sympathetic as Grime and Loosepine, who acquiesce with such ready grace in the denial of precedence, and so effortlessly make it unimportant. The author's own attachment to them has gone far to offset the weakness of his plot ; he should have realized his very great gift for character drawing, and allowed it to influence his conduct of that plot, or else employed it on more rewarding material.

Sir Gowther is another romance in which, despite the limitations of his talent and the great improbabilities of his subject, the author achieves the effect of an entirely sympathetic character. Sir Gowther, whose unlucky mother was got with child by the same fiend who fathered Merlin, is superhuman not only in strength and prowess but also in evil-doing. The story of his unregenerate career, his abject misery when his origin is made known to him, the penance the pope laid on him, and his rehabilitation is not very skilfully told. Nevertheless Gowther attracts our attention, and even admiration, from the moment he comes into the world with a load of ill-fate upon him such as even the Greek tragic poets seldom devised. The reason for this effect is partly the injustice of visiting upon him the burden of a piece of inhuman malice, partly the noble simplicity which the issue assumes in his mind as soon as he learns what he is. With no hesitation or repining he turns from the enormities of his past life and the hideous inheritance of his paternity, and sets out simply and honestly to purify himself of the diabolic. He shows no sign of self-pity or of any Oresteian resentment of the injustice that has declared him responsible for a circumstance in the creation of which he had no part. To us his misfortune seems monstrous, but the character of Gowther himself, by the sympathy which his admirable attitude attracts, is a permanent artistic achievement. If a man is to be the son of a demon, and if he is to purify himself, this is how we would have him behave.

Golagros and Gawane, a competent but not, at first sight, exceptional romance in a variety of the alliterative long line, affords an instance of felicity of another kind unusual in the romances. The story begins slowly and thinly, looking at first as if it is to be only the familiar glorification of Gawain's courtesy by contrast with the boorishness of Kay. While this impression lasts, the alliterative language, manipulated with agility, the rhetoric and the fine courtly air seem adornments too important for the tenuous account which occasions them. At length, however, the author plays his trump, for all the developments of plot and all the careful suggestions of character suddenly unite to create a dilemma both quite unusual and at least as natural in the circumstances of the times as many of those upon which the plots of the classical French tragedies were made to hang. Gawain gets the upper hand of Golagros in a fight ; but the honour of the latter will not allow him to yield, and the chivalry of Gawain will not allow him to take the customary step of killing Golagros. At once the intention behind the earlier effects becomes apparent, and we are obliged to concede that although these may have been over-elaborate and uneconomical they did nevertheless serve a functional purpose by preparing a *milieu* in which such conflict of principles could arise. The design and the dramatic situation are rare and noteworthy in mediæval literature. The weakness of their appearance in *Golagros and Gawane* comes from the slight story and its artificial theme, which prevent the reader from believing that there is much at stake at the critical moment.

Generydes and *Sir Launfal* have a common fault of treatment which consists in the fact that each is written in two ' keys ', one appropriate and the other wrong. In *Generydes* the change is made for the worse, in *Launfal* it rescues what would otherwise have been an unexceptional and possibly even a downright bad piece of writing. The brilliance of *Generydes* is to be found in the first impression the poet creates, and continues until his tone and intention suddenly and completely change. He opens in a courtly manner Chaucerian in both its maturity and its polish. A rhyme royal stanza used with much deftness carries his account easily along and unfolds a story thin and bloodless to be sure, but beautiful and artificial in the good sense of that word, from which any suggestion of close contact with popular sentiment or the full-blooded heartiness of the more ingenuous romances is excluded. This part of *Generydes* is an escape from reality into a well-bred world of courtly love where, if passion is wanting, at least the attitudes of passion are gracefully assumed. The impression of this early section of the romance is formal, stately and gracious. But the exigencies of the story throw Generydes into prison, his *gestes* begin, and with the change in matter comes a distinct change in key. At once the limitations of the author's gifts become apparent. He may have read *The Knight's Tale* and *Troilus* but he has not learned from them either how to reject irrelevant material or to preserve the courtly manner when handling vigorous or popular matter. After the change his romance becomes an indifferent collection of adventures, too rough to fit his beginning, too bookish to be any good as such. His credit comes from having been able to sustain the courtly manner with good effect as long as his matter did not make too great demands upon him.

Sir Launfal, conversely, makes a good end after a bad beginning. At the outset its author seems to labour under every one of the handicaps which the *lai* imposed upon its users. The development of a *lai* plot seems usually to have depended upon some marvel or miracle. At the same time the *lai* was too short to slur over the improbability of such a phenomenon by a show of circumstance, and the crucial marvel or miracle was likely to stand out naked and unrelieved in the story. By only one possible means could this difficulty be overcome—the writer had to cast off reality completely and write a story with a spell, an effect of magic or unreality in which the miracle or marvel would be acceptable. It must be held against the author of *Sir Launfal* that he began to do this only late in his poem, after a mealy-mouthed and sanctimonious opening in a court where Arthur is a choleric cuckold, and Guenevere, among other promiscuities, plays Potiphar's wife to Launfal's Joseph. The romance should have begun and been developed throughout in the exquisite tone of its ending : Launfal living in faery with a mistress whose worst-favoured serving-maid is lovelier than Guenevere, but coming back to the world from time to time, and waiting in a wood to joust with passing knights *to kepe hys armes fro the rustus*.

The exceptional quality of *The Erle of Tolous* is entirely in the subject of its story. This romance has great faults of structure, for its treatment is too extended and the emphasis is not skilfully controlled; in addition it is stylistically always unremarkable and sometimes incompetent. But however the author's art may have been at fault, the instinct which prompted his choice of this story and determined his particular conception of it [1] was both original and sure. It tells, with exceptional delicacy, how Earl Bernard fell in love with the empress and she with him, and how they conducted themselves with decency and devotion until the emperor died and they were able to marry. Generations of the more decorous novelists have accustomed the modern reader to such situations, and indeed nowadays this one will probably be thought dull. But such a plot and such a sober and sympathetic treatment were, to say the least, uncommon in the Middle Ages, and the judgement which singled them out was bravely and independently exercised.

The author of *Le Bone Florence of Rome* is exceptional in that, quite incidentally to his main moral purpose, and despite the many faults which relate his work to the inartistic specimens of the romance tradition, he produces from time to time situations and passages of poetry in the real heroic mode. The most striking of the shortcomings of his romance are those of presentation of material. In form *Le Bone Florence* is protracted, episodic and ill-connected. It captures the imagination only where the author deals with the classical situations of chivalry. He knows men and their behaviour; this knowledge serves him well as long as the hagiological element in his story does not interfere. In his best moments he indulges his feeling for splendid effects, conveys them with efficient expression, and shows a true conception of heroic poetry, as in this lament for a dead emperor by his men :

> Who schall us now geve londes or lythe,
> Hawkys or howndes, or stedys stythe,
> As he was wont to doo ?   (ll. 841–3)

---

[1] See Laura Hibbard, *Mediæval Romance in England*, 40–2.

or in this noble answer when another emperor releases a prisoner of war and tries to extract a promise of peace from him in return for his liberty :

> Syr, when y come into the towne
> I and my men muste be bowne
> To greve bothe thyn and thee.   (ll. 952–4)

The emperor's response to such heroic defiance is correspondingly fine. ' Do so, strike on ! ' he says, and lets the knight go. The faults of this romance are many and grievous, but its moments of exaltation are very fine.

The same is true in a general sense of the much more important *Partonope of Blois*.[1] Of this romance the most serious artistic fault is its excessive length. The story itself is already long ; in addition the characters talk endlessly, with endless analogies and comparisons, on every possible point however trifling, and to their talk the author has added lengthy opinions and comments of his own. By no means all or even much of this talk is dull ; generally it is a very interesting revelation of the mediæval mentality. But added to the passages in which material traditionally expanded in the romances is developed at length, it makes the treatment of *Partonope* too extended. The two kinds of inflation, one conventional and the other personal in origin, have swollen this romance beyond the limits within which its story could be profitably treated. It now moves too slowly ; the primary interest in the narrative is lost, and the discursive interest which replaces it is not a fully satisfactory artistic substitute. Not even the English translator's extremely capable verse, rarely faltering, never in itself tedious, deftly accommodated to high, middle and low subjects, can overcome the disadvantages of the story's prolixity. Therefore the effect of the sum of the many very good passages in this romance is not as great as it ought to be. The descriptions of tournaments and hunting scenes and battles and magic castles and magic boats, the finest a romancer could produce, clearly visualized and skilfully conducted, are too many and too long. The conversations and reflections and discussions are always interesting in themselves, but they hobble the narrative.

[1] EETS(ES) 109, ed. A. T. Boedtker (London 1912).

The first redeeming permanent quality of *Partonope* is the author's understanding of human motives, which comes near to equalling that of Chaucer in its penetration. Partonope himself, Melior whom he loves, and even the minor characters are made not only to act but also to develop throughout the story in the most natural way. None of them is too good or too perfect to be real. The principals, whose characters are drawn in the greatest detail, behave in engagingly human ways. Partonope, something of a young rascal in his readiness to take advantage of the situation in which he first meets Melior, and none too considerate of her afterwards, manfully accepts the chastening lesson he has brought on himself, and contrives to regain his self-respect and our affection in the end, not only by displaying all the courage and prowess expected of a romance hero, but also by suffering considerable heart-searching for his early mistake in discretion and by showing, in his treatment of another girl who has fallen in love with him, that his character has improved with experience. Melior, the heroine, is the author's triumph. The daughter and heiress of the throne of ' Constantine the noble ', she chooses Partonope as her consort with the help both of the fabled Byzantine powers of magic and of a senate humanly pompous in its deliberations. By the former means she causes him to be brought first to her palace and then to her actual chamber where, however, he appears to upset her plans by seducing her. Such an anticipation of an eventual relationship is usually excused in the romances as no more than pardonably hasty, and here the balance of sympathy is preserved by setting Melior's indiscretion against the opportunism of Partonope on the same occasion. In any case Melior still has all her magic and does not need our sympathy. But Partonope, influenced by his mother, and by the King of France his kinsman, who have, understandably, other plans for him and fail to appreciate the highly dubious connexion he intends, is persuaded to violate a condition which Melior has laid upon him. At once her magic falls from her, she is exposed to the querulous reproaches of her council for her original headstrong conduct, and becomes an ordinary, helpless woman, very much in love and faced with the anxiety that the man to whom she was too readily generous, and who has already failed her once, will fail her again.

In this use of magic to help him develop a woman's character the author of *Partonope* has shown how at least one conventional feature of the romances can be turned to good artistic account.   He gives further evidence of his artistic perception in other ways.   His descriptions of battles are tedious by their length, but uncommonly credible in themselves and relatively free of the excess of exaggeration to be found in the conventional romances.   Partonope is a good knight and a brave one, but he never wins his encounters by the absurdly wide margin to which we grow accustomed elsewhere ; things are often touch and go with him.   Most striking of all is this author's treatment of the Saracens, whom he depicts as rational human beings and even admirable ones at times.   He holds by the conventions of courtly love, but never lets them make his characters into puppets.   In fact he measures everything human in his story by his own knowledge of life.   It is, for instance, evident that his own experience has given him a considerable insight into the hearts of lovers, and perhaps it is on the grounds of this experience that he asserts that love can

> Make eche man hys mastere vse :
> Knyghtes shame to refuse,
> Clerkes to love well clergye.   (ll. 4454–6)

That it was unhappy seems to have served to imprint it the more firmly upon his memory.[1]   He is remarkable in his times

---

[1] The reasons he finds for this lack of success may be taken as an illustration of one late fourteenth- or early fifteenth-century point of view about courtly love.

> In þo dayes wele wote ye
> Men wonne her ladies in dyuers degre,
> Some with manhode and chevalry,
> Some þrow beaute and curtesy,
> Some with faire speche and richesse,
> Some þrow strength, some be largesse.
> All þat is go withouten nay,
> The worlde is turned anoþer way,
> For neyþer richesse ne beaute
> Ne fayre speche in no degre
> May make a man his love to wynne,
> They be so sore aferde to synne.
> Of fredame, curteisy, ne of largesse
> They take noone hiede, for holynesse

for many features of his art ; the pity is that he did not limit the size of his work.

Guy of Warwick [1] and the Fillingham *Sir Firumbras* [2] are perfect foils to the reflectiveness and sensibility of *Partonope*.

> Hath so caught hem in his service
> Of wordly lustes now in no Wise
> Take they hiede, but only to wyrche
> þat they may pleace God and his chirche.
> For eueryday yerly they rise,
> To chirche they gone to here servise
> Of God, and hardly þere they be
> Til it be noone, for dame chastite
> Governeth now hem in such wise
> From knelyng hem luste not ones to Rise.
> To go to her dyner haue they none haste ;
> They Reke neuer how longe they faste.
> Of ffresshe array take they none hiede ;
> They go cloþed in homely wede.
> They wole not swere neuer an othe
> But ' nay ' or ' yee, it is sothe '.
> But in olde tyme ladies wolde
> Haue mercy on lovers þat in cares colde
> Loved and for love had grete diseace.
> Some tyme ladies such folk wolde pleace;
> But in þes dayes it is noþing so.
> For be a lovere neuer so wo,
> His lady list not hym make chiere,
> For his compleynt þei wole not here
> Neþer be speche neþer letter writyng :
> They wole not rede it for no þing.
> All þat men sey they take in grief ;
> I trow chastite hath made hem defe. (ll. 9664–705.)

I do not know of any general reform of feminine morals at the turn of the century. It may be either that the author's own case moved him to these dismal conclusions, or that on the strength of what he read he was assuming a greater freedom of conduct in the past than the general uniformity of human behaviour in these matters from age to age would justify.

[1] EETS(ES) 25, 26, 42, 49, 59, ed. J. Zupitza (London 1875, 1876, 1883, 1887, 1891). The fifteenth-century version, nos. 25 and 26, is superior to the versions found in the Auchinleck and Caius MSS. ; the story is substantially the same in all three. *Reinbrun Gij Sone of Warwike* which is copied as a separate romance in the Auchinleck MS. belongs to the larger work and is properly included in it in the Cambridge MS.

[2] EETS 198, ed. M. I. O'Sullivan (London 1934). The MS. is now B.M. Additional 37492.

Guy of Warwick illustrates the extent of their difference, for its length is equal to that of *Partonope,* yet its unreflective strength and unremitting action carry it to its conclusion without flagging. The faults of *Guy* and *Sir Firumbras* correspond remarkably to the virtues of *Partonope.* They are rough in texture where it is smooth, excessively simple at times in their development of character, bald in their descriptions of marvels, frankly popular where *Partonope* is subtle, artificial and courtly. Neither has any of the literary finish that distinguishes *Partonope.* Their excellence lies in their great vitality, and their best moments occur when this vitality acts upon material perfectly suited to express it, and is thus fully communicated.

The fragmentary *Sir Firumbras,* like the Bodley version,[1] keeps much of the old *chansons de geste* about it. Feats of arms are enormously exaggerated; the Franks bring miracles about by prayer and relics, the Saracens by magic arts. The latter rant and rage and break their gods in the approved manner but, once christened, become as gentle as the *douzepers.* The courtly love convention is not observed. Men and women behave naturally to one another; Floripas calls Guy 'My lord'; she is his equal in courage and in counsel, but as a lover he is the master. In this mixed material there are faults of treatment in the form of inconsistencies, especially when a traditional turn of subject conflicts with the author's general inclination to treat character on the human level. For instance, the Saracen king smashes his idols and forswears Mahounry in a moment of pique with his gods, but when Charlemagne captures him he prefers death to forsaking his religion. The first action comes from the convention; the second may come from the author's invention. But such inconsistency is simply evidence of an incomplete digestion of material which may in part have been caused by the very rapidity of the pace, and it does not seriously offend; it is glossed over by the remarkable energy to which this romance owes much of its effect. The author's whole creative power seems concentrated upon the simple account of events. He hardly ever pauses for description; his narrative is swift,

---

[1] See above, 15–16.

economical, heavily outlined, with no pauses for reflection, for every incident leads breathlessly to the next. But as a result of his conception of the story, out of this account the principal characters emerge as healthy, extrovert, full of life and remarkably young. Now and then there is buffoonery at the expense of the Saracens, but otherwise the tone is always sympathetic, and once or twice it rises to a heroic level. The effect of the whole is pleasantly cool, brisk and exciting, marked by an individuality wanting in the Bodley version.

The same rapidity of movement characterizes *Guy of Warwick*. This is a story reduced to its bare essentials of incident, without reflection, comment or criticism. One of the reasons for its great and prolonged success must lie in this fact, and in the consequent ease with which the uncomplicated action could pass through the laziest mind, stimulate it slightly, and immediately give place to another event. Such extravagant speed of movement is the product of a highly developed special skill. The author of the Cambridge version rises once to the creation of poetry when he describes Guy's knighting,[1] and his fluency is perhaps a shade more literary than that of the authors of the other versions, but all are well able to maintain control of the construction of this long story : all the versions are remarkable for dextrous compilation. The connexions between adventures are logical and probable within the subject ; one springs out of another, and the same characters as they reappear after long intervals conform to the impressions which they made in their earlier entrances. They are in fact well developed as far as their parts in the story are concerned. Even Guy's surprising renunciation of the world is fully motivated by mediæval standards. To make himself a worthy match for Felice he first pursued a career of adventure for pure glory. But as he achieved fame and greatness it came home to him how selfish were his motives, and how for the gratification of one man and one woman many men were killed. Yet God spared him. Now in gratitude for that divine forbearance he would renounce everything he had won, including the woman, and use his great strength and skill in arms only for others. It was this that he had

[1] ll. 387–422.

in mind when after the renunciation he was asked by a
Saracen king

> Whi artow þus iuel ydiȝt ?...
> A feble lord þou seruest, so þenkeþ me,

and answered in veiled language

> A wel gode lord [ar] þan serue[d] y :
> Wiþ him was no blame.
> Wel michel honour he me dede,
> And grete worþschipe in eueri stede,
> & sore ich haue him grame[d] ;
> And þerfore icham þus ydiȝt
> To cri him merci day & niȝt
> Til we be frendes same.   (Auchinleck vers. st. 85)

Rough this may be, and mediæval in the sense that the modern
world has largely discarded the concepts which it embodies.
But for all that its effect is the effect of the whole romance in
any of its versions, strong, vital and lofty in tone. No amount
of essentially improbable incident can destroy the principles
upon which the story of Guy of Warwick was founded,
the chivalry by which its personages govern their conduct, the
decent loyalty in keeping faith and friendship by which the
author clearly set great store, or the unremitting vigour of his
whole composition.

Two great ' historical ' romances, *Richard Cœur de Lion* [1]
and *The Life of Alisaunder* [2] (or *Kyng Alisaunder*) are as
strongly written as *Guy* or *Firumbras*, but find time occasionally
to linger and elaborate the developments of particular incidents
or to suggest effects additional to the simple narrative. The
two are very similar in tone and treatment, and it sometimes
looks as if one of them might be modelled upon the other. In
each case the cohesion of the story comes from the personality
of the hero, who is a compound of marvels, marvellously
begotten and born. *Richard Cœur de Lion* does not, however,
get far beyond this starting point, for not only the unity of
this romance but also most of its effects and its power to
interest comes from Richard's character, fierce, arrogant and

---

[1] Ed. H. Weber, *Metrical Romances* II (Edinburgh 1810).
[2] *Op. cit.* I.

over-impulsive, but decent, kind and passionately fair-minded. The romance has his qualities of violence, ardent patriotism and militant crusading fervour. Its nationalism, directed against all foreigners but most against the French, should be compared with that of *Guy of Warwick*, which is the partisanship of fiction, not related to actuality.

> Frensche men arn arwe and feynte . . .
> Whenne they sitte at the taverne
> Ther they be stoute and sterne
> Bostful wurdes for to crake
> And off her dedes yelping make . . .
> But when they come to the myster
> And see men begynne strokes dele
> Anon they ginne to turne her hele
> And gunne to drawen in her hornes
> As a snayl among the thornes—
> (*Richard* ll. 3821–37)

But the impulse which prompted these lines does not stop here where it might be no more than blustering ; it goes farther and deeper by reflecting a growing national strength, self-confidence and self-respect transferred from the plane of action to that of composition, and shows itself finely in the moment of the poem when the crusaders first see the Saracen forces :

> As snowgh lygges on the mountaynes
> Behelyd were hylles and playnes
> With hawberk bryghte and helmes clere.
> Off trumpes and off tabourere
> To here the noyse it was wundyr ;
> As though the world above and undyr
> Scholde falle, so ferde the soun. (ll. 5585–91)

Not a word of surprise or anxiety follows this sight, but simply

> Our Crystene men maden hem boun.

There is only one departure from this strong treatment, in Richard's intrigue with the King of Almayn's daughter, and that seems to have been introduced mainly to give him an opportunity of scoring off her father. Commonly violent feeling predominates, either on the national level against the

French or more generally against the enemies of Christendom. This violence, which appears to proceed from the author's conception of Richard's character and his relation to the circumstances of his reign, is the means by which the romance acquires unity of effect. The subject, strongly apprehended in these terms, is successfully communicated in a capable octosyllabic prosody which, at the cost of a certain liberty with rhyme, largely avoids inversion and padding.

In *Alisaunder* the unifying emotion is not aggressiveness but wonderment. Like the story of Troy, that of Alexander could as good as guarantee success by the glamour with which it was endowed. The present version has the look of having been written while the story of Alexander was still fresh and marvellous, and had not yet become ' so comune '. Its author has lost his heart to the hero, and is carried without flagging through an enormous, sprawling account of his life by his unfalteringly enthusiastic devotion to him. His faults, which are of structure, are directly related to his intention and material. He is determined to be inclusive in his treatment, but the four stages in Alexander's career, his birth and growth, his Persian wars, his Indian expedition and his *affaire* with Candace and death differ greatly not only in quality but also in value to the story-teller. They are by no means all equally interesting or important ; the second section has only one moment of excitement in thousands of lines and the last is trivial by comparison with the others. His account of Alexander's birth, however, is superior to that in the alliterative version, and the Indian expedition is more than simply a succession of Plinian marvels ; this author has made it into a story of lonely, frightened men venturing out against their better judgement beyond the edge of the known world. Perhaps one's acquaintance with Xenophon introduces an element of unfairness into the opinion that the section on the wars with Darius is dull ; although it is always energetic, graphic writing it understandably fails to equal a contemporary reporter's account in its hold upon the imagination. But even here, where the romance-writer's effects seem less good, it is evident that he took great pleasure in the magical contact with antiquity, and his enthusiasm for his subject, labouring to supply defects of knowledge, actually improves his technique and empowers it to create grand, spectacular effects. So Darius hears that the Greeks are coming :

> Darie the soudan, maister of kyng
> Is strongly anoied of this tidying.
> He is yset in a verger
> And with him mony a kayser,
> Alle of Jude into Mount Taryn
> And of Affrik, to the cite Garryn ;
> Ther was mony a sarsyn
> And long-berdet Barbaryn.
> Bytweone Tygre and Eufraten
> Saten alle this hethen men. (ll. 1918–27)

Let us not underestimate the load of associations, emotional and imaginative, which these lines and the names in them carried for the man who wrote them and saw in his imagination the picture of the Great King's assembly. All the material he handled was rare and exciting to him, and his communication of his response to it is still part of the persuasive power of his romance.

At times this romance reveals a distinctly poetic tendency, which is allowed most liberty in the verses by which the various sections are marked off. These verses, lyrical, gnomic and bucolic by turns like the illuminations in some books of hours, are commonly unrelated to the story, and are put without compunction not only to a mechanical but also to an external, decorative use :

> In tyme of heruest mery it is ynough ;
> Peres and apples hongeth on bough.
> The hayward bloweth mery his horne ;
> In eueryche felde ripe is corne ;
> The grapes hongen on the vyne.
> Swete is trewe loue and fyne. (ll. 5754–9) [1]

---

[1] See also ll. 139–44, 457–63, 796–801, 911–20, 1241–6, 1575–8, 1844–8, 2049–56, 2547–50, 2901–6, 3293–8, 4060–5, 4290–3, 4748–55, 5210–3. The same use is found in *Richard Cœur de Lion* ll. 3731–43. It is possible that such verses were meant to be sung in the intervals of reciting or reading aloud. Alternately they may, like similar passages in the alliterative romances, e.g. in *Sir Gawain and the Green Knight*, the *Morte Arthur*, *Seige of Jerusalem* and *The Gest Hystoriale of the Destruction of Troy*, have a rhetorical origin. In the alliterative poems the gnomic element is somewhat less common and there is generally more attempt to relate the passages in question to the story.

It cannot have been difficult to make pretty verses when, as here, their length and theme were unrestricted. But the same tendency to poetry is otherwise, if less clearly, reflected in sudden felicitous imagery, in attachment to richly circumstantial description, and in readiness to be imaginatively excited by anything spectacular. We must set against the faults of order and structure which the romance contains this quick imagination and its particular manifestation as an enthusiastic response to the ancient material.

Time and again the attempt to explain or understand the effect of a romance leads back to the relation of the author to his subject. In certain especially attractive romances, as we pass from the simplest to the more complicated kinds, this becomes increasingly apparent. Seven romances, *Lai la Freine*,[1] *Gamelyn*,[2] *King Horn*,[3] *Havelok*,[4] *Floris and Blaunche-flur*,[5] *Beues of Hamptoun* [6] and *William of Palerne*,[7] which differ widely in subject, treatment and technique, all have this in common, that despite undeniably serious faults of material, conception and execution, they possess to a very high degree the power of engaging not only the interest but also the sympathy and affection of the reader. The external means by which such attraction takes place are various and often hard to identify. The attraction of the romance for the reader seems to reflect an original attraction which its subject held for the author, and which was strong enough to survive his shortcomings as an artist, and to be communicated in his composition, again with sufficient force to make the reader overlook the technical faults of that composition. Some such attraction must probably be posited in all creative writing except hack work. Its exceptional quality in these seven romances, however, is the strength which makes it almost their principal feature, and the variety of forms which it assumes, all of a kind to have an emotional effect on the reader not

---

[1] Ed. H. Weber, *Metrical Romances* I (Edinburgh 1810).
[2] Ed. W. W. Skeat, *The Complete Works of Geoffrey Chaucer* IV and V (Oxford 1894 and ff.).
[3] Ed. J. Hall, *King Horn, A Middle English Romance* (Oxford 1901).
[4] EETS(ES) 4, ed. W. W. Skeat (London 1868).
[5] EETS 14, ed. J. R. Lumby, re-ed. G. H. McKnight (London 1901).
[6] EETS(ES) 46, 48, 65, ed. E. Koelbing (London 1885–94).
[7] EETS(ES) 1, ed. W. W. Skeat (London 1867).

limited by the passage of time and change of circumstances. An elementary example of this effect is afforded by *Lai la Freine*, a technically unremarkable little story of exposure and recognition which evidently attracted the author, and still appeals to the reader, by its simplification of the issues of life. In the world of this story offence is committed from a simple motive ; it is simply repented, readily forgiven. No memory of malice lingers after the forgiveness. The good ending erases evil, and the loser bears no resentment. This romance corresponds to the essential formula of escape fiction by its insistence on the fundamental ' good nature ', of life and attracts by reflecting the author's conception of this.

The attraction, revealed by an expression of the author's personality through his subject-matter or personages, takes a wide variety of forms. In *Floris and Blauncheflur* it consists in the reflection of the author's imaginative experience of the complete and single-minded love of the couple. In all other respects, except the whole-heartedness of this experience, the romance is disappointing. It recalls the story of Aucassin and Nicolette, but technically it is much inferior to the famous *chantefable*, for it wants both the narrative skill and the poetry of the French story. It is formless and rambling, and stylistically poor as well ; it is plainer and less poetic than the French version ; it fails to create any background to set off or enhance its central theme. Nevertheless that central theme is treated with assurance and judgement. The author seems to have been instinctively aware of the direction which his development of it should take. He was attracted, as anyone fenced in by the circumstances of reality is likely to be, by the opportunity for escape into a less restricted existence which the story of the abandon of the two lovers afforded. Perhaps instinctively he took pains to make such escape easier by avoiding the suggestion of any conflict between fantasy and actuality in the circumstances of his story. The lovers do not flaunt their selfishness, but simply ignore, as the reader must ignore, anything that ought to make them considerate of others. They never make an act of defiance of morality like that in which Aucassin expresses his preference for the splendid company of the damned, and thus avoid uncomfortable moral questions. They are blindly wanting in concern for anything but each other's love.

> Non oþer heuene hi ne bede
> Bute eure swich lif to lede.
> (Cambridge vers. ll. 553–4)

Despite its artistic shortcomings the romance conveys the strong attraction of this beautiful, amoral fantasy of love opposed by no considerations other than the physical obstacles which separate lovers.

The effect of *The Tale of Gamelyn* is a less rarefied, plainer and homelier one of unpolished, honest artlessness. This romance has no literary pretensions or courtly airs of any kind, and yet it gives an impression of quality. Its author thinks like a yeoman, with a yeoman's appreciation of all that goes to make up solid worth. He is violent in his opinions, for he is confident of his sense of values, violently anti-clerical, strong for the under-dog, passionately loyal to the king and fierce against the local oppressors who maladminister the king's justice. His own personality responds ingenuously to his material, and merges with it so that his characters convey his opinions in a lively, natural manner ; indeed the good dialogue that they speak is one of the more effective features of his story. His account of a successful struggle against oppression is made attractive finally by his own forthright honesty reflected in his treatment of every situation. Again he escapes, and draws the reader with him, into an easier world of simple motives and simplified issues.

Despite its setting in courts, *King Horn* is much less polished in structure and expression than *Gamelyn*. It has almost no technical merit, for its author had very little notion of trying for an effect but was sufficiently occupied with the exigencies of simply moving his story on. This story is loosely episodic, distorted by gratuitous duplication, inartistically expressed in a prosody which sometimes looks and possibly is incompetent. By no standards can *King Horn* be called great, yet it is decidedly attractive. It engages our sympathy and affection, and thus enables an imaginative surrender despite the absurdities which arise in it out of disregard for narrative structure and out of inadequate motivation, for it possesses a pleasing ingenuousness which indeed might not have survived a higher degree of literary cultivation, but is nevertheless distinct from the crudity of the execution. The attraction of this romance consists in being completely natural, first in reflecting the author's enthusiasm for the hero, then in its pleasure in the triumph of right, then in its description of a society where behaviour is open and direct, where action follows hard upon impulse and the emotions are not concealed behind a ritual of polite conventions. This simplicity of relationships which *King Horn* offers as its escape often shows itself openly, best perhaps in Rymenhild's wooing of Horn:

> An euen & amorewe
> For þe ich habbe sorewe
> Þat y haue no reste
> Ne slepe me ne lyste.
> Horn þou shalt wel swyþe
> Mi longe serewe lyþe;
> Þou shalt wyþoute striue
> Habbe me to wyue.
> Horn haue of me reuþe
> & plyht me þi treuþe,
>
> (Harleian vers. ll. 407–16)

or in the beautifully natural expression of gratitude which Horn addresses to the boat that saved his life, so primitive that it reads like an incantation:

> Nou ship by þe flode
> Haue dayes gode;
> By þe see brynke
> No water þe adrynke;
> Softe mote þou sterye
> Þat water þe ne derye.
>
> (Harleian vers. ll. 143–8)

Havelok the Dane resembles *King Horn* somewhat in the nature of its appeal, but is at the same time much less uncouth. The text has suffered scribal maltreatment, but still shows pretty clearly that the style of the original, though unadorned and homely, was mature and competent and reflected a well-defined attitude of the author to his subject. But the success of *Havelok* at engaging the interest and affection of the reader does not depend on any relative superiority of style. It comes from the author's evident attachment to his main character and his pleasure in contemplating the experiences of that character. Havelok, like Candide, is an example of the young man confronted with situations for which his experience has not prepared him, but which his personality enables him to meet and master successfully. Such a character, a tried device of story-telling, is perennially appealing, especially if, like Havelok, he is made further attractive by his diffidence. Much of Havelok's charm is due to the fact that he is never over-confident, or even fully sure of himself, and much of the appeal of the romance comes from the author's evident pleasure in this simple conception, the success of which is more than great enough to compensate for the somewhat obvious patterns of the story and the artistic shortcomings of its presentation.

In something of the same way *Beues of Hamptoun* has a better effect than its component material would seem to warrant, for this almost formless story, with its miracles and marvels, ranting Saracens and dragons, is told without any polish or skill in a style generously padded and tagged, with little sense of poetic or narrative art, and still the romance is more than merely readable. As with *Horn* and *Havelok* we tolerate its artistic crudity [1] for the sake of the company of the hero and the heroine, Beues and Iosiane, who reflect the warm humanity of the imagination that created them. Beues, whose adventures give the story such cohesion as it possesses, is wholly admirable without being a prig. The author knows too much to make him perfect, or even perfectly dignified ; once at least he touches him with ridicule, when Beues fights his way into the court where the villain rules who killed his father and married his mother, and that mother puts an end to his plans of rough justice by seizing hold of his ear. The suggestion of immaturity in this check seems to enhance the admirable qualities of Beues in the same way that Havelok's diffidence makes him a more attractive character. This treatment was probably instinctive in the author rather than

[1] For a remarkable exception to this general state, see above, 10–11.

calculated, but in either case it is part of his general good taste in all but literary matters, and his story, for all its acquiescence in every excess and absurdity to which the romances were addicted, is strong, clean and wholesome in effect.

The alliterative romance of *William of Palerne* differs from the six with which I group it in almost every respect except that it has to an even greater extent than any of them this characteristic of engaging the interest and affection of the reader. In artistic quality it is considerably above the average romance ; the narrative is conducted circumstantially, the characters are well developed, the author writes his own experience of life into his descriptions, and he uses a good, plain style of the alliterative long line with a freedom and skill that increase as he goes on. He gives plenty of evidence of the exercise of discrimination in the selection of detail, especially in electing to use as gracious ornaments some of the outward rituals of the courtly love convention while rejecting its fundamental principles of service and adultery. The greatest fault of *William of Palerne* is that one of the main circumstances of the story, the disguise of the bearskins assumed by William and Meliors in their flight, is an offence against simple physical probability so outrageous that by comparison with it even the benevolent werewolf who has so much to do with the development of the plot seems credible and acceptable. Precisely because this disguise is a physical improbability and not a supernatural one it is hard to swallow, for it can be tested, and the marvellous cannot. The concept of the disguise, and the predicaments which it conjures up in the imagination are ludicrous, undignified and indecorous to such an extent that they are capable of destroying the effectiveness of the story as such. Fortunately, however, *William of Palerne* relies for its effect less upon the story than upon the appeal of the breadth of humanity that it generally displays. For this reason it seems to have more sensibility, substance and dignity than the general run of the romances. Its characters expand under a painstakingly sensitive treatment that seems to spring from a happy and unembittered understanding of human nature. This pleasant wisdom shows itself particularly in the treatment of Melior's love for William ; her sense

of the risk she has taken in running away with him is finely
expressed, and her fear, when at length he recovers his inheritance and comes to greatness, that she will lose him now
that their hard times are over, is one of the finest pieces
of lover's psychology in the romances. The author reveals,
throughout the romance, a lively sense of proportion, by
developing little touches of the grotesque, especially applied
to William. It is conceivable that a keen sense of the ridiculous
on his part, turned to irony, is responsible for the acceptance
of the disguise theme which looks to us like his most serious
error of taste and judgement. Elsewhere his humour unmistakably acts as an element of balance. With all its improbabilities *William of Palerne* is enjoyable. It attracts by
its breadth, which ranges across human experience from a
sun-dappled glade where two lovers, having shaken off the
pursuit, hide for an idyllic interval, to the blank ruin of his
native Sicily that William finds when he comes home. This
romance contains work too good for its material.

At the opposite pole to these romances whose success is
emotional and is to be ascribed first to the temperament and
personality of the author and only secondly to his artistic
ability, there are five romances of great virtuosity in which
the relation between the technical ability displayed and the
evident artistic intention of the authors seems an unusual
one for the *genre*. These five works, all to a greater or a less
degree outside the normal tradition of the romances, can best
be described as curiosities.

Three of them, *The Awntyrs of Arthure at the Terne Wathe-*
leyne,[1] *Syre Gawene and the Carle of Carelyle* [1] and *The Jeaste*
of Syr Gawayne,[1] late minor developments of the Arthurian
legend, are distinguished by too much talent and too little art.
The virtuosity of *The Awntyrs* is the least remarkable, for it is
purely one of prosody. Its story is weak and meagre, and
scarcely begins to move in the first half of the romance. It
could be an imitation of *Sir Gawain and the Green Knight*,
but the point is hardly worth considering, for the story in
the *Awntyrs* hardly comes to matter at all; what holds the
attention for as long as it is held is the verbal resource
displayed in the use of its alliterative rhyming stanza. In

---

[1] Ed. F. Madden, *Syr Gawayne* (London 1839).

dialogue or in the static moments of the romance it practically smothers the sense ; even at its least objectionable, in description of action, it has a strong retarding effect, as in this hunting scene.

> Vndir þose bewes þay bade, þose beryns so bolde,
> To bekire at þose barrayne in bankis so bare ;
> Thay keste of þaire copills, in clyffes so calde ;
> They recomforthed þaire kenettis to kele þam of care ;
> Þare myght hirdmen, hendely forsothe, herdis byhalde,
> Herkyn huntynge with hornnes, in holtis so hare . . .
> With fresche hundis and felle, felonsly þay fare.
> > Þay questede and quellys
> > By frythis and fellis
> > Þat þe dere dwellys
> > & darkys and darys. (ll. 39–50)

It seems most probable that the author of this romance was conscious of the derivative nature of his story and felt compelled to make its treatment novel in at least one respect ; he contrived, however, to be original only in his excess. The thin little thread of narrative is soon lost among the masses of well ordered words ; their novel effect wears off, and only the boredom is left, for fear of which the author apparently strained his ingenuity so misguidedly in the first instance.

The two other Gawain romances are singular not in their style so much as in intention and effect. *Syre Gawene and the Carle of Carelyle* is a burlesque and principally remarkable as such. The attitude of the author of this romance to his subject is healthy, but the work itself is technically poor, cheap and coarse-fibred. The originality of treatment consists in making Gawain, Kay and Bishop Baldwin the under-dogs for once, powerless in the hands of an ' aluisch mon ' to whose whims they must conform. But aside from this unusual circumstance, which indeed is most fully developed by the adaptor, the romance has no merit. *The Jeaste of Syr Gawayne* is equally singular among English treatments of the Arthurian legend in showing Gawain as a profligate, the debaucher of a young girl, using the advantage of his superior prowess in arms to avoid getting his due from her kinsmen. The workmanship of this romance is merely ordinary, and the effect of

3

the innovation is discordant now as it probably was when it was made. The authors of these two romances have taken the grave step of departing from the traditional treatments of their subjects and have thus asserted their independence of judgement. The virtuosity of both works consists in the remarkable innovations, made without the aid of English models, which they represent.

The virtuosity of *Athelston*, however, consists in the violent character of the effect which it achieves. This striking and early romance, most vigorously and efficiently composed, depends for the turn of its story upon one of the least artistic, and at the same time commonest conventions of behaviour to be found in the romances, that a man must readily believe evil of those whom he ought to trust the most, however untrustworthy his informant may be. In *Athelston* the king listens to charges of treason made against one of his sworn brothers and then will neither let anyone stand surety for the accused man nor let him clear himself. With that artistic limitation the cruel story of the consequences is a most successful exercise in the horrific, consciously designed and deliberately achieved. It is as brutal as *Titus Andronicus* and more intensely effective because it is not made diffuse by rhetorical inflation. It is a terribly efficient romance, a masterpiece of concentrated effect, but that effect is horrific.

These romances are curiosities because the virtuosity of their authors was misapplied. Chaucer's *Sir Thopas* is also a curiosity, not indeed for this reason, but because the virtuosity with which it is composed derives from a unique understanding of the nature and quality of the popular romances, because while it parodies the romances it is in itself, as far as it goes, quite a normal one by the standards of *Torrent of Portyngale* or *Sir Eglamour of Artois*, and because it is so good as a parody that its superlative badness makes it almost unreadable. Few writers in the past have left to posterity so seemingly devastating a comment upon a contemporary literary form, and few have had such an effect, after the lapse of centuries, as Chaucer has here achieved, for *Sir Thopas*, however it was received in its own time, must have diminished many a modern student's ability to enjoy the romances by setting afoot an exaggerated notion of the extent to which the

absurdities that it parodies occur in them. Yet the issue is
by no means as simple as might seem to be the case, for clearly,
in order to have so fully at his command the material of this
literary kind, Chaucer must have had more than a superficial
acquaintance with it ; he must have steeped himself in the
romances and have read or listened to the worst as carefully
as the best.

The most cnclusive evidence of Chaucer's understanding
of the roma ices is possibly not those successful specimens
which he composed, but the six hundred lines of the fragmentary *Squire's Tale*. There are several possible explanations
of its unfinished condition. It may be Chaucer thought that,
as he had set out to treat it, the story would be too long for
his purpose ; possibly, by including so many threads in the
plot, he had set himself a task of unravelling too complicated
for his taste or his leisure ; possibly he ceased to be interested
in the material or amused by it. But one point is clear ;
Chaucer was here playing his game of transforming a literary
genre, not by changing its nature but by improving its use,
by heightening to the superlative degree its characteristic
qualities, and his method shows how perfectly he understood
these. He has made the setting as remote as was possible in
the world he knew, raised the splendour of the condition of
the characters to a fabulous level, suggested the richest and
most royal surroundings to be found in any romance, concentrated a wealth of marvel and magic in its short space, and
given this a distinct quality of novelty, and set the stage for
a love story not natural and straightforward but courtly and
dramatic. This heightening, evidently reflecting a desire to gain
effect by intensifying those qualities by which the romances
afforded an escape from reality, suggests not only that he had
studied their nature, but also that he accepted the *genre* as
legitimate, and as one in which artistic success was possible.

In conjunction with this evidence must be taken the fact
that the pilgrims who hear *Sir Thopas* do not know it for a
parody. The Host's criticisms of its ' lewedness ' and ' drasty
speche ' and ' drasty rymyng ' are quite off the point, for
technically it is very clever. From these considerations it
seems probable that within the framework of the *Canterbury
Tales* Chaucer intended *Sir Thopas* to stand as a romance,

but a very bad one. It is also probable that he gave no external clues to its parodic nature because the personal audience for which he intended that effect was capable of recognizing it for what it was without a key, and because, understanding the romances as a class of literature rather better than the modern scholars who have attempted to trace the allusions in *Sir Thopas*, he appreciated and sympathized with their purpose and intended no wholesale condemnation of the *genre* but only a caricature of its absurdities. I am sure he did not, when he composed *Sir Thopas*, care for the thought, if indeed he entertained it at all, that it might have an improving effect upon the subsequent development of the romances, but that he was primarily concerned with the pleasure he obtained from the exercise of virtuosity in assembling such a concentration of excesses of absurdities of subject, style and structure from the romances that scarcely a line of *Sir Thopas* fails to contain one of them.

It would not, however, do to take this riot of absurd reminiscence seriously as a romance ; indeed it is almost impossible to read, for the actual story is scarcely developed to the point where it begins to have meaning, and the allusions and echoes are a constant distraction. Doubtless the writing of *Sir Thopas* gave Chaucer all the pleasure which people with a gift of mimicry get from exercising their talent ; it may also be that his habit of irony moved him to intensify his enjoyment of the act of parody by keeping it to himself, and concealing the greater joke beneath the ostensible but lesser one of the poor figure he cuts as the teller. Meanwhile the technical brilliance of *Sir Thopas* cannot be overstated for, as a romance, it is so bad that only supreme craftsmanship could have produced it. It is, however, to be taken as a criticism not of the romances generally but of their more serious faults of conception and execution.

It is virtuosity, hardly to be compared with that displayed in *Sir Thopas*, but nevertheless appreciable, and also directed to good use, which distinguishes six striking romances, *The Gest Hystoriale of the Destruction of Troy*,[1] *The Siege of Jerusalem*,[2]

---

[1] EETS 39, 56, ed. G. A. Panton and D. Donaldson (London 1869, 1874).

[2] EETS 1d8, ed. E. Koelbing and M. Day (London 1931).

the *Alliterative Alexander Fragments*,[1] *The Seven Sages of Rome*,[2] *The Clerk's Tale of Griselda* and *The Man of Law's Tale of Constance*. In each of these, by a *tour de force*, exceptional talent has contrived to wrest some measure of success from unlikely material or to arrange material, in itself unexceptional, in a remarkable and successful way. In the alliterative poems the difficulty to be overcome was one of incongruity between the classical subject-matter and the equally ancient but vastly remote Germanic prosody; in the *Seven Sages* the problem of sustaining a succession of conflicting moral points by a series of *exempla* demanded great and unfailing ingenuity; in *Griselda* and *Constance* the author set out to treat on the human and dramatic level stories which were in the first place scarcely naturalistic, and in the second undramatic because they were based on ancient beliefs or legends from which all operative motives and explanations of conduct had been lost, and of which only the uncomprehended but traditionally fixed stories remained. In all these romances there is work of great brilliance which at moments approaches very near to complete success.

In the three alliterative poems this approach takes the form of an effect of singular richness that is the product of the application of a deliberate, leisured, reflective and recapitulative attitude of mind as well as medium to remote and incongruous material. That attitude seems partly to be induced by the prosody, for the Middle English alliterative long line has commonly the effect of bringing the writer's subject close up to his eye for minute examination. His presentation of detail can therefore, if he chooses, be prolonged and intimate, is with difficulty detached and made impartial, and is swift only when some kind of violence is implicit in the subject. We are accustomed to such a development of limited and local subjects, or subjects patriotically viewed, or to close studies of the single individual. But the employment of the alliterative long line for grand, remote and complicated themes has remarkable and often very fine results, which can have been produced only by a considerable effort of adjustment in which the virtuosity of the writers displays itself.

[1] EETS(ES) 1, 31, 47, ed. W. W. Skeat (London 1867, 1878, 1886).
[2] EETS 191, ed. K. Brunner (London 1932).

It would be too much to expect of the author of the *Gest Hystoriale* that he should have succeeded in making this adjustment with uniform success throughout the fourteen thousand lines of his work. Like most of the mediæval writers on Troy he laboured under an excessive reverence for his material which made him unwilling to shorten his account ; inevitably it is unremarkable in parts. He did, however, contrive by avoiding a wide or general treatment of his subject and by limiting himself to a single train of narrative, to indulge the tendencies of elaboration inherent in his medium. The effec. of this type of treatment upon the whole vast story is not altogether good, for in consequence the story itself fails to be well defined. But the good result of the indirect narration, the patterned embroidery of detail, is that the romance seems highly polished and cultured, artificial and formal, intensely rhetorical. Although these qualities can be stylistically explained, they probably owe as much of their origin to the author's conception of his subject, his sense of its importance, and the general nature of his response to it, as to the prosody he used. His formal descriptions [1] are carefully designed both to create a particular local effect and to heighten and magnify the whole work. His rhetoric is not always well calculated ; at times it is altogether too stilted ; twice at least it degenerates into gymnastics of prosody that defeat the purpose for which they were intended.[2] Nevertheless the predominant effect of the romance is one of a consciousness of the magnitude and antiquity of the subject expressed in a rich and elaborate treatment of detail.

The weaknesses of the author of the *Gest Hystoriale* consisted in obscuring his story by undue local elaboration, in an emotional response that expressed itself more in the superficialities of treatment than in any profounder artistic conception of his subject,[3] and in technical inadequacies as a result of which even his local effects are at times unsuccessful. The

---

[1] For example those at ll. 1055–63, 2732–9, 4029–41, 1629 ff. and 3019 ff.

[2] For instance, in the report of the returning embassy (ll. 2032 ff.) and in the catalogue of ships (ll. 4048 ff.).

[3] His description of Helen of Troy, for instance, is that of a rhetorician only (ll. 3019 ff.), and affords an interesting comparison with that of Iosiane in *Beues of Hamptoun* (see above, 10–11).

virtuosity of the author of the *Siege of Jerusalem* consisted in the mastery of details and small touches of communication, and in employing great resources of the alliterating vocabulary in their execution. His conception of his subject is curious ; out of ancient history he has made a close, personal, intensely partisan experience of which his treatment seems to emphasize the limited and local nature. We cannot deny him the right to transform his material in this way, but he is open to reproach for indulging in an excessive display of his linguistic and prosodic virtuosity of a kind incongruous with his subject. Inevitably the effect of his romance is confusingly mixed. His close attachment to his subject is evident and admirable, and one must sympathize with his desire to develop it in the richest and most elaborate manner that he could command. Unfortunately, however, the ornate quality of his language seems to transfer itself into the personalities of his main characters in the reader's mind, and thus although they speak strong and war-like words, they seem to have an old-maidish, fussy air when they ought to be most dignified. Titus and Vespasian as crusading Christian knights, brave and capable general officers speaking a stilted and precious language, a strong story weakened by excessive insistence on detail, these are the effects which mix to form the impression that this romance is an example of talent mis-directed and misspent. And yet, when we isolate the ex-pression of the romance from the subject which it sets out to communicate, our impression of the author's virtuosity is confirmed anew.

The Alliterative Alexander Fragments [1] are the most success-ful of the attempts at adjustment between ancient classical material and the alliterative long line. The effect of strange-ness produced by this combination of the flavour of classical antiquity with a restricted and regional mode is in their case an agreeable one. The adaptors (or adaptor) of the A and B fragments, to which *The Wars of Alexander*, fragment C is,

---

[1] The convention of the subject requires us to regard these as the vestiges of a romance. Their incomplete condition prevents us from considering the question of structure in them ; this limitation is, however, relatively unimportant because the original material would almost certainly have dictated the arrangement of the matter.

perhaps because of its subject, inferior, have shown good literary judgement in using their medium unobtrusively and soberly, but with a dignity and sense of importance befitting the subject. They avoided embroidery and elaboration and kept their writing, free from aspirations to poetic effects, on the level of competent narrative verse ; at the most they allowed it to light up once or twice with an austere Lucretian gleam.[1] Such effects are, however, less important than the general mastery of the subject matter, the grave, almost philosophical interest in this for its own sake, the judicious extraction of dramatic or spectacular effects from it, and the exceptional moderation in the use of a poetic medium inclined to extravagance which are displayed generally in these fragments and particularly in A and B.

The brilliance of *The Seven Sages of Rome* consists in its arrangement and design, and in the skilful manipulation of material of a wide variety of kinds so that it shall all make one single point. The work has no merits of expression ; its verse is unprepossessing, even threadbare, without polish or poetry or any kind of elegance. Probably there did once exist a version at least correctly versified, but just as probably the expression in that version was entirely plain and un-adorned. This material, however, needed no ornament. Its strength was in its point, and the success with which that point is made time and again makes *The Seven Sages* the highest literary development of the *exemplum* type in the Middle Ages. The author employed a situation in which a vacillating emperor is drawn two ways, by a deceitful and murderous wife, and by his seven wise counsellors. The issue at stake is whether his son, whom the empress hates, shall be executed on the ground of her accusations or not. The successive stories are told by the counsellors and by the woman for and against the boy respectively, the first purpose of the counsellors being to gain time and the second to dissuade the emperor from trusting his wife. This fiction is useful until the alterna-tion of arguments by *exempla* is under way ; the anxiety of the sages, sharpened by the woman's hatred, communicates itself to the reader. But soon he, like the emperor, begins to be less concerned with the boy's fate than with the next story.

[1] For example in *Alexander and Dindimus* ll. 922 ff.

' Let both the boy and the woman wait ; a good *raconteur* is worth more than either.'

> Quaþ þemperour, ' In alle maner
> þat ilche tale iche moste her '.

The woman's hatred and the emperor's weathercock mind are both no more than necessary machinery to set the story afoot and keep it moving. Even the conclusion is like a concession to a lower level of interest.

The stories were what mattered. The important element in an *exemplum* was the strength with which it made its point ; if this was not acutely driven home the story was nothing. *Exempia* used for religious teaching did not always fulfil this condition, for in their case it was too easy to invoke spiritual or moral laws to intensify their import. The stories in *The Seven Sages* can invoke no such external aid, for in most of them wrong or worldly wisdom triumphs, and the point which must emerge by their unaided efforts is ' Look how right has failed to prevail here ; see that it does not similarly fail in your case '. Wrong triumphs over obtuseness or complacency, and the consequences of that obtuseness or complacency are generally so final and overwhelming that they condemn it more than any formal reproof could have done. So morality is saved, and meanwhile there is opportunity for an extended display of knavery which is both praiseworthy, in view of the end which it serves, and at the same time exciting and interesting in the way that evil is— however deplorably—more exciting and interesting than good. Although the stories in *The Seven Sages* generally have aristocratic personages, they group themselves with the *fabliaux* in this respect, that the only ' moral ' principle upon which they rely is a hard shrewdness, and that their target is not so much vice as stupidity. The plan by which they are joined is ingenious but not quite convincingly carried out ; the virtuosity of *The Seven Sages* consists not in its execution but in its first conception as a means by which, without impropriety, the subject of the triumph of evil could be developed, and then in the complete and unfailing mastery of emphasis by which, in each of these stories, the point is made by no other means than the resources of the narrative itself.

3*

The Man of Law's Tale of Constance and *The Clerk's Tale of Griselda* display another kind of virtuosity than that of construction—a mastery of persuasive rhetorical and poetic craftsmanship to express an instinctively right poetic apprehension, as a result of which stories at best indifferent are treated in such a way that their inherent faults are minimized, or that the reader's attention is distracted from them. *The Man of Law's Tale* recounts a succession of miraculous preservations of the kind which, on the lower levels of *Octauian* or *Emare* stood out from the other contents of those romances as glaring improbabilities. The Constance story as Chaucer tells it depends entirely upon the credibility of these preservations for its existence. If Chaucer had failed to acknowledge this fact, or alternatively had placed too much emphasis on their sensational character, they would have offended not only the modern reader but doubtless also such of Chaucer's contemporaries as did not cultivate the purely extravagant for its own sake. The mastery of his treatment consists in two points. First, he neither denied nor emphasized the miraculous quality of Constance's two voyages, but explained them briefly, in the only possible way, as manifestations of a divine providence, in itself so remarkable that no single instance of its operation need give rise to wonderment. Then, having made this concession to probability, he proceeded to use every artistic device at his command to win attention over from the improbability of his story to its emotional quality. The tone of the narrative is one of extreme piety ; good and bad qualities are depicted with skilfully simplified exaggeration ; the pathetic element in Constance's character and experiences is kept constantly to the fore. Where this would not draw attention to the improbable the story is made circumstantial in order to give a sympathetic reality to Constance [1] ; where too much affectation of reality would be inadvisable, sonorous or highly pitched rhetorical devices are employed.

> I pray yow alle my labour to relesse—
> I may nat telle hir wo until tomorwe,
> I am so wery for to speke of sorwe. (ll. 1069–71)

---

[1] A good instance of this trick occurs at ll. 645 ff.

As a final inducement to the suspension of disbelief the verse is made as smooth and effortless as was within the author's power. Nothing is to stand in the way of the pathetic experience of observing

> So benigne a creature
> Falle in disese and in mysaventure. (ll. 615-16)

To speculate why Chaucer, who was evidently aware that as narrative this story was hardly convincing at any point, should have chosen to use it, does not belong to the present study. One inference, however, is tempting. Is it possible that Chaucer cared as much for the pleasure of exercising his gifts as for the works that these produced? He may have found that the challenge of a plot like that of the Constance legend was hard to resist, and may have enjoyed the struggle with its indifferent material. However that may be, it is correct to say that none of his considerable success with *The Man of Law's Tale* was inevitable or inherent in the material, and that he avoided failure in his treatment not by disguising the weakness of the story but by acknowledging it, developing it in the only possible direction which it allowed, and thus actually turning the story to artistic account.

Nevertheless the considerable effort which this undertaking required of him is evident in the lack of moderation generally which characterizes *The Man of Law's Tale*. Its tone is rhetorical and strenuous, its effect artificial, the human beings in it are distorted and unreal. This is not equally true of *The Clerk's Tale of Griselda*, which is told in a tone much more even and subdued. The improbability in *The Clerk's Tale*, although of another kind, is almost as great as that which governs the adventures of Constance, but while in the latter case a succession of incredible circumstances, beginning with the Sowdan's remarkable infatuation for a woman whom he has never seen and ending with a preposterous duplication of the first fantastic voyage, are all necessary to the action, in *The Clerk's Tale* one major improbability only, not of circumstance but of character, is essential to the plot, namely the capricious and wayward behaviour of the Marquess. That improbability is a very serious one of which Chaucer was well aware; in order to remove it he devoted the first thousand

lines of his story not to Griselda, whose submission is the
ostensible subject of the romance, but to Walter's character
and behaviour, and especially to his sudden, freakish impulse
to test a wife whom it was needless to try.

He attempts this task by two separate means, by suggesting
motivation and by the direction of emphasis. The first of
these is only moderately successful. Chaucer insists on
Walter's caprice, on the wilful and arbitrary impulses which
moved him to his three improbable actions of marrying a
woman of the people, concealing her identity from his subjects
and testing not her fidelity, which might have been understandable, but her submission. For this waywardness he
suggests two explanations which would actually be mutually
exclusive, first that Walter was a creature governed by
impulse and incapable of resisting the extravagant notion of
the moment, *But on his lust present was al his thoght* (line 80),
and that his conduct was accordingly irresponsible, and
secondly, that the testing proper was a kind of obsession
which he could not resist, and which fascinated him into acts
of cruelty that horrified him even while he was committing
them :

> But wel unnethes thilke word he spak
> But wente his wey, for routhe and for pitee.
>
> (ll. 892–3)

Chaucer was, however, probably instinctively aware that such
explanations could not be fully convincing, for he employed
also a much more successful device, both brilliant and
extremely simple, of changing the emphasis of the presentation from a naturalistic one in terms of motives to an ethical
one in which Walter's actions are not glossed over or minimized,
but are expressly judged and condemned. By examining the
morality of the Marquess's behaviour Chaucer avoids the
question why the man should have wished to act in such a
fashion at all :

> As for me I seye that yvele it sit
> To assaye a wyf whan that it is no nede,
> And putten hire in angwyssh and in drede.
>
> (ll. 460–2) [1]

---

[1] Cf. also ll. 621, 696–7, 785.

It is this dextrous shift of emphasis and not the half-hearted attempts at motivation which saves *The Clerk's Tale* from the failure with which the nature of its intractable old story, governed by the vestiges of long-forgotten folk-lore, threatened it. Moreover, the moralizing tone of the romance is doubly useful, for it fits the clerkly teller's character ; out of this aptness there develops an air of mingled authority and condemnation upon which the acceptance of the story finally rests. If this was achieved by design, then the whole scheme was indeed brilliant ; we accept the quite improbable story on the authority of its soberly formal narrator.

Brilliance is not, however, enough to guarantee the artistic success of a literary effort ; in addition there is needed not only that correspondence between purpose and achievement which conveys a sense of fulfilment in the artist and satisfaction in the reader, and some of that quality of universality which makes it unnecessary to apologize or make allowances for a work on historical grounds, but also a freedom from those signs of strain which show themselves when an artist's material has made excessive demands upon him, either because he has misunderstood it and is handling it improperly, or because it is intrinsically unsuited to use in the form in question. Any sign of such strain is inevitably detrimental to the effect of a work, whatever the author's gifts. It is then possible for genuinely successful romances to display less virtuosity and brilliance than is found in works which, because of faults of technique or mistakes of intention or material shortcomings, fall short of success. I have, for instance, consigned several of Chaucer's romances to the middle class which neither fully succeeds nor fails, and yet they contain immeasurably greater felicities of execution than can be found or matched in the writings of most other authors of the times. It is the whole effect which must be considered in judging a romance, and a work in which this effect is enhanced by a sense of the effortlessness that accompanies the tranquillity of fulfilment is to be preferred to one in which a conflict between the author and his subject or medium is evident, or is not fully resolved.

The Stanzaic Morte Arthur [1] is a case in point. Never once

---

[1] EETS(ES) 88, ed. J. D. Bruce (London 1903).

in its four thousand lines does it attain to brilliance, yet its effect is so unmistakably one of fulfilment and of harmony between intention and result that it must be regarded as a success. It is, however, the only one of the successful romances which does not succeed by more than just this quality of sober competence ; each of the others adds to this effect of completeness and fulfilment an impression of great talent profitably exercised. In *The Alliterative Morte Arthur* [1] and *Sir Gawain and the Green Knight* [2] there are further signs of greatness added to this sense of fulfilment and ease of achievement in the shape of a splendidly rich elaboration of imagery, as well as strength of both writing and conception ; in *Sir Perceval* [3] and *Ywain and Gawain* [4] and *Sir Orfeo* [5] there is a delicate fantasy of escape into a world of the imagination ; in *The Franklin's Tale of Dorigen* the human side of romantic fiction is expressed with unparalleled skill ; in *Sir Degrevant* [6] the originality and courage of the treatment of subject are fully justified by the result ; in *The Knight's Tale of Palamon and Arcite* and *The Squire of Low Degree* [7] there are two perfectly   complementary   idealizations   of   the   theme   of chivalry.   These exceptional features would not, however, be enough to make successful the effects of the romances in which they occur ; they must be founded upon a performance of unbroken strength which not only ensures a uniform and harmonious effect but also preserves the particular spell of each romance, whether this is simply belief suspended, or something more magical and marvellous than that.

The Stanzaic Morte Arthur then represents not so much the lowest as the simplest kind of success in the surviving romances. Its content is not original and generally retains the structural form which the material had before the adaptor took it in

---

[1] EETS 8, ed. E. Brock (London 1898).

[2] Ed. J. R. R. Tolkien and E. V. Gordon (Oxford 1936).

[3] Ed. J. O. Halliwell, *Thornton Romances* Camden Soc. 30 (London 1844).

[4] Ed. J. Ritson, *Ancient English Metrical Romances* I (London 1802).

[5] Ed. K. Sisam, *Fourteenth Century Prose and Verse* (Oxford 1933).

[6] Ed. J. O. Halliwell, *op. cit.* Since this study was made an edition has appeared by L. F. Casson, EETS 221 London 1949).

[7] Ed. J. Ritson, *Ancient English Metrical Romances* III (London 1802).

hand. Its medium is an alternately rhyming stanza of eight four-stress lines,[1] unremarkable in itself. In each of these apparently unexceptional features there is, however, an advantage to be discerned which may have played no small part in the success of the final whole effect. The traditional subject gives the romance the quality of a set piece ; it becomes a revisiting of tried familiar regions of the fancy, where the response and the enjoyment are assured by long and pleasurable association. Its predetermined narrative form frees the author from any anxieties about construction and allows him to concentrate them upon restatement. The stanza form, half-way, as it were, between the dangerous tail rhyme type and the simple octosyllabic, shares the good qualities and avoids the dangers of both, for its pace is steadier and stronger than that of the tail rhyme stanza, and it is more poetic by nature than the octosyllabic.

Out of these features emerges the quality of this romance ; it is a succession of related incidents from the fund of Arthurian story, selected with an eye to a particular effect, told in a tone chosen to support this effect and in a medium which well conveys it. As a quiet, allusive rather than explicit retreatment of an old story this romance is outstanding. By its delicacy of touch, by its practice of sketching rather than full drawing, by the lovely semi-lyrical flow of the stanza, and by a deliberate, artificial thinness of voice, it contrives to be what is very rare indeed in its *genre* in the Middle Ages— a romance with an effect very like that which Morris and Swinburne half imitated, half created to their own *ideas* of romance. This effect, uncommon and sustained, will not have been achieved by accident. The slow, unsubstantial, shadowy figures, who never complete themselves and yet haunt us, owe their existence to a special view of the legend both romantic and poetic. This *Morte Arthur* should properly not be compared with those parts of Malory's work which cover the same material, for the two are separated by a fundamental difference of conception. When the catastrophe comes at last, when their world topples about them, Malory's knights are bewildered to the point of frenzy ; they lash out like

---

[1] *abababab*, but the patterns *ababbaba* or *ababcbcb* also occur and there are some stanzas of less than eight lines.

maddened beasts, or like wounded Oliver at Roncesveaux,
or because it relieves them to strike. Their stature is great,
and as their civil wars were both raging and flamboyant so
their final piety is extreme. But such strength is not to be
found in *The Stanzaic Morte Arthur*. Its author seems to have
seen his subjects as plaintive, querulous failures refined only
by the spasmodic reawakening of chivalry in them. They
feel no sense of doom such as might have stirred them to
heroic greatness, and even no strong regret for the passing of
an age ; they are merely stung to irritability by a consciousness
of defeat and frustration.

Whether this view of the Arthurian close is a valid one or
not hardly matters here. The important point for us is the
steadiness with which it is maintained and expresses itself in
The Stanzaic Morte Arthur. It was the choice of its author to
see his subject in half-tones, and with no great stirring of
emotion. As the Maid of Ascalot lies dead Gawain remarks
of her :

> For sothe dethe was to vnhende
> Whan he wold thus fayre a thinge
> Thus yonge oute of the world do wend.
>
> (ll. 1001–3)

To call death *vnhende*, ' ungracious ', is perfectly typical not
only of Gawain but also of the poet's detachment and of the
terms by which he measures conduct. He sets great store by
the knightly attitudes and little by the sources from which
they originated. He is seldom deeply moved ; once only,
when the Maid of Ascalot is struck with love for Lancelot,
does he appear to share the emotion of the subject :

> Vp than Rose þat mayden stille
> And to hyr chamber wente she tho ;
> Downe vppon hir bedde she felle,
> That nighe hyr herte brast in two.
>
> (ll. 185–8)

This flush of warmth, the greatest in the poem, is only
momentary, and is kept in check throughout by caution and
restraint. Lancelot sees what has happened and follows her,

carefully taking her brother along to avoid compromising not the girl but himself :

> He satte hym downe for the maydens sake
> Vpon hyr bedde there she lay,
> Courtessely to hyr he spake
> For to comforte þat fayre may ;
> In hyr Armys she gan hym take
> And these wordis ganne she say :
> ' Sir, bot yif that ye it make,
> Saff my lyff no leche may '.   (ll. 193–200)

In response to this pathetic appeal Lancelot gives her what is undoubtedly the coldest comfort a man can give a woman : *For me ne giff the nothynge Ille*, ' You must not make yourself unhappy over me '.

Yet a *Morte Arthur* thus conceived and executed is neither disagreeable nor unsatisfactory. The many contradictions inherent in the accumulated material of the Arthur legend confuse the issues so completely in any case that no moral point of view could be consistently maintained with regard to it. The only possible conceptions will be artistic ones, and they will be determined, as was apparently the case here, by the quality of the effect which the material originally had upon the author, and by the nature of his response to it. In *The Stanzaic Morte Arthur* the effect and the response were romantic and melancholy ; they were also, which concerns our literary judgement of the romance more, successfully sustained throughout its length, and fully in harmony with the material as far as one can judge. The effect is then legitimately subdued, haunting and sad ; artistically it combines a rare detachment with its sense of *fin de siècle*.

No two treatments of a similar theme could differ more in intention, execution and effect than do *The Stanzaic* and *The Alliterative Morte Arthur*. In the latter there is no trace or suggestion of melancholy or defeat. It is written with the robust mentality of strong men who look back upon another age which was also strong. It is passionately attached and partisan where the stanzaic version is detached. Above all it is heroic, not romantic, and comes in its richness of treatment, its high seriousness and dignity, its stately splendour

of colour and imagery and its concept of its subject nearer to
the epic level than any of the other romances. Its success is
to be ascribed not merely to a satisfactory fulfilment of the
author's intention with regard to his material, but also to
various technical expressions of his genius.

He too has made the most of the advantage of dealing
with a known story by concentrating in his detailed development upon single incidents and merely sketching in the
prescribed arrangement by which these are connected. He
has assessed the value of the material with great discrimination
and distributed the emphasis among it in such a way that
almost every detail of his romance glorifies Arthur either
directly or by reflection. The principal means by which this
glorification is carried out is description. Applied to inanimate
objects the quality of this description is nearly as high as that
in *Sir Gawain and the Green Knight,* and when its subject is
action it is both stronger and less polished. It lacks the
delicate effect of *cloisonné* which in *Sir Gawain* seems to come
from the poet's especially clear and precise vision. But by
way of compensation the description in the *Morte Arthur* is
more robust and red-blooded, a little coarser in texture and a
great deal stronger. Both the description of the Green
Knight when he rides into Arthur's hall and of the giant
of the Mount are excellent of their respective kinds, but
that of the Green Knight does not induce the same
personal sense of mingled awe and horror as does that of
the giant :

> His fax and his foretoppe   was filterede togeders,
> And owte of his face fome   ane half fote large ;
> His frount and his forheuede,   alle was it ouer
> As the felle of a froske,   and fraknede it semede,
> Huke nebbyde as a hawke,   and a hore berde
> And herede to the hole eyghne   with hyngande browes ;
> Harske as a hunde fische,   hardly who so lukez
> So was the hyde of that hulke   hally al ouer. (ll. 1078–85)

An excess of strength and exuberance went into this kind of
description, and as a result it sometimes spreads and sprawls,
or goes on a shade too long ; but the great momentum carries
the reader over such rough passages. On the whole the

technique is well suited to the author's intention. The principal difference between this romance and *Sir Gawain and the Green Knight* is, however, to be explained in terms not of technique of detail but of the relative sizes of the two subjects. That of the *Morte Arthur* is large, multiplex, European, designedly scaled to the heroic size, and in consequence treated with less intimacy and more detachment than the close, limited and personal theme of *Sir Gawain*.

The heroic tone of *The Alliterative Morte Arthur* is set and sustained with more delicacy than these remarks might suggest. Its combination of manliness and sensibility is indicated in the description of Arthur's ride along the river bank with his companions on the way to fight the giant of St. Michael's Mount.[1] A suggestion of roughness, possibly not artless, is present in this description to enable the practical man with no time for poetry, the huntsman and the wildfowler to enjoy it without embarrassment or sense of a sacrifice of decorum, and yet the emotional effect is one of not only whole-hearted enjoyment but also understanding appreciation of Nature.

In proper heroic circumstances this poet shows his emotion without embarrassment or restraint. Some of it will be lost upon us because of the weakening and disappearance of associations with time ; for instance, our response to the suggestion in a knightly pedigree ' of Alexandire blode, ouerlynge of kynges ' is very unlikely to resemble that of a poet and a public whose passion for associating themselves with antiquity made such words a strong evocative symbol

---

[1] ll. 920–32.

Thane they roode by that ryuer,　that rynnyd so swythe
Thare the ryndez ouerrechez　with realle bowghez.
The roo and the raynedere　reklesse thare ronnene,
In ranez and in rosers　to ryotte thame seluene ;
The frithez ware floreschte　with flourez fulle many,
Wyth fawcouns and fesantez　of ferlyche hewez ;
Alle the feulez thare fleschez,　that flyez with wengez,
ffore thare galede the gowke　one greuez fulle lowde,
Wyth alkyne gladchipe　thay gladdene theme seluene ;
Of the nyghtgale notez　the noisez was swette,
They threpide wyth the throstilles,　thre hundreth at ones !
That whate swowynge of watyre,　and syngynge of byrdez
It myghte salue hyme of sore,　that sounde was neuere.

for them.   But the material more common to past and present,
the more active expressions of noble and knightly conduct,
can still move us.   Some of these, in the *Morte Arthur*, are
highly dramatic.   As Arthur's party is hard-pressed in the
last battle a young knight, Sir Idrus, while he fights in the
king's bodyguard, sees his father being borne down some
distance away but refuses to leave Arthur's side and go to the
aid of the man who, he protests, himself

> Commande me kyndly   with knyghtly wordes
> That I schulde lelely one the lenge,   and one noo lede elles ;
> I salle hys commandement holde,   ȝif Criste wil me thole !
> He es eldare thane I,   and ende salle we bothene ;
> He salle ferkke before,   and I salle come aftyre.
>
> (ll. 4148–52)

The wry callousness of the last two lines here is not a super-
fluous conceit but a sign of the poet's own deep response to
the situation and character he has created, ironic because
that character professes to dismiss emotion when emotion is
at its strongest.   The situation belongs to the standard
pattern of heroic poetry in which a man is torn between two
loyalties and makes his choice only at great cost.

On occasions when the drawing of characters to the heroic
scale is combined with great emotional issues, the effect of the
poem becomes magnificently spectacular and dramatic.   The
highest moment of this kind is the death of Gawain in that
same last battle.   Gawain and Modred fight and Gawain gets
the better of his opponent ; he beats him down and falls upon
him to unlace his gorget and cut his throat and end all Arthur's
troubles.

> He schokkes owtte a schorte knyfe   schethede with siluere
> And scholde haue slottede hyme in   bot no slytte happenede ;
> His hand sleppid and slode   o slante one the mayles
> And the tother slely   slynges hym vndire :
> With a trenchande knyfe   the traytoure hym hyttes.
>
> (ll. 3852–6)

Thus Gawain dies.   A Frisian adventurer in Modred's company
asks who the dead man was and Modred himself, raised

momentarily to the heroic stature of his victim, gives him a fine tribute ; then

That traytour alls tite   teris lete he falle,
Turnes hym furthe tite,   and talkes no more,
Went wepand awaye,   and weries the stowndys
That euer his werdes ware wroghte   siche wandrethe to wyrke :
Whene he thoghte on this thynge,   it thirllede his herte ;
ffor sake of his sybb blode   sygheande he rydys ;
When that renayede renke   remembirde hym seluene
Of reuerence and ryotes   of the Rownde Table
He remyd and repent hyme   of alle his rewthe werkes.

(ll. 3886–94)

The fine fatality of this encounter, and the manner in which Gawain dead had more power than Gawain living to turn Modred from his purpose, is part of the climax of destruction, the heroic calamity to which this poem rises. At the same time the tone of the closing episodes is strong and sound ; the world will not end nor will England perish when Arthur dies, although many men will grieve for him. The whole of *The Alliterative Morte Arthur* is sustained by the strength from which that healthy state of mind derives. From the first line to the last it is alive with its author's uncomplicated and enthusiastic response to his material, it is made swift and compelling by the force of his expression, and enriched with pageantry by his pictorial talent. In the end the effect is heroic as it is in none of the other romances.

Sir Gawain and the Green Knight, related in tradition of both subject and medium to *The Alliterative Morte Arthur*, differs from it in almost every feature of its effect. In *Sir Gawain*, Arthur's court is set not on the edge of a Europe he will conquer but on the frontiers of Faery ; its subject is not the rise and fall of a great kingship but one single man's adventure, its medium not bold and free but comparatively restrained and trimmed, with a more strenuously disciplined prosody. In consequence *Sir Gawain* is never heroic as the *Morte Arthur* is heroic. Gawain is a brave knight and a true one, but his stature in the romance that belongs to him is less than that in the larger work where he must share the room. His adventures with the Green Knight are essentially of no great moment, both because little more than his own life could hang upon their outcome and also because that outcome can never really be in doubt ; even the simplest fourteenth-century listener must have known that Gawain could not actually lose his head in *this* affair. By way of compensation the finer and more cultivated technique of *Sir Gawain* has protected it against a too rough exuberance, given it elegance and polish not to be found in the *Morte Arthur*, and prevented the tendencies to luxuriance in the alliterative prosody from obscuring the plan.

Technically, in fact, *Sir Gawain* comes very near to the perfection of mediæval poetry as it occurs in the romances. Even the substitution of interest in the method of the *dénouement* for anxiety about the outcome contributes to this triumph, for it directs the author in his treatment to magnify his material to a size where it conveys a pictorial impression of a most unusual clarity. In large measure the success of this effect is also due to his exceptional powers of description ; he seems to outline every action or object clearly and to endow each picture, as it strikes the mind's eye, with a special distinctness, so that the effect of all is extremely vivid. In consequence the mind is not readily wearied in reading this romance ; the clarity of succeeding impressions seems to refresh the reader instead of exhausting his straining imagination as do the diffuse and ill-defined impressions created in some other romances.

The visual quality of *Sir Gawain* is of crucial importance to the necessary harmonization of two elements in its story, the everyday, human and dramatic one, and the formal, conventional one of magic. It is a fair inference from the treatment that the author found the rôle of the latter in the plot not greatly to his taste, for he scarcely developed Bercilak's enchantment by Morgne la Fay, or her motive in setting afoot the beheading challenge. Wherever, in fact, the magic influenced the conduct of the plot he treated it very quietly. Nevertheless it was absolutely necessary to the story and had somehow to be made convincing ; the author acknowledged this commitment, and fulfilled it by developing with the whole of his power as an artist not its function in the plot but its effect upon the minds of the people who are in contact with it. His success with this begging of the question is considerable ; nowhere else in the romances is the sense of uneasy fear of the supernatural as clearly and convincingly conveyed to the eye of the imagination as in the moment when the Green Knight gropes for his head among the feet of the bystanders who have just been kicking it about, or for that matter in the panic tangle of reasons to which Gawain appeals in refusing the importunate lady, not one of which would in fact have preserved him when it came to the point.[1] By hiding the necessary but embarrassingly improbable cause behind the vividly and pictorially perceptible and therefore credible effect, the author won acceptance for his material, satisfied his own acute sense of the probable, and to a large extent smoothed over the inevitable discrepancies between old conventional motifs and the naturalistic and human treatment of the subject which he preferred.

The only alternative to this treatment would have been to present the story entirely in the conventional manner as an artificial offshoot of the Arthurian legend in which the action was directed not by human motives but by the almost incomprehensible vestiges of ancient myths and rituals. Once the difficulty was overcome, however, and the means of making the story credible were devised, then the measures of expediency which constituted those means could themselves be cultivated for the sake of art, and the poet could hang upon his account circumstantial details which sped, not slowed it, while at the same time they increased the impression of reality conveyed. Thus these circumstantial details, the full and exact descriptions in which this poet revels, not only serve the vital purpose of supporting the less credible parts of the actual story but also become a pleasurable end in themselves for him. Not only does he, by their means, raise a story which, although dependent upon fewer improbabilities numerically than the average romance, is nevertheless far from credible, to a level where the mastery of treatment is such that it makes the general narrative less important than the particular incident before us at the moment. In addition,

---

[1] Gawain, the poet tells us, is saved from temptation not by the half-hearted mixture of expeditiousness and principle in his mind at the time, but by Mary whose knight he is. See line 1769, also 644 ff.

with his pictorial gift he develops a technique that achieves one of the main objects of the romance kind by conveying the idealization, not exaggeration or distortion of real life : the lavish setting of gold and silver and the filigree of both, and precious stones, against backgrounds of rich Eastern stuffs, the fine tall men and the women, none of whom is plain or ordinary unless she be hideous, the never-failing courage put in doubt only to be subsequently reaffirmed—in short, the full escape into the world of fantasy made at the same time to seem unlike an evasion by the presence of enough—but only enough—of the plain circumstances of life, the driving sleet on Gawain's journey, the fatigue of his charger, the misery of sleeping out in armour, the brightness of blood on snow. Every feature of this poet's success derives in the end from his instinct for the picturesque, the fine talent for seeing and describing which he possessed, and the discrimination in selection which he exercised. The men, the objects and the observations he puts into his romance have outgrown the story which was his subject ; their vivid imaginative existence is hardly due to this at all, but is the entire product of his fancy, just as the coherence, the good order and the decent limits of his subject were imposed by his taste. *Sir Gawain and the Green Knight* is remarkable for the small contribution made by the story and material to its success, and for the extent of the transformation of that material by the poet's imagination ; his brilliant achievement enriches the Arthurian legend in England.

In *Sir Gawain* the success comes principally from the poet's remarkable visualization of the action and setting of his story, and only to a lesser extent from the conceptions of conduct upon which the characters act. These are, to be sure, noble and gracious enough, and reflect a good knowledge of human behaviour, but beyond the degree to which they are heightened there is nothing particularly remarkable about them. The exceptional success of this romance comes from other sources than the principles of behaviour upon which its action is based.

Sir Perceval of Galles does, however, succeed in transporting the reader into a world of fantasy by developing an idea of behaviour delicately conceived and executed. The story is that of ' the young man slowly wise ' which has been variously developed in European literature by being given a religious and symbolical meaning in *Parzifal*, a satirical turn in *Candide*, and an idyllically naughty one in the *Daphnis and Chloe* of Longus. *Sir Perceval* is neither as profoundly and sonorously spiritual as the first, nor as disillusioned as the second nor as sportive as the third, but is distinguished principally by the author's constantly evident, sensitively humorous sympathy both for Perceval and for those wiser but sometimes less agreeable characters upon whom his *gaucheries* impinge. This sympathy and humour, and the impression of a humanely understanding author which they convey, are reflected in the tone, which is neither solemn nor flippant but gentle, kindly, and tinged throughout with ironic wisdom.

In consequence the story, told swiftly and gracefully, with considerable assurance, in a thin, lovely, half-laughing, half-lyrical strain, is a perfect escape into the ' golden world ', for it neither quite rejects the real one nor embraces that of the fantasy with too uncritical a readiness. It is in fact entirely mature even when most a romance. It can be no criticism of *Sir Perceval* to observe that it fails to achieve the greatness of *Parzifal* ; the intention in the English romance was quite a different one, and its author would probably have been most uncomfortable in the maudlin and mystical atmosphere of the German work, which, to the unsympathetic eye, could quite easily appear a welter of sentimental symbolism. If he had a philosophy it was simply to love mankind while he gently mocked all those outward forms of the knightly life by which the wild boy set such great if unthinking store, and which he occasionally failed to observe. ' Look ', says the author in effect, ' at Innocence confronted with the conventions ! '

Technically *Sir Perceval* is competent. The actual medium is a light, rapid, tail rhyme stanza, and the language that of the popular romances used with remarkable efficiency. There is a minimum of inversion and padding, and the verses generally seem to slip effortlessly into the rhymes. The expression into which these elements are shaped is simple, direct and graceful.

The slow revelation of Perceval's identity to those with whom he comes into contact, and the gradual fulfilment of undertakings which last the length of the story, preserve interest and act as unifying factors despite a certain disproportion in the elaboration of the material. The author's good sense of a dramatic situation encourages him to develop individual incidents to advantage, but even if he devotes to some of them more attention than the story warrants, he never fails to keep before us the principal unifying element of the romance, the development of the boy's personality. At his first appearance Perceval wins our interest and affection, and as our concern for him grows it takes the place of suspense about the outcome of his adventures.

It is not easy, either by analysing this romance to discover what elements have gone into its making, or, by reciting and insisting upon its excellences, to convey a just idea of the peculiar attraction which it exercises. Indeed the whole romance is so even in quality, and the language is everywhere so subservient to the content, that it is almost impossible to disengage passages for quotation. Probably the simplest explanation is the truest, that while the quality of technical execution of this romance is high it is also unobtrusive and never thrusts itself upon the reader, and that meanwhile the success of the romance is principally due to the great affection which the author evidently had for his subject, and to the manner in which this affection qualified his treatment by informing it with grace, wisdom and a humorous but delicate sympathy.

The success of *Ywain and Gawain* consists in the lovely spell which it creates. It has no moments of tedium, and no shortcomings as a romance. It never stumbles or pauses too long, but continues throughout its length with a graceful motion in verse which has an unwavering effect of lightly touched music. Here, 'more perfectly than in any other surviving example, the modern *idea* of the romance [1] is fulfilled. The subject is at once both original and typical, the movement of both story and medium is easy, gentle and smooth, and the effect is as magical as we would expect to find it in the perfect specimen. In *Sir Perceval* the spell was one created by the impression of a personality ; here it is the result of

[1] This is discussed by Dorothy Everett, ' A Characterization of the English Medieval Romances ', 104 ff.

treating a fantastic subject with great artistic sensitivity. Indeed that ability is hardly remarkable in view of the identity of the author of the original, but Chrétien was also lucky in a translator who saved much of the flavour of what lay under his hand. The perfect fluency of *Ywain and Gawain* bespeaks considerable literary skill, not only experienced and self-possessed but also well-bred enough to avoid both the pretentious vulgarities of over-adornment and the ignorant ones of meanness. The strongest quality of the writing in this romance is its constant appropriateness.

At the same time that it possesses these high technical distinctions, *Ywain and Gawain* has more substance than would be necessary for simple entertainment. The purpose of entertainment was certainly a real one to the author ; Ywain's adventures are knit into most ingenious sets of circumstances from which he is extricated, after considerable suspense, only by skilfully invented devices like the two separate sets of argument by which Lunet reconciles him to her mistress ; at the same time, however, the characters, lightly sketched and plausibly conceived, are also symbols designed to glorify knighthood in its most abstract and idealized conception. It is to fulfil this symbolism that Gawain figures in the romance, and fights Ywain.[1] Ywain has adventures with two sorts of enemies : he fights either knights as highly principled as himself whom circumstances or misunderstandings have made his enemies, or he fights ruffians who, whether giants or churls or false stewards, use unknightly weapons and fight unfairly in twos and threes against him. With these latter he cannot come to terms ; he destroys them, and on each victorious occasion he frees prisoners or rescues maidens— puts an end, in fact, to evil forces and to their malignant effect. The lion who aids him in such battles can on this level of interpretation be a symbol of the courage he discovers in himself on occasions when it seems impossible to win, at the same time as it is the grateful beast he has rescued, and able to discern and give due honour to royal blood. When Ywain fights against true knights, however, no such evil factor is

[1] On symbolism in the French romances see, for example, E. Vinaver, *The Works of Sir Thomas Malory* (Oxford 1947), lix–lxxxv, especially lxiv–lxvii.

involved, and he must actually make amends for killing the lord whose wife he himself marries, although they were made to fight by the compulsion of magic. When he finds himself at odds with Gawain, his friend and cousin and peer, over a quarrel that concerns neither of them, they fight long and hard but neither can beat the other down. True knightliness admits no superior, the poet is saying here, and with the assurance of this he is able to make each of the two, when he learns the identity of his opponent, eager to own himself beaten by his friend.

The presence of this symbolism shows clearly upon analysis, but what is not quite so clear is the precise need for it here. Most probably it grew first from the author's devotion to all persons and actions chivalrous, generous or courteous, which he desired to glorify. It makes, however, an indirect and perhaps unintended contribution to the effect of the romance by strengthening the story and by saving it from the suggestion of triviality. At the same time this symbolism, attached to the chivalric qualities in the principal characters, endows these otherwise simple figures with a sense of unexpressed significance that makes them harmonize with the subdued, subtle and magic-laden background. Indeed the whole workmanship of *Ywain and Gawain* is smoothly directed to maintaining the spell which this romance casts from the first moment of the suspension of disbelief. That spell is also remarkable in this sense that, although it is unique in its nature among the English romances it nevertheless carries the suggestion that here we have the true and ideal effect of the romance kind. Differences spring to mind at once—the lavish effect of *Partonope*, created in part by the use of splendid Byzantine magical machinery, the dangerous faery world of *Sir Orfeo*, probable and credible despite the crudities of technique in that romance. But possibly the explanation is that *Ywain and Gawain* answers to an *idea* of the romance by its relative freedom from the faults of many of the other outstanding specimens, for its faint, gentle and yet unfailing magic comes principally from the sureness of touch and taste with which it is presented.

The spell of the faery world of *Sir Orfeo* has much more vitality ; indeed, if this were not the case, the technical shortcomings of the romance might deny it success. Superficially it is a strange mixture of moments of great roughness or banality and moments of sensitivity. None of its faults is serious, but their number is not small, and it would not be hard to find resemblances between the expression in *Sir Orfeo* and that in some of the notable failures among the romances. However, the power of *Sir Orfeo* to win the suspension of disbelief is apparently not dependent upon technicalities of expression, but exists without reference to such faults, and can dazzle the reader, as it were, out of seeing them. Indeed no other romance conveys so strong an impression of contact with another existence older, colder and less happy than our own, sinister in the chill of its beauty, and able to ' take ', that is to lay its compulsion upon mortals in their unguarded moments.[1] The success of *Sir Orfeo* comes partly from this sense of contact which heightens the imaginative tension, partly from the victory of the warm world of flesh and blood over faery which Orfeo's recovery of his wife constitutes, and partly from the simple clarity of the issue by which the mortal characters in the romance are made good and loyal while a boundless suggestion of unexplored evil is ascribed to the other world and its inhabitants. The beginning of this contrast, and of the conflict as well, is the author's ability to develop and maintain the sense of contact with faery which, either by its direct effect on the story, or by the suspense it creates, or by the sense of liberation and relief that we feel when it is dispelled, makes an essential contribution to the success of the work.

He builds this effect up slowly over half the length of the romance. The first suggestion of it appears in the mention of the time when those other-world people can ' take ', an ' vndrentide '

> In þe comessing of May
> When miri and hot is þe day ; (ll. 57–8)

in such a perilous moment Queen Heurodis goes out into an

---

[1] As far as the Wife of Bath was concerned this world of faery was a fable. But there were men of the Middle Ages who either believed in it, or held it a fable worth believing and maintaining. Cf. Maistre Wace, *Roman de Rou et des Ducs de Normandie*, ed. H. Andersen (Heilbronn 1879), ll. 6409–20, and Giraldus Cambrensis, *Itinerarium Kambriae* Liber I, Cap. VIII (Rolls Series 1868, *Giraldi Cambrensi Opera* vi, 75 ff.).

orchard to sleep, and disaster overtakes her, for when she
awakens she is nearer mad than sane :

> Euer sche held in o cri
> And wold vp and owy. (ll. 95–6)

When Orfeo learns that she has been marked for taking he
determines to keep her by force of arms, although she tells
him that this will be no use, and so it proves :

> Amiddes hem ful riȝt
> Þe quen was oway ytuiȝt,
> Wiþ fairi forþ ynome ;
> Men wist neuer wher sche was bicome. (ll. 191–4)

Gradually, from the suggestion to the threat, and thence to
the action, the impression of imminent evil has grown.
Orfeo has now felt the power of this hostile race, and its
strength is signified in his condition after Heurodis disappears.
But although it is evil it is also beautiful ; its fascination
introduces bright poetry into Orfeo's wanderings far from the
habitations of men, when he comes to see

> Oft in hot vndertides
> Þe king o fairy wiþ his rout
> Com to hunt him al about,
> Wiþ dim cri and bloweing ;
> And houndes also wiþ him berking ;
> Ac no best þai no nome,
> No neuer he nist whider þai bicome.
> And oþer while he miȝt him se
> As a gret ost bi him te
> Wele atourned ten hundred kniȝtes,
> Ich yarmed to his riȝtes,
> Of countenaunce stout and fers,
> Wiþ mani desplaid baners,
> And ich his swerd ydrawe hold,
> Ac neuer he nist whider þai wold.
> And oþer while he seiȝe oþer þing :
> Kniȝtes and leuedis com daunceing
> In queynt atire, gisely,
> Queynt pas and softly ;
> Tabours and trunpes ȝede hem bi
> And al maner menstraci. (ll. 282–302)

Even to the modern imagination this is effective ; it must have been full of uncanny suggestion for a mediæval audience, a vivid and alarming picture of creatures not quite the same as mortal men, whose hunting noises are ' dim cri and bloweing ', who dance ' Queynt pas and softly ', who marshal their armed knights only for show, and who lack the power to take life. To this picture there is added a suggestion of the envy of these creatures for ordinary human beings, and the reason why they take them ; the mysterious huntsman cannot kill, but the

> Sexti leuedis . . .
> Gentil and iolif as brid on ris,

the mortal women who have been carried off, never fail when they cast their hawks at waterfowl.

As Orfeo follows this party of ladies into the other-world the sense of danger mounts again ; it is confirmed, and the mask of beauty is stripped from faery when in the courtyard of the palace Orfeo sees a horror, the figures of the taken mortals in the attitudes of their moments of capture. Now the open conflict between Orfeo and the evil forces begins ; he emerges victorious when he rebukes the king for failing to honour his promise :

> ʒete were it a wele fouler þing
> To here a lesing of þi mouþe . . .
> Nedes þou most þi word hold. (ll. 464–8)

At this moment the power and the spell of faery break, the evil beauty finally falls away, and thereafter a sense of relief from anxiety and oppressiveness, of *blitheness* in the mediæval sense of the word develops in the romance until it reaches its climax in the final recognition of Orfeo.

A most gifted artist has been engaged upon *Sir Orfeo*, who has used the popular elements to great advantage, and with an understanding of artistic possibilities not generally brought to bear upon them. He has quite transformed the classical subject ; there is no critical point in comparing his story with the Ovidian account, for it differs now in kind, and of its kind it is very good. The success of the romance depends upon the presence of the faery element in it, but that element is never other than a servant to the general effect of the work ; it is important only as it affects Orfeo and his party. The peril of the other-world mounts and threatens until the moment when Orfeo wins back his wife ; then its absence is a relief which continues to be felt until the end. From the extent of that relief we can discover how uncannily strong it was. But the spell of *Sir Orfeo* is the fascination of the danger from that world and the conflict with it, rather than of a romantic escape into it.

In *Sir Perceval, Ywain and Gawain* and *Sir Orfeo* the comparative simplicity of the treatment makes the invitation to an escape into fantasy direct and uncomplicated. Its nature differs in each case, but the effects of the three romances are alike in possessing a quality of unsubstantiality which seems to originate not so much in the subjects, or even in the improbability of the stories, as in the single, simple intention of each author to produce one particular effect and to interpret all his material in terms of this effect. It is the fulfilment of this intention which is primarily responsible for the success of these stories, and their setting in the land of romance, or the magic and marvels upon which their plots depend, are in reality incidental and contributory features.

In this respect these romances invite comparison with *The Franklin's Tale of Dorigen* which contrives to succeed as a romance despite the apparent absence of such a simple intention. In every respect except its plot *The Franklin's Tale* is the last word in the cultivated literature of the fourteenth century. The expression is as highly polished as that of any of Chaucer's writing, and highly artificial at the same time, for scarcely a line of this romance wants the mark of the rhetorician's art. *Amour courtois* is developed in a manner calculated to appeal to both courtly and bourgeois taste ; [1] two *compleyntes* are included in the text for poetic colouring, and one of these contains an imposing collection of *exempla*. The characters are finely and richly drawn, and the splendour of the setting in which they move is repeatedly suggested. There is, in fact, no thing or person in this romance where

[1] See, for example, ll. 792 ff., 922.

meanness of any kind might be discerned ; the personages, the material objects, and the writing are made to appear as quietly perfect as the author can devise. As if to complete this *embarras de richesse* he raises the fashionable issue of *maistrie*, of sovereignty in marriage, and finally puts the question to which the romance gives rise for debate in the best manner. Indeed it seems from his own attitude to *The Franklin's Tale* that Chaucer was proud of his achievement in these respects.[1]

But all this rhetoric and fashionable conventionality and the repeated departures from the simple strain of the story which it involved might easily have smothered the delicate spirit by which this romance lives and succeeds in obtaining the willing suspension of our disbelief. Cultured and cosmopolitan and touched with the Petrarcan renaissance though *The Franklin's Tale* may be, its undoubted success comes not at all from these qualities, but from what by the nature of the plot must be the first and most natural and the simplest feature of the story, the essential fineness of character, which we would call decency, of Arveragus and Dorigen. To Chaucer the development of this quality in them may have seemed simply an obvious and necessary part of his work, a secondary effect as it were. Yet the dilemma in which the plot of the romance reaches its climax depends for the credibility of its solution entirely upon the skilful preparation of their characters.

Fortunately Chaucer found both energy and talent to spare for developing this side of *The Franklin's Tale* despite his evident preoccupation with the externals of presentation. In the earlier part of the romance, the discussion of *maistrie* and the promises which husband and wife make to each other not only serve the external controversy of which the story seems to be a part but also effectively prepare for the later behaviour of the two married lovers. Thus the slow movement of the story in its early stages is not to be ascribed to incompetence or to dilution but to the need of preparing for the classically perplexing choice that Dorigen is eventually obliged to make. An instance of most skilful psychological preparation to this end is to be found as if in anticipation of

---

[1] See, for example, the disclaimers at ll. 716 ff., 890, 1266 ff.

4

the actual promise when Dorigen, meditating in her husband's absence,

> Is ther no ship, of so manye as I se
> Wol bryngen hom my lord ?

looks down at the rocks off the coast and reflects that

> An hundred thousand bodyes of mankynde
> Han rokkes slayn.

It seems thenceforward as if these rocks and their threat to her husband obsess her, preoccupy her subconsciously until ' in pleye ' she promises :

> Looke what day that endelong Britayne
> Ye remoeve alle the rokkes, stoon by stoon . . .
> Thanne wol I love yow best of any man.[1]

One is inclined to take for granted, in the case of Chaucer, the fine workmanship implicit in such preparation, but to have created in the course of it characters who not only promote the development of the story but are so wholly likable that they take command of it was the decisive stroke of genius for this romance, whether it was designed or instinctive. It is entirely upon the appeal of these two and of Dorigen in particular, for we see more of her, that the success of *The Franklin's Tale* depends. Their fine decency and uprightness, so infectiously admirable that it communicates itself to the unscrupulous squire and to the necromancing clerk, and so enlivens what might otherwise have been an artificial *dénouement*, is vastly more attractive than any parade of literary accomplishments could possibly be.

Dorigen and Arveragus might easily have become prigs ; that Chaucer avoids this pitfall speaks for his essentially fine taste. They have our sympathy at once ; it grows into anxiety for Dorigen when her friends, after her husband's departure, succeed in persuading her to ' go out and enjoy herself ', into indignation when she is exposed to the squire's importunity, and into dismay when his trick looks like

---

[1] For the development of this effect see ll. 854–94 and 992–7.

succeeding. Part of the sympathy that both husband and wife arouse seems to originate in a sense that they are alone in a world either indifferent to their fate or actively against them. No one can help them with their problem once it has come to a head. Admiration for the standard of honour they set themselves, affection for their entirely attractive integrity, and anxiety about the outcome of their problem are factors more important to the success of *The Franklin's Tale* than the show of rhetoric, the learnedly allusive prolixity and the generally fashionable quality of its treatment. It is as if in this romance Chaucer had been trying to better the external form of the kind but had been led back to the centre of his art by the characters of his story. The rhetoric of *The Franklin's Tale* may commend it to the historian of such matters, but the behaviour of Dorigen and her husband in their predicament is what makes it attractive to the common reader.

The success of *The Franklin's Tale* begins and ends on the human side, for the real action in this romance takes place in the minds of the personages and could stand alone without the show for which Chaucer has made it an occasion. On the other hand, a romance in which the action was principally physical, and was given a more or less violent external form by the simplicity of its conflicts between desires or between desires and circumstances, might well lend itself to a much greater extent to the splendid and ornate kind of treatment, and indeed actually benefit from such a presentation. This is certainly the case with *The Knight's Tale of Palamon and Arcite* in which the glittering exterior of the world of chivalry is splendidly displayed by verbal resource. Chaucer's mastery of every trick of language known in his day is the most important single factor in the success of this courtly work ; here he has suited manner perfectly to matter. Indeed the rhetoric as he applies it either to description for effects of enrichment, or to the expression of emotion, presumably for emphasis, is entirely successful. The effect of the setting thus achieved is one of superlatively lavish splendour, and the emotions are so little complicated that the rhetoric not only does them no harm but actually increases our sense of their importance and probability.

The whole strength of *The Knight's Tale* is crustaceous, external and superficial.   The action of the story could hardly have been more successfully designed to fit without pinching into the conventions which shape its every situation, knightly, amatory, stylistic or of any other kind.   To observe this is not to condemn the romance in any way but simply to draw attention to the channel into which Chaucer's creative energy was here directed.   He evidently saw that this material would best be presented by concentration upon the perfection of its outward form, and by this means he made of a pretentious and inflated renaissance ' epic ' a romance externally so near perfection that only the closest scrutiny reveals its internal defects.

Indeed it is partly because of the actual defects in the story that Chaucer's creative efforts could express themselves so readily in form and style.   Because he was not obliged to expend any effort upon the characters of Palamon and Arcite, but had only to pour them into the handy moulds of the courtly love convention, he could devote himself to making their behaviour within that convention exquisitely correct [1] and describe it with equally exquisite finish ; because Emilye scarcely speaks she never cracks the surface of her too perfect heroine's beauty ;   because Chaucer could help his plot along with a coincidence which ill-sustains examination (he calls it *destinee*, to be sure) and by a blatant *deus ex machina*, he enjoyed a greater freedom to be circumstantial in those parts of the story where the going was better ;   and because the essential action, the rivalry of the two young men, was so slight and simple by nature that it scarcely admitted of development, he was free to parade his classical learning, his amateur philosophizing, his astronomical lore and his finely detailed descriptions of great mediæval occasions to their full advantage without harm to the story. But by these same tokens *The Knight's Tale* is almost all show ;   it awakens little emotion and the bright pictures which it leaves in the memory are cold.   There is little to choose, for instance, between Palamon and Arcite ; it is not even easy to keep them distinct in one's mind until Arcite individualizes himself by first disregarding Palamon's prior

[1] Except, of course, in the marriage with which the romance ends.

claim and then treating him with great knightliness. In all probability Chaucer cared greatly for neither, and his invocation of divine favouritism to decide the final outcome indicates his lack of interest in that outcome.

Because, however, it is early apparent to the reader that this romance is not to be an emotional experience, but is an adventure in perfecting the outward shows of chivalry at their most splendid, and in courtly love at its most correctly conventional, he takes little account of such shortcomings. For the effect of *The Knight's Tale* is dazzling ; it truly deserves its name. To the eye it offers a feast of images splendidly chivalric, to the ear some of the noblest verse that Chaucer wrote, and to the mind an exceptionally smooth mixture of ancient matter and mediæval conception. It is genuinely of no consequence that the characters are shallow, the plot wanting in verisimilitude or the emotion slight. They serve by affording the occasion for the spectacle which Chaucer set out to provide.

Yet, for all the superficiality of *The Knight's Tale* it is founded upon chivalry, and could hardly have kept its kind and quality without the strength and the cohesive factor afforded by the underlying conception of the order of knighthood. The Earl's advice to Guy of Warwick when he dubbed him *and bad hym become a good knyʒt* [1] applies in all the romances ; the only variable factor is the degree to which this is taken for granted or brought out into the open and emphasized, and the particular literary and narrative form in which the *good*ness expresses itself. This is strikingly true of the two remaining successes among the romances, *Sir Degrevant* and *The Squire of Low Degree* which, with *The Knight's Tale*, constitute the finest artistic expressions of the spirit of chivalry in mediæval English poetry. In each of these three a different aspect of this institution and of its effects is presented. *The Knight's Tale* displays both its gorgeous trappings and the stately patterns of its etiquette and formalities, heightened to a splendour far removed from the sober piety of the knighting of Guy ; *Sir Degrevant* shows the plainer social aspects of knighthood and how it might in particular influence the relations of two men whose estates

[1] EETS(ES) 25, 26 (Cambridge vers.), line 420.

marched with one another ; *The Squire of Low Degree* is a poetic and idealized expression of the life and setting of romantic chivalry, not glittering like *The Knight's Tale*, but softly and richly lambent in its effects.

Sir Degrevant is not poetic in this way ; it is set in English fields and deer-parks and substantial country houses full of good food and drink and furnishings just a shade too rare and expensive. Its author gives Degrevant a perfunctory connexion with Arthur's court and the Round Table which seems relatively unimportant ;[1] indeed his story is much more appropriate to a real fourteenth or fifteenth century than to a legendary Arthurian one, for there is not a single wonder or marvel in it from beginning to end. Every one of its actions is not only possible but probable in the light of the opening circumstances and the characters. The story deals with a feud between two gentlemen, Sir Degrevant and the Earl his neighbour, and with the complication of motives that results when Degrevant and the Earl's daughter Myldore fall in love. Nothing lofty or grand comes of such elements, but they do make a warmly human and entirely credible story, with a sharp contrast well expressed between the Earl, peppery and ineffective to the point of caricature, and Degrevant, ready to steal every trick from the older man but always careful not to insult as well as beat him. Degrevant, for all his hard hitting, is a likable, decent fellow, and they fight in this romance more as they do in *Chevy Chase* than in the conventional romance wars against Emperor or Saracen. The love affair, made exciting by the risk with which it is conducted, is very close to life in some of its touches. The effect of this romance, supported by skilful construction, a tone perfectly maintained, characters realistically conceived and developed, and a tolerably incisive narrative, is entirely good and persuasive.

[1] See ll. 17–32 in the version printed by Halliwell from Cambridge MS. Ff.i.6. I do not find the elaborate explanation of the author's intention at this point, given by the most recent editor of the romance (L. F. Casson, *The Romance of Sir Degrevant*, EETS 221 (London 1949), lxxi), entirely convincing ; it seems to me that the connexion was conventionally made, as if to give the romance location or authority. I do not see that it influences the treatment in any respect.

Despite his stanza form, which takes a very little of the edge off his story-telling, the author of *Sir Degrevant* has very considerable narrative gifts. He has visualized his subject magnificently and reproduces the circumstances of life as he sees them, with no distortion and with no other emphasis than the plot demands, as a series of warm, bright pictures that shift and change constantly with the changing scene and action. The impression is one of hard fighting and riding in a lovely countryside, and of a pair of pleasant young lovers both with faults enough not to be insipid. An impressive array of sources has been found for the situations in this romance, and a theory of its genesis constructed which denies the author any originality of invention, and leaves him little merit except his ingenuity at piecing together his borrowings.[1] Yet the effect of the romance is admittedly good ;[2] I find it also to be most unusual, if not unique in kind among the surviving romances. There is a paradox in this lack of originality producing a good and even a novel effect. But fortunately the question whether or not this romance is an unoriginal composite is unessential ; whichever alternative is correct it is the author's apprehension of his subject that has made his romance a full artistic success. Not only has *Sir Degrevant* the only story among all the surviving romances which might with no difficulty have been invented out of contemporary ' real life ' materials, but it is also wholly conceived, as few other romances were conceived, in terms of actuality. If, indeed, the various situations were actually copied and not invented, then an exceptionally fine discrimination operated in their selection and fusion. But originality of invention or the lack of it does not affect, and must be sharply distinguished from, originality of conception ; this in *Sir Degrevant* is so great that it can easily explain any possible contradictions between the material and the effect of the romance.

The chivalry of Sir Degrevant and of the Earl is not that of *lai* or legend, but that of the highly fed landowners of the later Middle Ages who would so readily fight to safeguard estates or honour, or even out of sheer excess of energy, but who could be persuaded by their womenfolk, when things

[1] Casson, *op. cit.* lxii–lxxii.　　　　[2] *Ib.* lxxiii–lxxv.

had gone far enough, that they were not behaving sensibly. The world of the Pastons, and the Pastons themselves had they been a little less put upon and more aggressive, might have afforded material for a story very like this one ; their mentality is often reflected in it. They would have respected Degrevant for being a man of substance :

> There was sesyd in hys hand
> A thousand poundus worth off land,
> Off rentes well settand,
> And muchlle delle more ;
>
> An houndered plows in demaynus,
> ffayere parkes inwyth haynus,
> Grett herdus in the playnus,
> Wyth muchelle tame store ;
>
> Castelos wyth heygh wallus,
> Chambors wyth noble hallus,
> ffayer stedes in the stallus,
> Lyard and soore.   (ll. 65–76)

And some of their neighbours might have stood models for the Earl who

> Hade a grete spyt of the knyght
> That was so hardy and wyght,
> And thought howe he best myght
> That dowghty to grode.   (ll. 101–4)

The Earl's envy is the beginning of the story, for he gives vent to it by raiding Degrevant's estates, slaughtering his deer by the score, drawing his rivers and killing his foresters. Degrevant, away at the holy wars in Spain, comes home directly his steward informs him of this outrage. At once the difference of this romance is made manifest ; Degrevant's first act is to repair the damage and fit his tenants out anew with ploughs and seed corn ; his second to write to the Earl demanding compensation. In the average romance he would never have sent the letter, or otherwise delayed before striking back. But the author of this romance has examined every situation he presents in terms of the corresponding actuality, and, in consequence, Degrevant behaves like a man who would prefer, if it can be managed, to live at peace with his neighbours.

On these same terms of actuality, heightened to be sure, but nevertheless entirely credible, the whole romance, including the love story, is developed. Myldore has no scruples about deceiving her father, going against his interest and pledging herself to his enemy, but unlike the romance heroines she does not lose touch with practical reality completely, but puts off Degrevant's impetuous love-making.

> ' Leff thou well, withouten lette,
> The ferste tyme y the mette
> Myn hert on the was sette
>   And my love on the ly3th.
>
> I thou3the never to have non
> Lord nothur lemman
> Bot onely the allon,
>   Caysere ne kny3th . . .
>
> fforthy, syre, hald the stylle
> Whyle thou get my fadyr wylle.'
>   (ll. 1521–34)

The consequences of her sound sense are a settlement of the feud and a marriage both advantageous and romantic. This is very close to the real world in which a solid backing of property and rents and sound management was necessary to maintain the fine externals of the knightly life, and where a girl might think twice before she risked losing the advantages of a marriage both ' good ' and founded on affection by too ready compliance.

Yet *Sir Degrevant*, if it were necessary to prove this point, is a romance by any of the definitions. The quality of its success in this kind is best judged by its effect. It rings with the horns of the raiding huntsmen, their bold talk while Degrevant and his men lie in ambush so hard by that they can hear every boastful word ; it is made dramatic by the sudden meeting of the lovers in the Earl's orchard, Degrevant

4*

' ryally arayd ', appearing suddenly before Myldore as she goes
to chapel, and she

> Sche come in a vyolet
> With why3the perl overfret
> And saphyrus therinne isett
>   On everyche a syde.   (ll. 625–8)

The pert lady-in-waiting who goes between them is more
practically minded than Lunet ; the tournament where
Degrevant beats Myldore's royal suitor and quite discourages
his suit is as splendid as any in the romances and more credible
than most ; the fight in the moonlight where, the intrigue
discovered, her father's men lie in ambush for Degrevant as
he comes with his squire to visit her, is more fraught with
suspense and danger than the run of such encounters ; the
lavish wedding and the many children are the conventional
turn.   The difference of artistic quality between *Sir Degrevant*
and the inferior romances supposed to have been its originals,
and its superior power to suspend disbelief, come not only
from the more closely knit construction and the consequent
unity of effect, or from the author's vigorous narrative gifts,
but also from the verisimilitude of subject and treatment that
originate in the author's sense of proportion and in his apprehension of his plot in terms of real life.   Like the love affair
the whole romance is a successful combination of sense and
abandonment subjected to the heightening which is characteristic of the romances.

The Squire of Low Degree, the last of the successes and
probably one of the latest of the surviving mediæval romances,
is unique in its manner of achieving a corresponding enhance-
ment of its subject, and an imaginative response, by sheer
profusion of poetry.   It is a beautiful romance, in a delicate
and tender mood set by the opening verses and never marred :

> It was a squyer of lowe degre
> That loved the kings doughter of Hungre.
> The squir was curteous and hend,
> Ech man him loved and was his friend ;
> He served the kyng, her father dere
> Fully the tyme of seven yere,

> For he was marshall of his hall
> And set the lords both great and small.
> An hardy man he was, and wight
> Both in batayle and in fyght ;
> But ever he was styll mornyng,
> And no man wyste for what thyng ;
> And all was for that lady,
> The kynges doughter of Hungry. (ll. 1–14)

The most striking feature of this romance is the manner in which the emphasis is laid almost entirely upon the moods of the various situations and hardly at all upon the narrative. The story turns on a series of surprises which, since we have not been prepared for them, seem discrepant. The squire hides his devotion for seven years, but is at once accepted when he declares it ; he is in mortal fear of discovery and the king's anger, but receives the latter's ready blessing when the secret is betrayed ; the king is deeply attached to his daughter, but he torments her by letting her mourn the squire for seven years when he could end her grief with two words. The characters, except that of the king, are scarcely developed, and the method of narration is to move rapidly over incidents which cover large periods of time, and slowly over moments where there is opportunity for poetic elaboration. There is little pretence at realism of any kind in this romance ; every-thing is devoted to the creation of poetic effects. The author appears to have written not for an audience anxious to gape at marvels, but for one which, like himself, enjoyed the con-templation of the more picturesque attitudes of romantic chivalry. Battles and tournaments interested him no more than did marvels and magic ; he loved graceful living, gentle manners and gracious behaviour. To ensure that nothing distracted from such subjects he gave the romance an air of artificiality by formalized design in both description and plot.

The date of *The Squire of Low Degree* is hard to fix with assurance, but certain of the qualities which its remarkable author bestowed upon it suggest that chronological or other circumstances enabled him to stand away from the romance *genre* and to select only those of its features which suited the effect that he designed, and that he was not carried along by the full stream of the tradition. There is in his romance at

least one outright rebellion against.the common practice to
support such an inference.   The false steward bears slander to
the king about the squire ; by the easygoing motivation of the
majority of the romances the king would have believed it, but
here he refuses :

> I may not beleve it should be so ;
> Hath he be so bonayre and benynge,
> And served me syth i was yynge,
> And redy with me in every nede,
> Bothe true of word, and eke of dede ;
> I may not beleve, by nyght nor day
> My doughter dere he wyll betraye.   (ll. 356–62)

As a result of the author's eclecticism this romance may be
called ' composite ', but the selection is never uncritical.
Only those externals of the convention find a place in it
which allow the author the poetic development of certain
moods, and each of these moods must have a potential beauty.
Only once is he defeated in this economy, for to sustain the
plot he is obliged to develop the character of the king who
keeps the secret of the squire's life for the seven years during
which his daughter mourns.   Perforce the king becomes an
ironist, a man both cruel and kindly, who indulges the sense
of power that his control of the happiness of the two lovers
gives.

Otherwise the characters and even the story are only
ancillary to the poetry of this romance.   A great part of the
thousand lines of *The Squire of Low Degree* are memorable
verse.   The man who composed them could write as well as
Chaucer, if in a slighter vein and within narrower limits.
Even when he is engaged in covering the ground of the
narrative he can throw off graceful passages both fluent and
apt, in which the emotion of the story shines through the
clear language.

There is, for instance, the graceful and pathetic talk of the
two lovers while the false steward waits in ambush to trap
and kill the squire :

> Come i am full pryvely
> To take my leave of you, lady,   (ll. 569–70) .

says the squire, and the princess by whose command he is setting out to win name and fame tells him

> It is for the worshyp of us two ;
> Though you be come of symple kynne
> Thus my loue, syr, may ye wynne
> If ye have grace of victory. (ll. 610–13)

In their world a man *may* rise from low degree to marry the king's daughter ; that is one convention of the romances. But another is that there shall be men who do not wish him well. And so here

> Ryght as they talked thus, in fere,
> Theyr enemyes approched nere and nere. (ll. 637–8)

In a moment swords and knives are out ; there is a brawl in the dark passage outside the door where the lovers whispered, and when the fight is over a body is thrown into the princess's room dressed in her lover's clothes. Seven years she cherishes it and her grief, and when the time she promised to wait is over, she makes a renunciation of life : she will become an anchoress. However, she never takes this dreadful step, for her father, who has overheard her grieving, breaks in upon her.

> Lady, he sayd, be of good chere,
> Your love lyveth and is here. (ll. 1051–2)

The most striking poetry in the romance is not, however, to be found in these frequent but incidental moments when simple words become charged with emotion, but in the deliberate poetic embroidery of situations and relationships for which the story provides the canvas. Of this the outstanding example is the passage of some hundred lines in which the king, who knows all the while that the grief which his daughter is trying to hide from him is needless and that she will have her lover in the end, nevertheless offers her diversion and consolation. There are few passages in all mediæval poetry as beautiful as this in which the ironic play of his fancy is recorded :

> Than shall ye go to your evensong
> With tenours and trebles among ;
> Threscore of copes, of damaske bryght
> Full of perles they shal be pyght ;
> Your aulter clothes of taffata
> And your sicles all of taffetra.
> Your sensours shal be of golde
> Endent with asure many a folde.
> Your quere nor organ songe shall wante,
> With countre note, and dyscant,
> The other halfe on orgayns playeng,
> With yonge chyldren full fare syngyng. (ll. 781–92)

Lightly the king changes the moods with which, benevolently cruel, he masks his irony :

> An hundreth knightes, truly tolde
> Shal play with bowles in alayes colde
> Your disease to drive awaie ;
> To se the fisshes in poles plaie,
> And then walke in arbere up and downe. (ll. 803–7)

Or if this fails to disperse her melancholy she shall go to the waterside where

> A barge shall mete you, full ryght,
> With twenty four ores full bryght,
> With trompettes and with claryowne
> The fresshe water to rowe up and downe.
> Than shall ye go to the salte fome
> Your maner to se, or ye come home,
> With eighty shyppes of large towre,
> With dromedaryes of great honour
> And carackes with sayles two,
> The sweftest that on water may goo,
> With galyes good upon the haven,
> With eighty ores at the fore staven.
> Your maryners shall synge arowe
> Hey how and rumby lowe. (ll. 811–24)

Knowing that his daughter's grief is needless, and indeed not expecting to diminish it, he indulges his fancy by offering her' what seems to him, as a connoisseur of situations, the perfect consolation.

Upon such play of the fancy, here extended but evident everywhere in the romance, and always sharpened by the situation of the moment, *The Squire of Low Degree* depends for its effect, and not upon yet another development of all the old knightly situations, the narration of which was ending its almost three-hundred-year-old vogue. This romance is, to be sure, set in the world of chivalry, and the squire himself is as brave and as knightly as the best of his predecessors. But too many knights and squires before him have ridden to do ' great chyvalry ' in Portugal and Spain, in Tuscany and Lombardy, and at the Holy Sepulchre. Not his knightly deeds, nor even the story of his love are the source of the interest of this romance ; it captures the imagination by the poet's originally idealized picture of a world in which the squire might have lived, the lovely objects of sense that it contains, the gentle manners and the gracious lives of those who inhabit it. The story has its beginning in the chivalry upon which all the romances by their nature and definition relied, but its fulfilment in the romantic imagination of a rare poet.

The remarkable individuality of the good and bad romances both, and the variety of methods employed in those which have any artistic merit at all to induce the escape into the imaginative world of fiction, do not conceal that the main excellence of the kind consists in achieving the ' willing suspension of disbelief ', and that all the artistic virtues of the romances were directed, according to the gifts of their various authors, to this end, however obscurely or imperfectly conceived. By virtue of their purpose of entertainment the romances belong in the tradition of development of European narrative fiction which began already with the end of the classical Latin period [1] and continues to this day. A long, slow process of adjustment created many external differences between the romances and their more modern equivalents in

[1] Cf. C. S. Lewis, *The Allegory of Love* (London 1936), especially 75–6, 82.

this tradition. The range of subject was widened to include matter other than knightly ; authors began to discover empirically or by inference from other *genres* that a greater number of human experiences, including those with unhappy issues, was capable of artistic treatment and acceptable to the public ; the extent of the artistic experience within the attainment of fiction was thus both broadened and deepened ; prose began to be more widely employed as a medium until its use for fiction largely supplanted that of verse ; and a changed conception of the physical world narrowed the boundaries of probability within which the authors would be obliged to confine the occurrences of their stories. Such changes meant the end of the romance *genre* as such, but to notice them only emphasizes the continuity of the essential purpose of narrative fiction which that *genre* possessed, and confirms the two assumptions upon which the present evaluation has been based. The examination of the romances has borne out, first, that many of the qualities because of which the modern reader may object to them are actually not essential to them at all, and second, that the qualities of permanent appeal and permanent artistic success, the ' excellences proper to the kind ', are, broadly speaking, those of all narrative fiction.

In the romances, then, artistic success appears to depend on excellences of two kinds, of conception and of presentation. The excellences of conception will be produced by the author's capability of sympathy, by which he is able to ' enter into ' or apprehend emotionally his story, and to make its characters more than merely symbols in an exercise of narration, and equally by the power of his imagination to visualize clearly, in artistically significant relationships, the persons, motives, action and settings which he undertakes to describe. The excellences of presentation will depend upon his ability to select and arrange material so that its external form answers to and conveys his conception of it, and so that a generally ' persuasive ' effect is achieved ; they will also be governed by his possession of the command of language needed for efficient literary communication or to add to the ' persuasive ' power of what he writes. The measure of artistic success in the romances is not then their conformity to any *idea* of form or conception or expression, but the extent to which, by means determined in the temperament of their authors, they can enlist the imaginative co-operation of the reader, and satisfy his desire for the escape into fantasy. Artistic failure, conversely, is not the product of the specifically mediæval circumstances by which, in addition to the narrative purpose, the *genre* is defined, or of any obscure change by which something which was once ' good ' or ' popular ' has since become inartistic and bad, but of incompetence or lack of cultivation in the individual authors.

These general conclusions bear upon the definitions by means of which the romance as a literary kind has been identified. In the most important study of these definitions [1] it has been argued that, properly speaking, the contemporary effect of the romances was not, as has been maintained, to appeal to ' the sort of imagination that possesses the mystery and spell of everything remote and unattainable ' or to ' the imagination which found special glamour in the remote or impossible ' ; [2] and that the characteristic quality of the romances was, in the first place, not their remoteness from real life but actually their ' modernity ' ; [3] that although the marvellous was often a part of the subject-matter of a romance, it was most frequently treated in a bald, matter-of-fact way ; [4] that the authors who employed it by no means necessarily obtained ' romantic ' effects from it, but that when ' glamour ' was a quality of the treatment this was ' the gift of the artist ' and not a property of the *genre* ; [5] and that the principal attraction of the romances for their contemporaries was the opportunity that they afforded of an ' escape from the failures or partial successes of life as it was lived by showing . . . that life idealized '.[6]

The results of the present examination of the romances seem partly to bear out and partly to modify these contentions. ' Romantic ' effects of ' glamour ' and remoteness are not, it seems, essential features of the romance *genre*. What is, however, necessary to the literary excellence of the romances, and was necessary at the time of their composition,

[1] Dorothy Everett, ' A Characterization of the English Medieval Romances ' 98–121.

[2] *Ib.* 104–5.   [3] *Ib.* 101–4.   [4] *Ib.* 108–9.
[5] *Ib.* 111–13.   [6] *Ib.* 105–6.

is the ability of the author to induce in his public, by some means, a ready surrender to the experience of fiction. He may indeed find that the nature of his material enables him to fulfil this requirement best by creating a spell of wonder and mystery, or by setting his romance in an enchanted country, or simply in that distant past which excited the mediæval imagination as much as it can excite our own, although the forms of expression of this excitement may differ. But equally his own apprehension of the subject may suggest other means of making his account persuasive, or may even in exceptional cases contain such means. By whatever effect the imaginative surrender is induced, that particular effect itself cannot be an essential quality of the *genre* ; it is no more than the particular device of the artist to make his creation persuasive, and therefore an *accident* that belongs outside the definition of the *genre*. As to the question of ' remoteness ' or ' modernity ', it would seem that all artistically good romances must have been essentially remote from real life even at the time of their composition, not because they reproduced in fiction worlds distant in time or place, but because they were in fact successful fiction. Again, it is necessary to guard against confusing the heightening which enabled escape with the particular means of achieving heightening. I do not think it would be correct to associate the quality of naturalism with the romances as a *genre*. The accident that their authors lacked a highly developed historical sense and therefore translated the past into contemporary terms, or that in order to suggest the *dernier cri* they would dress a knight of the remote Arthurian past in the very newest styles of fourteenth-century armour does not affect the issue. The charm, the contemporary success and the permanent excellence of the romances consist in affording experience of a world of fantasy essentially unreal in some respect ; this world must be somehow remote from actuality even though its details of setting may in occasional instances be, whether anachronistically or not, those of the time of composition.

The romances concern the student of literature because they illustrate an important stage in the development of narrative fiction, and the mediævalist because in the course of their literary evaluation he may observe the state of literary cultivation in his period and the effect of the presence or absence of this upon the results of creative activity. They seem to me also interesting because they are human documents. In every case, whatever the backgrounds of a romance, its continental or native sources, the simple or complicated circumstances of its authorship, or its connexions with other romances, it should never be merely a dry historical specimen. It represents both the stuff of human activity and the creative imagination by which the apprehension of this is given artistic forms. Changes in time, society, beliefs and language may indeed have set up barriers between us and the romances, but we ought to be aware that they remain essentially close to us by virtue of the common and unchanging humanity whose life and aspirations they reflect, and upon which all literature in the last analysis relies for its interest. It is not merely unnaturally academic to neglect this side of the romances ; it is also dangerous because it inclines us to reduce positive and vital qualities to abstractions, formulæ of ' convention ' and ' tradition ' which may conceal from us the strong individuality of most of the romances and the high literary quality of a few of them.

PART II

THE MIDDLE ENGLISH RELIGIOUS LYRICS

THE study of the Middle English religious lyrics both has its own special problems and is made more difficult by the common circumstances which interfere with the easy appreciation of Middle English poetry in general. The remoteness of these lyrics from modern times has created differences of language generally and of poetic diction in particular, which can be serious obstacles to our appreciation of them. By our ignorance of the exact circumstances of their preservation and of the extent to which the surviving specimens represent the whole production in this kind, we seem to be prevented from generalizing with any assurance about the *genre*, and seem obliged to limit the application of our inferences to such poems as have been preserved, or else to hedge them about with burdensome qualifications. Most of the surviving material is anonymous, a fact which forces upon us an approach quite different from the unexacting, intimate, often gossipy biographical criticism that has always been fashionable in the study of English poetry. Indeed, if we are to be able to recover with any degree of success the experience recorded in these poems, we must subject ourselves to an extended and complicated discipline easy enough to appreciate in theory but by no means easy to maintain.

We have, for instance, first of all to make an adjustment of language by which we allow the Middle English poet the same liberty of difference that we would grant to a poet who is writing in a foreign tongue. We must in no circumstances be offended by the differences between his English and our own. In theory this should be easy enough ; in practice it is very hard, for the suggestion of incompetence, of broken English, of faltering, unassured expression is difficult to avoid. It lurks in the bristling orthography of *Nu yh she blostme sprynge*, in the *d* and the inversion of *My gostly fader, I me confesse*, in the phonology of *I stale a cosse*, in the double negative, the omitted relative pronoun, the *he* form of the feminine pronoun, the change of construction in mid-sentence, the loss of rhymes through dialect confusion in transmission, and any number of similar features which quite improperly but very readily suggest crude and incompetent workmanship. Such differences between Middle and Modern English are great enough to make the unqualified comparison of the older with the more recent poetry improper, but not great enough to keep the impropriety of the comparison constantly before our minds. We have, in addition, to make allowances for the differences in poetic diction between the poetry of mediæval England and that of more recent periods by admitting the principle that the effect of poetry is largely created by the associations which the reader attaches to the words and phrases of a poem, and that these associations will inevitably differ in different ages, however similar in appearance or even in literal meaning the words that evoke them may have remained. James Ryman, the fifteenth-century author of carols, could write without evident impropriety of the Eucharist *In virgyne Mary this brede was bake*, but today the line is offensive. It is, to be sure, an extreme instance of difference of response, but the many other less glaring examples will be more dangerous, for we may easily miss them altogether and simply regard the poems in which they occur as bad.

When we have made these adjustments we are further compelled by the question of the preservation of these lyrics to refrain from generalizing with too much freedom or confidence in terms of the surviving specimens about the whole *genre*. It may be, as has been argued, that the majority of the religious lyrics composed during the Middle English period have survived, but nothing can rule out the possibility that more or greater religious verse was composed in that period than has been left to us. All judgements of the subject, therefore, and the generalizations formed upon them, can be no more than tentative when once they are made to extend beyond the known specimens considered as relatively isolated survivals.

The anonymity of most of these specimens imposes a further restriction upon our criticism of them. Modern students have generally been schooled, either consciously or unconsciously by the influence of their critical environment, to look in a poem for its author, and then in the personality of that author for elements of temperament or experience which may help to explain the poem.   There seems no general reason why lyric poetry, when it is actually the product of an intensely personal function, should not be examined in the light of the temperament, character and life of the poet if such an examination increases our knowledge of the experience he·seeks to communicate.   If, however, we have become accustomed to this critical method, it is only natural to find difficult or even unrewarding the study of poetry about which no external information is available, to which no name and often no exact date is attached, and which is often too short to afford material for speculation about its author.   We have then to guard against allowing the anonymity of Middle English poetry, and the impossibility of obtaining any help other than that afforded by its own lines for interpreting a poem, to influence us either knowingly or unconsciously by diminishing our interest in it or affecting our opinion of its ' weight ' or ' substance '.   We are obliged to forego biographical glosses and begin our study of the experience communicated in the poem with its text, and to confine it to that text and its effect upon us.   I do not think that this principle would be disputed : the difficulty is rather not to forget it or the need that it imposes on us of adjusting our attitude.

Even if as critics we are vigilant enough to protect ourselves unremittingly against the possibility of error on all these counts, there remain æsthetic considerations which particularly increase the difficulty of appreciating the Middle English religious lyrics.   The first and simpler of these consists of a misunderstanding that can originate in the very term ' lyric ', a word which seems to have been quite properly used within the very wide meaning permitted by modern usage to describe the collections of this kind of poetry, but which seems quite often to have a special significance whereby a ' lyric ' poem must conform to a kind of *idea* of poetry characterized by intensity of feeling and a special type of poetic language. When this word is understood in such a limited sense there is a serious danger of larger misconceptions ; the *idea* which it

signifies will be used as a standard of measurement for material
to which it cannot fairly be applied, and the result will be
either disappointment or confusion. It is necessary, then, to
allow the term ' lyric ' its wider meaning when it is used in
connexion with Middle English poetry, in order to avoid such
perplexity.

The second æsthetic circumstance has more serious
implications. It resolves itself into the question ' What are
we to establish as the criterion of success in the Middle English
religious lyrics ? ' The problem expressed in this question is
a special one related to the subject-matter of this poetry.
Suppose, for instance, that we accept the principle that the
success of a poetic composition is to be measured by the extent
to which the author has carried out his intention. We must
then first determine as exactly as we can what that intention
was, what effect the poet wished to create, and what was the
particular nature of the lesson or emotion or experience that
he wished to communicate. This may have been primarily
religious, and the author may have set little store by poetic
or æsthetic obligations of the kind which, according to our
concept of poetry, he incurred by using verse as his medium.
Can we then allow that if he has fulfilled his intention he has
written a good poem, or, more strictly, a good religious lyric ?
It seems inevitably logical that the next stage in our criticism
ought to be an examination of the poet's intention itself to
ascertain in the first place whether it was poetic, and then
whether it was permanently or only temporarily valid, trivial
or great.

Our judgements on such questions will be very seriously
affected in two respects by the differences in time and background which separate us from the Middle English religious
poet. In the first place he would not have admitted that the
validity of his subject, or its self-sufficiency, was in any way
open to question. His assurance on this point must be allowed
as a factor in our consideration of his work. In the second
place we ourselves have often to overcome an antipathy, open
or subconscious, to his religious subject. Not only modern
agnostics, but modern Christians as well can for a variety
of particular reasons fail to be sympathetic to the religion
of the Middle Ages. The difficulty with religious poetry

which such lack of sympathy can create makes dangerous all personal judgements on questions of value which arise out of this subject-matter. We ought for these two reasons to refrain from applying criteria of validity to the subject-matter of the Middle English lyrics. Instead we may consider whether in particular instances it has been poetically treated, whether the effect of a poem is likely to have been good in its own time, and whether it is capable of arousing emotion in the reader of today. With our attention directed to the treatment rather than to the subject, we may then profitably examine in detail the artistic gifts and the poetic technique of the author, and inquire how these were related to the subject and perhaps affected by its special nature.

Taken by itself any one of the restrictions upon our criticism of the religious lyrics assembled above must seem obvious ; together they become a formidable and exacting discipline which it will not be possible for anyone to observe without occasional lapses. To collect them emphasizes the complexity of the problem which the study of Middle English lyric poetry and the religious lyric in particular sets us, and incidentally is a safeguard against the patronizing attitude to the Middle Ages which is so easy to assume, and which, more than any other single factor, darkens our understanding of their literature.

In the case of the Middle English religious lyric in particular these restrictions determine our point of view as critics. Beyond requiring sincerity in its artistic treatment, we cannot well undertake the acceptance or rejection of a religious subject. We may, however, examine the peculiar relation of the subject to poetry in general, and to the poetic experience communicated in a particular lyric. The form which the experience takes as religion may throw light upon the author's intention ; the discovery of that intention will in turn indicate the technical means by which the poet achieves his communication, the intensity of the effect he has created, and the connexion between the success of his poem as such and its efficacy as an exercise of a religious function. In general terms, the quality of the Middle English religious lyrics is to be accounted for by a study of the manner in which the poet's consciousness that he was treating a great and sacred subject, which to him had a completely independent importance, affected his attitude to what he wrote as poetry. This attitude is best revealed by studying the Middle English religious lyrics according to the types of religious activity which they represent or reflect. Such a study at once throws into prominence certain types of poetic or creative activity and illustrates them with characteristic specimens both good and bad. At the same time it constitutes, in my opinion, a necessary preliminary to the examination of this poetry according to either the specific themes with which it deals or the prosodic forms in which it is cast.

Two main religious functions, a moral and a devotional one, are represented in the surviving Middle English lyrics. These can, however, profitably be subdivided. In the first kind, for instance, there are elementary moralizing lyrics where the intention of the poet was evidently no more than to produce ethical or religious teaching of an uncomplicated kind. Then there is moral verse of a less simply admonitory character, often concerned with illustrating the precept in question by examples or appeals to the emotion or the imagination of the reader. Among the devotional lyrics, *prima facie* of a higher artistic order, there is simple prayer in verse which can be good or bad without its function of worship being affected, and there is poetry devotional and meditative in the sense that the *Imitation of Christ* is meditative, where the function of worship is carried out not by formal verbal prayer but by contemplation. In this second kind the artistic and the religious success are related; both depend on the power of the poem to produce in the reader the emotion which the author wished to convey. In all cases the determination of the religious function of a lyric explains and illustrates its author's artistic purpose or lack of one, and directs attention to his particular gifts of language, feeling and imagination. In doing so it illustrates, if not the circumstances, at least the processes by which Middle English religious poetry was produced and thus contributes materially to the understanding of a difficult subject.

The simple moralizing lyrics are artistically the least complicated of the religious poems. As a rule their effect upon the modern reader is not strong; they lack the immediacy

of subject from which, when they were composed, that effect
drew its strength. This obstacle to our appreciation of them is
unfortunate. To form a truer impression of their contemporary
effect we ought to try to revive the instancy of their communication to the man of, say, the fourteenth century who
heard or read them. In his religion hell-fire was a reality as it
rarely is in the comfortable Anglicanism of the modern
Englishman, and his sense of sin was genuine and terrifying.
He devoutly believed, when he remembered to think in such
terms, that this world *Hit nis but fantum and feiri*, and that
to attach himself to it was to embrace the trivial and transitory
good at the cost of losing the great and permanent. His moral
sense was close to his imagination, excited it, and was in turn
sharpened or at least made more lively by the pictures of
awful consequences that his imagination could call up. His
state of mind was then vastly more receptive to these moral
lyrics than is that of the common reader of today, and in
consequence their effect upon him could be considerable, even
violent.

The exact nature of this effect can be determined with some
accuracy, again in terms of the mediæval religious mentality.
The man who, in his normal way, might be comfortably
unconcerned about the preacher's ' Four Last Things ',
death, judgement, heaven and hell, would be reminded of them
with something of a shock. His unconcern, promoted not so
much by indifference as by natural forgetfulness, would be
replaced by painful uneasiness, by a disconcerting awareness
that possibly these injunctions applied to himself. This
state of mind would lead him to examine his conscience and
to find, inevitably, that his spiritual condition left something
to be desired. Such a sense of his shortcomings and of their
possible consequences would intensify the force with which
the unanswerable moral teaching of his religion came home
to him. The necessary conditions for this logically self-
contained process are the faith which we may assume in any
mediæval man who was prepared to read or listen to moral
verse, and the sense of spiritual imperfection which would
probably be found in such a man. The process of being
subjected to this effect might be uncomfortable but could
also be exciting, perhaps in something of the way that

evangelical revivalism seems to be exciting, and might well take place in subjects not normally disposed to a lively piety.

The poet's manner of achieving his effect was, in the majority of the surviving moral poems, simply to apply in verse, as emphatically as he could, the conventional homiletic material. Any number of the usual themes might be introduced ; the commonest would be reminders of the transitoriness of worldly pleasure and glory,

> Arthur and Ector þat we dredde
> Deth haþ leid hem wonderly lowe—

of the inconstancy of fortune, and of mortality in general. While the author could clearly rely upon obtaining a general success from the force of his moral arguments, the further intensity of his effects would depend upon the manner in which he expressed those arguments. An important element of his success would be the power of persuasion upon which the classical rhetoricians set such store, the ability to convince not only by the logic of the subject, but by the telling presentation of that logic. A simple form of this rhetorical science was undoubtedly part of the technique of preaching in the Middle Ages and could be applied direct to moral versifying. Indeed much of the simple moralizing verse of the Middle English period looks as if the authors believed that this power to convince by argument was an essential feature of their work.

The so-called ' Vernon Series ' of fourteenth-century moral poems [1] very well illustrates both the excellences and the shortcomings of the simply moralizing lyrics. It is, meanwhile, remarkable for the very high level of performance which the poems that comprise it maintain, not only technically, but also in the manner of presenting their moral teaching. All show unfailing competence in these respects. Each of the best examples [2] looks as if it were the product of a well-balanced mentality, thinking smoothly and expressing its thoughts fluently, economically, and at times even with originality. There is unmistakable evidence, not only in

---

[1] Carleton Brown, *Religious Lyrics of the Fourteenth Century* (Oxford 1924) 125–208

[2] C.B. *XIV* nos. 101, 103, 104, 106, 110, 117, 120, for instance.

the correctness of the poetic form but also in the method of
presenting the material, that the treatment was intended to
be poetic, at least up to a point. The preacher often sweetens
the opening of his lesson by the use of the vision fiction,
of a ' lettre of loue . . . wrytyn on a wall,' [1] of a bird taken by a
merlin and preaching mercy to its captor,[2] of a forced leave-
taking,[3] or of a man making a prayer of confession ;[4] once he
illustrates his moral point with a specific reference to greatness
past and faded,[5] another time he quotes Solomon and
Socrates for authority [6] and, perhaps most effectively of all,
either sets his poem in actual topical circumstances [7] or relates
it to them.[8]   But thinking of a treatment as poetic does not
make it so ; and there is never a flash of inspiration in any
of these poems.   It is easy to conceive that the author or
authors of the ' Vernon Series ' thought of these devices as a
part of their rhetoric ; certainly they use them in a fashion
both perfunctory and unsustained.   The real quality of the
poems is revealed when the preacher speaks with undisguised
voice, either from scriptural authority,

> In a Pistel þat poul wrouȝt
> I fond hit writen & seide riht þis,[9]

or else relying simply on the point of what he has to say for
conviction.[10] This outright preaching, into which all the lyrics
of the Series sooner or later fall, is by no means unskilful.
The direct address adopted by all these lyrics, whether they
make their perfunctory appeal to the poetic imagination or
not, is generally searching and powerful.   Sometimes it is
raised to an almost philosophical level of conception, detached
and yet moving :

> I wolde witen of sum wys wiht
> Witterly what þis world were :
> Hit fareþ as a foules fliht,
> Now is hit henne, now is hit here.[11]

---

[1] C.B. *XIV* no. 105.   [2] *Ib*. no. 95.   [3] *Ib*. no. 97.
[4] *Ib*. no. 107.   [5] *Ib*. no. 100, ll. 93–4.
[6] *Ib*. no. 101, ll. 73, 85.   [7] *Ib*. no. 96.   [8] *Ib*. no. 113.
[9] *Ib*. no. 100, ll. 1–2.   [10] E.g. *Ib*. nos. 102, 103, 108, 109.
[11] *Ib*. no. 106.

The strong, the great and the glorious are cut off in their prime, the sun and the streams and the winds keep their courses, and no man comprehends the whole plan, for ' þis world fareþ as a Fantasy '. Generations come and go and are forgotten, and our fate will be the same :

> So schul men þenken vs no-þing on
> Þat nou han þe ocupacions.

Man's strength is nothing in itself, and a source of vexation to him because he cannot keep it. Who dares to say what a man is or where his spirit goes when he dies like the beasts of the field ?

> Dyeþ mon, and beestes dye,
> And al is on Ocasion ;
> And alle o deþ, hos boþe drye,
> And han on Incarnacion.

Nothing distinguishes man but the little wit that he employs to increase his own perplexity :

> For þus men stumble & sere heore witte
> And meueþ maters mony and fele ;
> Summe leeueþ on him, sum leueþ on hit,
> As children leorneþ for to spele.
> But non seoþ non þat abit
> Whon stilly deþ wol on hym stele.

Only rarely, however, does even such a relatively serene and contemplative poetic emotion transform the sermon of the simple moralizing verse. The majority of lyrics in which this religious function is expressed gives the general impression that their authors made no more than formal and perfunctory concessions to what they probably thought of as the frivolous tastes of those for whom they intended their work.[1] The matter, they surely believed, was strong enough, and needed only to be communicated with point and emphasis to convince by its own force as moral teaching. There is little greatness in these lyrics, and only very rarely any imaginative or creative excitement. The preaching mission was a primarily

[1] See M. Dominica Legge, *Anglo-Norman in The Cloisters* (Edinburgh 1950), 128 ff., for an analogous attitude.

intellectual function in which, in these instances, imagination and the creative activity played at best only an ancillary part.

The clue to the attitude of these moral poets to their audiences is to be found in that mission to preach and convert. As teachers of ethics they seldom consciously included themselves among those to whom their admonitions applied. They seem to have written from the superior point of view of men who were and knew themselves regenerate. That assumption of superiority, never expressed but often reflected in their writing, accounts for the repellent coldness of much of this poetry, for no show of self-righteousness is ever quite attractive in any age. The exceptions, poems not complacently predicatory, but written by men conscious that what they wrote applied to themselves, serve to emphasize the importance of the poet's attitude in this respect to the success of his poem, for the transformation of moral verse into divine poetry seems to take place at the point where the poet apprehends his moral lesson in terms of his own salvation and experiences it emotionally.

> Louerd, þu clepedest me
> An ich nagt ne ansuarede þe
> Bute wordes scloe and sclepie :
> ' Þole yet ! þole a litel ! '
> Bute ' yiet ' and ' yiet ' was endelis,
> And ' þole a litel ' a long wey is.[1]

This poem, of a quality exceptional among the English moral verse of three centuries, although it is a translation of a passage from Augustine's *Confessions*, is worth more than all the elaboration of precept and principle that went to make the ' Vernon Series '. To have seen how those few lines in the great book were a unity, to have cast them into poetic form, making the abstract expression of the original concrete, and to have done this briefly, intensely and beautifully were the work of a man who had either entered into the experience of the famous penitent in his imagination, or had himself experienced the same spiritual movement in his own right. However that may be, his poem was produced by a sincere poetic impulse and shows signs of an inspired creative imagination.

[1] C.B. *XIV* no. 5.   See also the note to the poem, 243–4.

The rarity of such examples among the surviving simple moral verse emphasizes that the difference between the latter and the less simply admonitory moral poetry is one of quality as well as of kind. In most of the simple preaching verse the concession to human frailty implied in the appeal to the imagination is perfunctory ; in the second class, which persuades by other means as well, it is more generous and whole-hearted, and suggests another point of view in the poets concerned. The personal application of the moral lesson is not merely understood but also felt ; the poets make a primary appeal to the imagination, and often their admonition to turn from the world is tinged with a nostalgic regret for that deceitfully lovely life from which man must detach himself or be damned. One thirteenth-century lyric, *Vbi Sount Qui Ante Nos Fuerount*,[1] excellently shows both the differences and the similarities in question. Like some of the simpler moral verse it consists of the two elements, the appeal to the imagination and the moral lesson. These appear at first sight to be distinct and separable, so that the success of the first, which is considerable, might look like an accomplished application of poetic virtuosity to the purpose of moral instruction. To a certain extent this opinion is probably correct ; there can be no question that the poetry was designed to lead to the sermon. Its subordination to the latter is, however, nothing like complete. In fact, at the moment of its expression the poetic side is supreme, and has taken emotional hold of the poet in a way it could not have done if it were a deliberate and calculated bait to catch readers. The effect that it creates survives and sweetens the rest of the poem :

> Uuere beþ þey biforen vs weren,
> Houndes ladden and hauekes beren
> And hadden feld and wode ?
> Þe riche leuedies in hoere bour,
> Þat wereden gold in hoere tressour
> Wiþ hoere briȝtte rode ;

---

[1] Carleton Brown, *English Lyrics of the Thirteenth Century* (Oxford 1932) no. 48.

> Eten and drounken and maden hem glad ;
> Hoere lif was al wiþ gamen I-lad.
> Men keneleden hem biforen,
> Þey beren hem wel swiþe heye—
> And in a twincling of on eye
> Hoere soules weren forloren.
>
> Were is þat lawing and þat song,
> Þat trayling and þat proude ʒong,
> Þo hauekes and þo houndes ?
> Al þat ioye is went away,
> Þat wele is comen te weylaway,
> To manie harde stoundes.   (ll. 1–18)

Moreover, although the point of separation between the two halves of the poem is distinct, the whole nevertheless proves to have an intellectual unity ; its second, moralizing portion could indeed stand alone, but gains immensely from the first part which, as well as preparing a suitable state of mind for the reception of the second, increases its significance.

The effect of this poem is then mixed, but nevertheless relatively successful ; it awakens not only fear of death but also a romantic sorrow for past splendours, in order to banish them with good counsel. Each half of the poem requires the other. The point of difference between this lyric and the more naïve moral versifying lies in the attitude of the author to his subject, which has excited his poetic imagination to the point where he himself has felt the romantic sorrow. This poetic emotion he has made a part of his lyric not in any perfunctory, off-hand manner, or spirit of exploitation, but sincerely, as if he has felt it himself. His poem as a whole then records an imaginative experience resolved in terms of moral counsel and not a sermon touched up with poetry. It is, incidentally, much more successful as a sermon because of its appeal to the imagination. For a modern reader the effect of the moral portion may be less intense than that of the *ubi sunt* stanzas, but the poem is notwithstanding this fact a spiritual unity, with its origin in the creative imagination.

Friar Thomas de Hales' *Love Ron* [1] is another illustration

---

[1] C.B. *XIII* no. 43.

of the difference between simple moral teaching in verse and the more refined treatment of moral lessons in which the imagination plays a principal part. Apparently the effect of this poem is difficult to appreciate, for it is often mis-understood. I do not find any ' erotic mysticism ' or any ' blending of the physical and the mystical ' in it.[1] Instead it answers quite directly to the formula of this second kind of moral poetry—a lesson of good counsel imaginatively apprehended and poetically expressed. Far from displaying the fervour which must burn in the mystic and warm by reflection even those who merely describe his experience,[2] the *Love Ron* is actually an artificial and elaborate structure of conceits, so much of a *jeu d'esprit* that one may wonder to what extent the author's emotion was personal and spiritual, and to what extent æsthetic. Friar Thomas is very talented ; he takes the usual elements, pill and sugar, and coats the one with the other very skilfully. His smooth and fluent verses are as good as anything written in English during the thirteenth century that has survived. An imaginative element more metaphysical than emotional preponderates in his poem and exercises itself in developing the conceit of the heavenly lover. But as that conceit is used here it is only a poet's fiction, not a mystic's idiom of thought. His ultimate purpose is his matter-of-fact moral lesson, and the expression of this becomes poetry as the poet is transported by his pleasure in the fluency of his own invention. That he had a great affection for his art is evident from the poem ; that he himself apprehended emotionally the moral lesson which he conveyed is perhaps not quite so certain. However that may be, his evident æsthetic pleasure in his creation is enough to set his poem above even the best of the plain moral verse and distinguish it by kind as well.

Generally the emotion in moral lyrics where the matter was imaginatively transformed is closer to that matter than to the means of its expression. There are instances where

---

[1] *Concise Cambridge History of English Literature* (Cambridge 1941) 31. Cf. also *The Cambridge History of English Literature* I (Cambridge 1907) 233.

[2] For a well-known instance, see Crashaw's *Hymn to the Name and Honour of the Admirable Saint Teresa.*

5

apparently the poetic emotion has originated in the excitement of contemplation of the moral subject. In such cases it is inevitable that the poet should associate himself closely with this subject and consider it in terms of his own life rather than as applied to a congregation which he addresses. Such contemplative emotion can have for its starting-point as simple a motive as the ' vanity of vanities ' of *Ecclesiastes*,

> We tyll þe erth, we tourne it to & fro,
> We labour ry3ht deuly with grete besynes,
> We dyge, we delue, we saw, we schere also,
> We geder þe corne home fore oþer mens ryches,
> We haue full seldome any restfull gladnes,
>> Bot labour in pouerte to þe tyme þat we dy3e—
>> 3it is oure labour not bot vanyte.[1]

Often it is aroused by the thought of age creeping upon the poet.[2] It finds its finest expression in concrete instances when the subject of contemplation is not a moral maxim impersonally conceived, but a reality with which the poet's day-to-day life has made him familiar.

The immediacy of such a subject seems to intensify the excitement of contemplation to a point where it takes control of the poem, awakens the author's creative faculty, and almost subordinates to the fulfilment of its own emotional existence the moral purpose by which we classify the poem, and which indeed may have been the original purpose of its composition. When the emotional experience has been turned into a lesson the poet seems to be resolving the moral problem in terms of himself, and to be thinking of his audience as no worse or less enlightened than he is. Illustrations of this process are afforded by two of the lovelier moral poems, *A Winter Song*[3] and *Lollai litel child whi wepistow so sore ?*,[4]

---

[1] Carleton Brown, *Religious Lyrics of the Fifteenth Century* (Oxford 1939) no. 151 ll. 71–7.

[2] As, for instance, in *Ib.* no. 148. Although this theme is probably universal it seems to have a special tradition in the Middle Ages beginning with the ' Elegies of Maximian ' (Baehrens, *Poetae Latini Minores* vol. v, 312 ff.) A direct English descendant of one of these is *Le Regre de Maximian*, C.B. *XIII* no. 51.

[3] C.B. *XIV* no. 9.   *Ib.* no. 28.

similar in tone, and between them very similar in their theme
and their treatment of this to Hopkins's *Goldengrove*. In the
first the particular melancholy of autumn leads the poet to
think of the general sadness of mankind :

> Wynter wakeneþ al my care,
> Nou þis leues waxeþ bare ;
> Ofte y sike & mourne sare
> When hit comeþ in my þoht
> Of þis worldes ioie hou hit geþ al to noht.

This is the ' You will weep and know why ', of the later
poet. The concept of mortality awakens sorrow and sets
the mood of the poem ; then the emotion takes an inward
and personal turn and applies the generality from which the
poet's grief arose to his own case.

> ' Al goþ bote godes wille,
> Alle we shule deye þah vs like ylle.'

In another age the corresponding emotion would have been a
form of *Weltschmerz* : life is brief and transitory, the moment
of its ending uncertain, our destination thereafter unknown.
In its mediæval expression a moving and sympathetic poem
emerges from what might have been a conventional piece of
moralizing. This poem for all its poignancy is, however,
weakened by commonplace expression in certain lines. The
inference is that the author was a man of more feeling than
art, who, while sincerely and deeply moved, failed to achieve
artistic perfection. Among the moral poetry, however, this
strong emotional quality is notable.

' The blight man was born for ' is the theme of *Lollai litel
child*. This lyric, a curiosity because it is the earliest of
the surviving *lullay* poems, because unlike all the others the
child in it is not the infant Christ but an ordinary baby, and
because it may be by an Anglo-Irish poet, a remote fore-
runner of Yeats and Colum and Gogarty, is itself poetically
very good. It communicates powerfully the reflective sadness
aroused by the thought of what a child may expect from life.
This effect is created principally by the tender and gentle
touch of the poet, his direct address to the child, which keeps

the tenderness constant, and his evidently genuine concern
both for the particular child of his poem and the generality
in question. His emotional and artistic sincerity result in a
plainness of expression entirely suited to his communication :

> Nedis mostou wepe, hit was iȝarkid þe ȝore
> Euer to lib in sorow, and sich and mourne euere,
> As þin eldren did er þis—

In its more successful moments the emotion of this poem is
so completely accessible even to the modern reader that there
is no need to make excuses for the occasional mediæval expressions which have lost their force with the passage of time, like

> Lollai, lollai, litil child, þe fote is in þe whele,

or this figure from the stage,

> Deth ssal com wiþ a blast vte of a wel dim horre ;

the poem is generally moving enough to carry us over them.

To recapture the emotional effect so completely is less easy
in the case of a special group of these moral lyrics, the
' mortality ' poems. These concern themselves in one way or
another with death in its physical aspects, and generally
spare us little in the treatment :

> Nu sal firrotien þine teit & þine tunke
> & al þat is wid-innen þe—þi liuerre & þi longe
> & þi þrote-bolle wid þat þu soncke—[1]

Their concern was not with the subject for its own sake but
with driving home the lesson of mortality by the grimmest
possible argument. The origin of this motive was probably
the sermon of the preacher of retreats, whose successors to
this day make a similar appeal to the morbid imagination ;
as a calculated preaching device systematically exploited it
is unattractive. Yet some of the poetic turns it was made
to serve in the Middle Ages justify themselves because in
them the poet dissociates himself somewhat from the simple
object of preaching the fear of death to an unregenerate
congregation, and instead himself experiences the emotion

[1] C.B. XIII no. 29 ll. 33–5.

in terms not simply of terror and revulsion, but also of splendour and awe, which he communicates as an experience of his own soul and salvation :

> Quid sum miser tunc dicturus ?
> Quem patronum rogaturus
> Dum vix justus sit securus ?

But only such exaltation will remove this mortality poetry from the grim banality of homily, and it is not, I fear, common in Middle English verse. The treatments of this subject of death take a variety of other forms.

An instance of no more than moderate success is *þene latemeste dai*,[1] bleak and graphic enough to have a powerful effect upon even the modern reader, but showing little use of imagination by its author except so far as he deliberately attempts to shock, and otherwise invokes the associative force of two common poetic motives, the *ubi sunt* theme and a reproach directed by the soul against the body. The author of this poem undoubtedly is aware of the application of his sermon to himself, but he does not become sufficiently detached from the preaching intention to achieve a poetic effect. The short poem called *Proprietates Mortis*,[2] which exists in several versions, comes nearer to achieving what we expect to find in poetry. Here too the teaching intention was evidently an influence on the author's attitude to his subject, but it is not directly expressed in the poem, which, in a description of the physical signs of death, by piling one detail of horror upon another, mounts to a cry of despair :

> Al to late, al to late
> Wanne þe bere ys ate gate !

While it is hardly possible to like this lyric one is compelled to admire it and to concede that its author has powerfully concentrated in it the raw material of the harrowing sermon.

Two less direct treatments of the same theme survive, which, although they may not be original with the poets whose versions we shall consider, certainly excited their

[1] C.B. *XIII* no. 29.
[2] *Ib.* no. 71. See also the editor's notes, 220–2.

creative faculties.   One of these is apparently the original of the second ' stanza ' in *Þer ie latemest dai* :

> If man him biðocte
> Inderlike & ofte
> Wu arde is te fore
> Fro bedde te flore,
> Wu reuful is te flitte
> Fro flore te pitte,
> Fro pitte te pine
> Ðat neure sal fine,
> I wene non sinne
> Sulde his herte winnen.[1]

Here the circumstance of dying is taken for granted and not elaborated ; instead the imagination of the poet turns to the less sensational if equally gloomy progress of the corpse, from whose point of view he extracts the pathos, to its grave and beyond.   The emotion of this poem is obtained with skilful economy :   the graphic words ' fore ' and ' flitte ' make us visualize this journey ' fro bedde te flore, . . . fro flore te pitte ', the leading epithets ' arde ' and ' reuful ' suggest the proper form of our response to the pictorial impressions, and then, when the required state of mind has been induced, comes the lesson.

Even more removed from the simple physical circumstances of death is a poem which in its probably earliest English form expressed an idea of some originality :

> Erþe toc of erþe erþe wyþ woh,
> Erþe oþer erþe to þe erþe droh,
> Erþe leyde erþe in erþene þroh—
> Þo heuede erþe of erþe erþe ynoh.[2]

These verses have been called a 'moralizing jingle ',[3] but the moral lesson which, by that description, ought to be trite and superficial, is actually a riddling conceit symbolically put, and the repetition of *erþe* contributes decidedly to the effect of the verses.   The theme is that there is a conflict within the natural world resolved by death.   Violently,

[1] C.B. *XIII* no. 13.   [2] *Ib.* no. 73.
[3] G. L. Brook, *The Harleian Lyrics* (Manchester 1948) 15.

wyþ woh, life is wrested from lifelessness; in compensation other life is drawn back to lifelessness again and enclosed within the universal element, whereby that element obtains satisfaction from itself and the conflict is in one instance resolved. The four hammering verses which express this idea contain another meaning in addition to the philosophical sense of the unity of existence : they also convey an uneasy emotional and personal significance in the image of ' erþene þroh ', from which, probably, the ' superficial ' moral lesson originates. The popularity of this theme [1] supports the opinion which ought to be formed from an appreciation of its meaning and emotional force, that its effect in its own time must have been intense. It may indeed not be a good poem, or even a poem at all in some strict senses of the word, but we ought to allow the poet his means of obtaining his effects, and recognize that he has forcefully transformed the *Memento homo quod cinis es et in cinem reverteris* which was his starting-point.

Erthe upon Erthe is probably too conceited to display the universality of its theme to advantage today. Two mortality poems addressed to beautiful women may possibly have a more permanent appeal. One, from the thirteenth century, evidently belongs to the mortality tradition at its simplest :

> Wen þe turuf is þi tuur,
> & þi put is þi bour,
> Þi wel & þi wite þrote
> ssulen wormes to note.
> Wat helpit þe þenne
> Al þe worilde wnne ? [2]

This piece of conventional moralization is given an original turn because the poet has limited his use of harrowing effects, and has had recourse instead to his own emotional apprehension of the poignancy of beauty decaying. The unassuming directness of his treatment, as well as all its limitations, become apparent if his intense little poem is

[1] See Hilda Murray, *The Middle English Poem Erthe upon Erthe*, EETS 141 (London 1911).
[2] C.B. *XIII* no. 30, and see notes, 191-2.

compared with a more pretentious and sophisticated mid-fifteenth-century development of a related theme in *A Mirror for Young Ladies at Their Toilet*.[1] In this poem the mirror speaks to the girl with the voice of death ; its words are polished and rhetorical, but as unkind and unsympathetic as if the poet took pleasure in the bitterness of his message. That they are in character does not diminish the coldness or soften his attitude. Neither the sustained figure of the talking mirror nor the polish of the treatment nor the one really memorable line,

> Shorte is thy sesoun here, thogh thou go gay,

make the poem attractive, but its force, and the manner in which its conception and treatment raise it artistically above the run of mediæval moral verse must be conceded ; it adds an imaginative element to the moral content and purpose, and its lesson is sharp and hard.

Very few of these moral lyrics can have in modern times anything like the effect that they must have achieved at the time of their composition. In modern appreciative criticism the word ' didactic ' is a bugbear ; it seems that the acceptance of a direct teaching function for poetry belongs to a tradition of criticism inadmissible nowadays, or at least, if this is not conceded, that we are inclined to require of poetry that professes to teach higher standards of artistic achievement than those by which we measure other work. Whether or not a different principle of criticism from that which we generally follow applies to the moral lyrics, these Middle English poems seldom approach poetic greatness or beauty. Their failure to do this may perhaps be ascribable to a theoretically necessary incompatibility between a didactic intention and creative activity, but it can also be more simply explained, for the absence of permanently moving qualities from the surviving examples may mean no more than that their authors wrote with a limited purpose which, in the religious circumstances of their times, they did achieve.

A further insight into these circumstances and the attitude which they formed in the Middle English religious poets is

[1] C.B. *XV* no. 152.

afforded by the devotional as distinct from moral poetry of the Middle English period. Middle English devotional poetry divides itself into two main kinds. The first is simply prayer in verse, and becomes poetry only on the few occasions when the sense and the emotion contained in it are expressed appropriately or beautifully enough to lift the commonplaces of worship beyond conventional utterance. Then the effect no longer depends merely upon a community of religion between author and public but is fortified by the communication of the worshipping poet's exaltation and the transportation of the reader. The second kind is devotional and meditative, and sets out to communicate a religious experience or to induce a state of devotion by other means than merely invoking the common symbols of worship that must even in the Middle Ages have been repeated so often as to become mere forms of words, and by relying on the effect that such forms of words must have among the devout. It extracts the devotional possibilities of sacred dogmas, situations or incidents by an actual effort of contemplation, and then communicates these with feeling.

Like the simply teaching moral poetry the first kind of devotional verse illustrates the attitude of a certain class of Middle English religious poets to their subject. These men evidently considered their religious topics to be emotionally self-sufficient, and capable of carrying the poems, while they regarded the verse in which they expressed them simply as a convenient medium, the use of which entailed no serious obligation, emotional or imaginative, to awaken a poetic response, but which might have the advantage of being more arresting, or more agreeable, or easier to use or to remember than prose. Indeed they may have adopted verse simply in imitation of the Franciscan tradition of making it serve religious ends. Some of them were certainly aware of its possibilities for embellishing their subject, and a few apparently strove for elegance of expression, but none of the authors of the surviving devotional poems, that are simply prayer in verse, appears to have recognized that in adopting verse he not only availed himself of certain advantages, but also exposed himself to certain hazards by awakening in the reader expectations of an emotional or

5*

imaginative treatment which, to obtain the fullest possible effect, he would be well advised to satisfy.

The hazards are of a different kind from those which applied in the moral poetry. There the danger was that the authors might, in the anxiety to make their moral points, fail to apprehend their subjects emotionally ; they were inclined to develop their lessons so as to persuade by rhetoric or by the preacher's arguments rather than by imaginative or other poetic means. The surviving devotional poetry is relatively free from this fault ; it displays an abundance of emotion, and its authors, of whose sincerity there seems to be little doubt, have apprehended personally what they had to communicate. The shortcoming of these devotional lyrics results from the confidence of the poets in the emotional effectiveness of their subjects and their consequent neglect or rejection of imaginative presentation. Having relegated the manner of their expression to a place of too little importance they produced devotional verse which as an expression of worship may be entirely admirable, but as poetry is unoriginal, uninspired, and, however fluent, seldom distinguished by either clarity of spirit or a genuinely direct and simple expression. Almost everything is wanting that would set the single poem artistically apart from its fellows. None is, strictly speaking, poetic in the sense of being the product of an artistic and creative as well as a simply religious spiritual movement.

The few partial successes make a poor showing, and even those few are outstanding only because of the poor company they keep.[1] They illustrate four styles which, with variations, were the basic media for prayer in verse in the English Middle Ages. Each has its advantages for the user, and each, in uninspired hands, is dangerous. The first, and possibly the most characteristically mediæval style, which borrows its idiom from the prose devotions of the early thirteenth century, is best represented by the thirteenth-century *Look on Me with Thy Sweet Eyes*[2] and a probably fourteenth-century *Prayer of the Five Wounds*.[3] Intimacy and an emphasis on

[1] They are : C.B. *XIII* no. 27 ; C.B. *XIV* no. 52 ; C.B. *XV* nos. 67, 68, 125, 141.

[2] C.B. *XIII* no. 27

[3] C.B. *XIV* no. 52.

the personal quality of the relationship, sweetness and tenderness are the distinguishing features of the lyrics in this style of prayer :

> Moder, loke one me
> Wid þine suete eyen,
> Reste & blisse gef þu me
> Mi lehedi, þen ic deyen.

Their simplicity is winning, and the more effective for seeming not artificial but natural and unpretentious, but as their expression and their concepts are the commonplaces of mediæval worship we may infer that no great poetic or creative activity attended their composition. The mood, the emotion and the words are the common property of the time ; only the act of expressing these in a particular combination and in a tolerably concise and compressed verse is original with the poet. At the best this style is tender, moving and sweet, at worst it is cloying to the point of insipidity.

The second style is a reflection of the idiom of fourteenth-century mysticism. A good example is the fifteenth-century lyric *Close in My Breast Thy Perfect Love*,[1] which resembles in the quality of its expression the devotional and meditative poems of the school of Rolle.[2] The characteristic of this style is its affectation of the language of the mystic, an air of great fervour real or assumed, a deliberate simplicity of vocabulary and a tendency to obscurity consequent upon the use of this vocabulary to communicate special meanings :

> Ihū, my luf, my ioy, my reste,
> Þi perfite luf close in my breste
> Þat I þe luf & neuer reste ;
> And mak me luf þe of al þinge best,
> And wounde my hert in þi luf fre,
> Þat I may reyne in ioy euer-more with þe.

---

[1] C.B. *XV* no. 67.

[2] See C.B. *XIV* nos. 77–86. Rolle's verse does not receive individual attention in this study because, in my opinion, it does not merit particular consideration *as poetry*. It seems to me principally important as a document of mysticism, with which phenomenon I am not here primarily concerned.

The run on the word *luf* is deliberate; *luf, ioy, reste* and *wounde my herte* have significances which the ordinary reader then or now might easily fail to attach to them, and much of the force of the communication is consequently in danger of being lost.

The third style of verse prayer is distinguished by a perfunctory concession to poetry; the writer opens with a poetic, often a secular figure from which he develops his prayer. For instance, he longs for Jesus

> As turtel þat longeþ boþe nyȝt & day
> For her loue is gone hyr froo,[1]

or he prays that the name of Christ

> Wedyr y ryde or gone
> In euery parell & in euery aduersite
> Be my defence aȝenste my mortall fone.[2]

The conception of these figures, of the languishing dove or of the knight beset by enemies is promising, but the poems do not fulfil their promise; they very soon lapse into what can even now be recognized with assurance as trite and commonplace expressions. The nature of formal prayer would probably be too well defined and inflexible to admit of the ready introduction of a sustained metaphor from without. I think that the poets themselves would have acknowledged this impossibility, and that they intended the tropes to be no more than quite secondary embellishments. If that is true they were surely mistaken in believing that an undeveloped poetic figure arbitrarily attached to a composition is anything else but detrimental to its quality.

Finally there is an evidently late style characterized by a dignified and lofty solemnity which, in one of the more striking instances at least, seems to derive its quality and possibly some of its specific aureate touches from its Latin original.[3] This style, which anticipates in several respects the present manner of formal worship, may well seem the most effective of the four to the modern reader. Even so it smacks of

---

[1] C.B. *XV* no. 68.   [2] *Ib.* no. 125.
[3] *Ib.* no. 141. See also the notes to the poem, 336–7.

pretentiousness, of pleasure taken in the artificiality of its language, of a preponderance of the intellectual over the poetic and creative faculties in its composition :

> All that to my helth y had of thi gyfte,
> Vnprofitably, as to thy sight hit semyd,
> I haue expendid thurgh dampnabill schyfte—
>
> That is to say, the tyme of my penaunce
> In vanitees, and in superfluite
> My body also, in pride and distaunce
> The grace of my baptyme ; but allthyng worldle,
> My lord, y haue louyd more than the,
> My redemptour, my noryssher and my conseruatour.

The second type of devotional poetry differs both in kind and in quality from that which is simply formal prayer in verse, but the difference in quality is usually a simple and predictable result of the difference in kind. It was observed above that this second sort of devotional poetry relied in part for its effect upon the religious exercise technically known as *meditation*, which is the intent contemplation of a religious subject for the purpose of inducing a devout state of mind. This meditation is a recognized form of worship which need not, although it sometimes does, include the actual formal address of prayer ; the excitement, or, if the term is preferred, the deepening of the spiritual state itself constitutes the worship.[1] It will at once be evident that poetry connected with this contemplative activity is by its nature more happily circumstanced than that which is concerned with the simple formal expression of worship, for the contemplative and meditative functions are activities of the imagination, and when they operate, that faculty, being wakened and alert, is

---

[1] It is perhaps advisable to observe here that there is no necessary connexion between the contemplative activity of meditation and mysticism. Most of the recognized exercises of the mystics begin with formal meditations, but the meditations themselves can be independently practised, with no view to the mystical experience. See *Catholic Encyclopedia* s. v PRAYER. The distinction is to be observed in the fact that the Church has always encouraged meditation, but has been chary of giving an indiscriminate blessing or unqualified encouragement to all those with mystical propensities.

more disposed to function in the poetic direction as well. There exists then a presumption that the devotional and meditative poetry will be artistically better than the simple devotional sort, and this presumption is borne out by the poems themselves.

The devotional and meditative poetry can accomplish its purpose of inducing a devout state of mind in a number of ways, each of which is determined by an attitude of the poet to his subject and his audience, and in its turn determines in part the effect of his poem upon both the contemporary and the modern reader. The simplest method is an express invitation extended by the poet to the reader to contemplate a particular religious subject and be devout accordingly. Such prompting of the audience is patently inartistic and derives either from a lack of literary experience or from the poet's mistrust of his own powers or the capabilities of his audience. The second method consists in a more or less faithful poetic treatment of the full-scale conventional meditative exercise authorized by the Church. The third, the first properly artistic method, is a description by the poet of his own emotional response to a religious subject, or of his apprehension of that subject in his own experience. This method produces very mixed results, some, as might be expected, quite conventional and unoriginal, some high in poetic quality. The first condition of success here seems to be that the poet's religious exaltation must to some extent take the form of a creative excitement, so that the religious experience is recorded in artistic terms. The fourth method is designed to bring the religious meaning of a subject of meditation home to the poet's audience by a direct, objective, often graphically descriptive account of it, in which its arresting and affective features are thrown into prominence, and the emphasis is generally so applied as to develop to the full the devotional possibilities of the subject. In this method the application of artistic principles to the subject remains in subordination to the religious intention. In the fifth method, artistically the highest, such a subordination of the artistic to the religious purpose is at least not marked, if it occurs at all. In this method the emphasis is at least equally on the artistic apprehension of the subject. The process of selection, rejection and arrangement by which this apprehension takes place is intensified to the point where a creative transformation of the subject occurs in the poet's fancy or his imagination.

The direct admonition to meditation which is the simplest and least artistic method of obtaining effect in this devotional and meditative poetry is not actually very often to be found in the surviving examples, and is seldom if ever employed to the exclusion of the other methods. Where the admonition or invitation does occur, however, it can, through its artistic crudity, affect adversely the poetic quality of the work in question by suggesting the catechist or novice-master. The extent to which a poem where it occurs is weakened by its presence depends upon how fundamental the device is to the structure and conception of that poem. A quite incidental intrusion,

> Who-so wele loue trewe
> Byhold ihū on þe croys,

or

> Who-so be proud in herte
> Þynk on god almyȝt
> And on his wowndys smerte [1]

need scarcely affect the quality of the poem in which it is made ; if, however, the admonition breaks the mood of the poem by gratuitous direction and comment it can be decidedly harmful.[2] Used as the opening of a poem it can weaken both the imaginative and emotional effects. The poet who wrote

> Abyde, gud men, & hald yhour pays
> And here what god himseluen says,
> Hyngand on þe rode [3]

was less of an artist than those who, treating the same subject, began directly with Christ's words. Those who had even less confidence in their audience, and maintained the attitude of the preceptor throughout the whole or a great part of their poems, sacrificed much of the imaginative response merely to

[1] C.B. *XV* no. 95 ll. 21–2, 31–3.   [2] C.B. *XIV* no. 57 ll. 25–8.
[3] *Ib.* no. 46.   Cf. C.B. *XV* no. 102.

be doubly sure of a docility which would not in any case have been refused by their readers. ' Man ', wrote one poet,

—Folwe seintt Bernardes trace
And loke in ihesu cristes face
How hee lut hys heued to þe
Swetlike for to kessen þe.[1]

To cite the authority may have strengthened the spiritual weight of his verses, but it weakens them as poetry and substitutes for the excitement of an imaginative experience the tedium of learning a lesson. The logical outcome of this method is moral poetry, for to extract the moral lesson from a subject of contemplation is the next step after the admonition to meditate upon that subject. The transition is well illustrated by a poem ascribed to Rolle [2] in which general guidance in meditation and outright moral instruction are thoroughly mixed. Neither is as clear or as forceful as it would be without the other, and the work in which the mixture appears has little poetic value. One of two inferences may be made from poems of the kind in which this explicit direction occurs: either that a man who could not rely upon getting an effect by the direct presentation of his subject was a poor artist or that he was not primarily an artist and that his principal aim was of another kind than artistic.

A variant of this method is found in a carol called *What More Could Christ Have Done ?* [3] where no express invitation to meditation is made, but where the lesson to be extracted is explicitly stated. Again we encounter the refusal to rely on the reader, not this time quite so openly evident, but still real enough to diminish, in every stanza, the chance of creating a mood by which the imagination and not the conscience of the reader may be most directly engaged. Conceivably such a consideration was unimportant to the author, who may have preferred an appeal to the conscience of his reader rather than to the warmer, gentler, and then as now probably more responsive imagination. His poem should be compared for

[1] C.B. *XIII* no. 69.
[2] C.B. *XIV* no. 86. Cf. ll. 1–4 with 5–24.
[3] C.B. *XV* no. 106. R. L. Greene, *The Early English Carols* (Oxford 1935) no. 333.

effect with *A Prayer by the Wounds against the Deadly Sins*,[1] in which the direction takes the form of prayers by the poet in his own person, in which he appeals by the several torments of Christ's passion for protection against particular sins. Here, although the author may have shared the opinion that it was better to be sure than to leave the nature of the response to the reader, he has at least achieved some success by making his prayers fit into the mood that his meditation has created.

The element of direction is usually present, but not always explicit, in those devotional and meditative poems which reflect formal exercises of meditation. The influence of a prescribed form of worship is important here ; in *The Matins of the Cross*,[2] for instance, the meditations for each devotional hour are accompanied by a prayer. Artistically, however, these prayers are sufficiently a part of the whole conception to add to the poetic as well as to the devotional effectiveness of the lyric. Another good example of this type of formal meditation is *The Hours of the Cross* [3] which reflects directly the communal devotional exercise of priest and congregation, when the former would read aloud the meditation :

> At þe time of matines, lord, þu were itake
> & of þine disciples sone were forsake ;
> Þe felle Iewes þe token in þat iche stounde,
> & ledden þe to Cayphas, þin handis harde ibounde,

whereupon the congregation responded :

> We onuren þe͘ crist & blissen þe with voys,
> For þu boutest þis werd with þin holi croys.

The close reflection of actual Church practice here is further evident from the relatively undeveloped quality of the various meditations and the absence of the marks of a private personality in them. Such elementary accounts of the subject may seem crude and ineffective to the modern reader ; he must remember the great evocative power they would have had for even the roughest mediæval man, and how he was trained by his religion to react to them with a considerable emotion.

[1] C.B. *XV* no. 62. [2] C.B. *XIV* no. 30. Cf. also no. 31.
[3] *Ib*. no. 55.

Technically or poetically more elaborate treatments have, however, survived ; *The Matins of the Cross*,[1] for instance, provides not one but several subjects for some of the devotional hours :

> At middai, ihesu, wit mild mode,
> þou spred þi bodi on þe rode,
>   To drau us all to heuen ;
> þat ilk time, lauerd, þou wild
> Tak flexs o þat maiden mild,
>   Thoru an angel steuen.[2]

The literary form of elaboration is well illustrated by one of the best specimens of Middle English devotional poetry, *Thy Blood Thou Shed for Me*.[3] This lyric incidentally begins and ends with a prayer, but concentrates in the body of the poem upon presenting the subject in an unadorned, unsensational manner so well regulated, so directly and competently employed, that it must be the product of considerable taste and discrimination. Two formal exercises in meditation on other subjects, *A Song of the Five Joys*[4] and *The Dolours of Our Lady*,[5] are marred by a religious sensationalism which the authors doubtless believed would enhance their effect, and are inferior in quality to *Thy Blood Thou Shed for Me*. It seems as if these authors, although they were not successful, did nevertheless regard their subjects as something like literary material and were ready to treat them poetically.

The most striking of the literary developments of a formal devotional exercise is, however, the oldest of the surviving specimens, *On God Vreisun of Vre Lefdi*,[6] which represents a much earlier form of the Bernardine tradition than the poems of this kind so far discussed. This poem, for all the uncouth effect of its language upon modern readers, is written in a highly cultivated literary dialect. It is less an outburst of spontaneous spirituality than a deliberate form of worship, a full-scale devotional exercise designed to arouse religious emotion. This will remain true notwithstanding its difference from the seventeenth-century prose which we

---

[1] Like C.B. *XIV* no. 34.
[2] ll. 70–5.
[3] C.B. *XV* no. 92 Cf. also no. 93 and no. 95.
[4] C.B. *XIV* no. 31.
[5] C.B. *XV* no. 94.
[6] C.B. *XIII* no. 3.

associate with prayer. I do not find the mystical experience reflected in it. Nor is it 'erotic'; [1] it would be better to replace that freely used epithet with the term 'sensuous', for this lyric uses every device of the eye and the ear at the disposal of poetry to achieve its effect. It is less rigidly formal than many of the later works that correspond to it, embraces a wider range of themes, and certainly rambles a little. Much of its formlessness is, however, to be ascribed to its want of stanzaic or strophic definition, but this formlessness is its most serious fault. The meditation, which is upon the joy of heaven and the mediatory and protective powers of the Virgin, gains much of its effect from the sensuous language. This poem can cast a spell. Its smooth lines have a murmurous sound, a polished syntactical flow; their effect is, in view of the subject, remarkably visual. At times it seems almost pre-Raphaelite :

> Al þin hird is ischrud mid hwite ciclatune,
> And alle heo beoð ikruned mid guldene krune ;
> Heo beoð so read so rose, so hwit so þe lilie,
> And euer-more heo beoð gled & singeð þuruhut murie. [2]

At other times the author identifies heaven with that perfect country which has haunted the fancy of many dreamers:

> Þer ðe neure deað ne come, ne herm ne sorinesse.
> Þer bloweð inne blisse blostmen hwite & reade,
> Þer ham neuer ne mei snou ne uorst iureden,
> Þer ne mei non ualuwen, uor þer is eche sumer,
> Ne non liuiinde þing woc þer nis ne ȝeomer. [3]

The extravagance of this conception, coming early in the poem, is artistically good and valid, for it establishes a mood of receptivity to the more earnest and instant problem of actually winning salvation that is treated in the later portion. Yet structurally this fine imaginative flowering is inferior to most of the work of a similar kind surviving from the fourteenth and fifteenth centuries ; the poet's fluent enthusiasm indeed enables him to create a state of devotion in the reader, but seems disinclined or unable to regulate and discipline itself. Consequently the effect of this poem, although intense in parts, is decidedly mixed.

[1] Cf. *op. cit.* xvii. [2] ll. 51–4. [3] ll. 36–40.

In the surviving devotional and meditative verse that reflects formal religious exercises the poetic effect depends then, other considerations apart, upon the attitude of the author to his audience and subject. As a first principle, the literary quality of this poetry seems to vary inversely with the amount of overt direction included in it, and with the importance of such direction to the poetic structure. Next it is affected by the elaboration of the poet's treatment, either by his development of the devotional technique itself, or by his use of poetic in addition to religious persuasion. Finally it is influenced by the obvious technical considerations of expression, structure, etc., which apply to all poetry.

The devotional and meditative poetry in which the poet communicates the mood of contemplation by recording his own emotional response to a religious subject differs in kind from both the solicitations to meditation and the formal exercises, for by definition it depends upon his attitude of mind and heart to his subject matter. The varieties of this kind of poetry are distinguished then simply by the nature of his emotion and the means by which it is expressed ; the relative excellence of the poems is further determined by the success of the communication.

In an inferior example, the early carol *Lovely Tear from Lovely Eye*,[1] the emotional attachment of the poet to his subject is evidently strong, but indifferently communicated. The inspiration which prompted this carol looks as if it might have come from an older piece which also contributed the burden ; but the poetic exaltation of this burden is not attained in the body of the carol. Only once does the emotion appear to have been apprehended in such a way that it informs the treatment ;

> I prud & kene,
> Þu meke an clene,
> Withouten wo or wile ;
> Þu art ded for me,
> & i liue þoru þe,
> So blissed be þat wile.

---

[1] C.B. *XIV* no. 69 : Greene no. 271.

Even there the effect of the contrast is neither as intense nor as concentrated as seems to have been intended. The possibilities of success might have been greater had the author developed only one of the two elements; either would certainly have suggested the other. Elsewhere too he seems to have groped for expression;

> Þi sorwe is more
> Þan mannis muth may telle

is certainly true of his own case. Moreover, his approach to the subject is too general; there is little co-ordination in his treatment of the incidents of the passion, and his emotion, in consequence of being ill-defined, appears to change character within the poem.

Such failure to define and establish a single effect is not, however, common among the poets who chose this kind of treatment. Generally they understood the effect they sought to create, and succeeded tolerably well in transmitting the emotion that fired them. Generally too their devotional excitement was attended by a poetic awakening. In *A Song of Sorrow for the Passion*,[1] for instance, not only is the movement of emotion considerable in itself,

> Hi sike, al wan hi singe,
> For sorue Þat hi se
> Wan 'hic wit wepinge
> Bi-holde a-pon Þe tre,

but it also sharpens the artist's powers of apprehension and enables him to create a fine pictorial effect, shaped by a well-developed sense of composition which makes his poem spectacular in the good sense of the word.

> Hey a-pon a dune
> As al folke hit se may,
> A mile wythute Þe tune
> A-bute Þe midday,
> Þe rode was op areride.

---

[1] C.B. *XIII* no. 64.

The quality of this poem is not uniform, but the emotion of the poet, who is intensely aware of the poignancy of his subject, is fully communicated :

> Þe naylis beit al to longe,
> Þe smyt his al to sleye,
> Þue bledis al to longe,
> Þe tre his al to heye.
> Þe stonis waxin wete—
> Allas ! ihesu mi suete,
> Feu frendis hafdis neye.

His apprehension of the subject makes these details into symbols charged with feeling, and is strong enough to glorify by the magic of poetry religious commonplaces too often invoked without emotion :

> He honge al of blode
> So hey apon þe rode
> Bitwixen þefis two—
> Hu soldi singe mor ?

Some such magical transformation is necessary before a religious lyric can be a good poem. The religious emotion must coincide and identify itself with a creative excitement. In *A Song of Sorrow for the Passion* such a union has taken place ; the poet has apprehended his experience artistically, and expressed it in poetry limited only by his gifts as an artist.

That union of religious and poetic emotion, the most important condition of success to religious poetry, is variously exemplified in four short poems, *The Mind of the Passion*,[1] *I Would Be Clad in Christis Skin*,[2] *Bless the Time the Apple Was Taken*,[3] and *I Have Set My Heart so High*,[4] which, although they are not among the best religious lyrics of the English Middle Ages, certainly belong with the most remarkable. Each of these four is a poetic expression of intense emotional experience generated in the poet by his meditation ; all reflect acts of worship of a profound kind, and in each not only a religious but also a poetic exaltation is to be

---

[1] C.B. *XIII* no. 56A.   [2] C.B. *XIV* no. 71.
[3] C.B. *XV* no. 83.   [4] C.B. *XIV* no. 129.

discerned. Their brevity is important ; they are like symbols to represent the force that produced them, or like glimpses into the minds of devout men who were also in some degree poets, and yearned for adequate means of expressing their devotion. The first, *The Mind of the Passion*, the least complicated both in form and in content, is an almost incoherent outcry of worship like the *saeta* with which the townsman of Seville in Holy Week greets the approach of the image of the saint of his quarter. The two English versions of this poem should be compared with the Latin which they evidently translate or reflect.[1] This is tranquilly prosaic, and they are breathless and exclamatory. Good poetry they are probably not, but religious emotion has possessed the creative faculty of their poets sufficiently to make them arresting. The second of these short poems, *I Would Be Clad in Christis Skin*, a poem of renunciation and taking refuge, like *The Mind of the Passion* seems to reflect a Latin original,[2] and in the same way its treatment is emotionally much more intense. Having borrowed the strong figure from which it is named, the poet developed this and made it more directly personal by coupling with it a simple and whole-hearted renunciation of the world. *Bless the Time the Apple Was Taken*, remarkable even in this company for the way it communicates the exultation of the author by the movement of its verse, has the rousing quality of a catch but is notwithstanding devout and spiritual. Its emotion centres in one of the great religious motives of the Middle Ages, the *O felix culpa, O necessarium peccatum ade* which formed a part of the Easter rejoicings of the mediæval Church.[3] The solemn liturgical jubilation has, however, here been translated into a less restrained and more personal joy so strong that it illuminates a no more than ordinary gift of expression. *I Have Set My Heart so High*, which communicates a more private and profound emotion, is probably from a literary point of view the best of these four poems. It is an intense

[1] C.B. *XIII* no. 211.

[2] C.B. *XIV* no. 267. The other source proposed by Brown (no. 268) seems unlikely upon closer examination.

[3] For another poetic use of the motive, see *Piers Plowman*, B-Text v line 490, and Skeat's note to the passage, EETS 67 (1877) 142

and poignant piece, approaching sublimity in the felicitous openings of its two stanzas, but marred by an anticlimatic close which suggests that the union of religious and poetic excitement is here still imperfect.

As much emotion, and a much more subtle art attended the creation of *Sunset on Calvary*,[1] which is to be classified with these four poems but is more beautiful and moving than any of them :

> Nou goth sonne vnder wod,—
> Me reweth, marie, þi faire Rode.
> Nou goþ sonne vnder tre,—
> Me reweþ, marie, þi sone and þe.

In this short lyric the fusion of devotional and creative activities is nearly complete. Its first effect is pictorial : the sun falling beneath an arm of the cross, and Mary's face, tear-stained and not beautiful now, raised to that cross. This is a triumph of selection. Two details only have been taken from a picture many times fully delineated, but they are most significant. The setting sun, the stark silhouettes against the light, the end of a long day of immeasurable unhappiness, these responses not only carry their own loads of feeling but can also set off trains of associations related to the most dramatic experience in the mind of the mediæval Christian. But the effect is not to be so simple or conventional ; the second detail evokes a special response, half impertinent, secular. *Me reweth, marie, þi faire Rode* is scarcely pious ; it is the poet's perennial regret for beauty destroyed. Yet its very incongruity intensifies the first emotion, adds to the total of feeling with which the poem is experienced, makes the whole situation human and immediate. That second detail is not simple in origin but must be traced to the *Book of Ruth* and the *Canticles*.[2] While this circumstance in no way increases the effectiveness of the poem, it is important to us as an illustration of a remarkably successful operation of combined religious and poetic activity.

From the modern point of view the best of the devotional and meditative poems which achieves its effect by the author's presentation of his own emotional experience of religious

---

[1] C.B. *XIII* no. 1.   [2] See *op. cit.* 165–6.

contemplation is the fifteenth-century poem *For Thy Sake Let the World Call Me Fool*.[1] This noble and lofty prayer is as good in every sense as anything of its kind written in the seventeenth century. Its sincerity is undeniable, and its effect is profound. Technically it is excellent ; its severely unadorned vocabulary and solemn, slow movement could not be better suited to the subject :

> —In thy blessyd wondes is the verey scole
> That must teche me with the worlde to be called a fole.
> O Ihesu, ihesu, ihesu, graunt that I may loue the soo
> Þat the wysdom of the worlde be cleene fro me A-goo.

There is here no denying the completeness of the communication, and no uneasy suspicion, probably improper but hard to avoid, of the presence of the Franciscan glibness of which the mediæval writers themselves have made one aware. Above all, the effect is sustained throughout the poem. If this piece were showier, or had more typically mediæval colour, it would be more famous.

Despite their arresting quality all but the last two of these poems have serious technical faults which no amount of sympathy ought to prevent us from remarking. They only partially succeed in establishing the effect which their authors evidently intended. *I Would Be Clad in Christis Skin* is good only in parts and commonplace elsewhere ; *The Mind of the Passion*, because of its poetically elementary nature, demands too much co-operation of the reader ; *Bless the Time the Apple Was Taken*, by its strange combination of matter and manner, seems to set itself singularly apart from the general run of its kind ; and in *I Have Set My Heart so High* the failure to sustain effect within the stanzas is so marked as to create a sense of anticlimax.

In the best examples of the next kind of devotional and meditative poetry, where the devotional significance of a particular religious occasion is brought home to the reader by an objective presentation of that occasion, such shortcomings are less often to be found. In these lyrics, artistically more advanced than the ones so far discussed, the authors, whatever their intentions and feelings may have been, refrain both from

[1] C.B. *XV* no. 98.

instruction and from openly expressing their own emotions, but achieve their devotional purpose and their poetic effect by selecting and arranging their material so as to endow it with significant form.   The best of them do not need to say

> Þi sorwe is more
> Þan mannis muth may telle ;

they enlist the eye and ear, and the imagination of the reader to help ' mannis muth ', and so not only awaken devotion in him, but also at times transport him by poetic means.

There appear to be two basic methods of objective presentation of the subject for devotion.   The first and more elementary of these consists in a simple narrative account, not particularly circumstantial, presented with little apparent selection for the sake of emphasis.   The surviving examples in this kind, *The Bargain of Judas* [1] and *The Journey of the Three Kings*,[2] apart from the attraction of the antique, have little to recommend them.   It is in fact not possible to discern any particular artistic intention in them.   Their authors evidently intended to increase religious knowledge and so devotion, and they may conceivably have been trying to make their subjects human and accessible, but in comparison with the poems in which the second method is employed, these two lyrics are quaint and feeble.

That second method, artistically much more advanced, assumes familiarity with the circumstances of the story, and is directed almost entirely to extracting by the selection of detail the greatest possible emotional effect from the subject, and to turning this emotion, by the skilful use of emphasis, into religious and devotional channels.   A striking illustration of this whole method of objective presentation is afforded by three of the *lullay* poems,[3] which differ in form but are all designed to induce the pathetic emotion, to evoke feelings of tenderness by whatever means their poets can devise.   Not only do they set out to awaken sympathy ; they also seek to intensify the normal response by drawing attention to the particular object, by pointing out the sensational contrast between the child's actual omnipotence and his helplessness

---

[1] C.B. *XIII* no. 25.   [2] *Ib.* no. 26.
[3] C.B. *XIV* no. 65 ; C.B. *XV* nos. 4, 5.

in his mother's arms. They are unashamedly sentimental, but for all that each of them succeeds in its effect by creating an awareness in the reader of the Christ-child's miserable humanity, and the magnitude of the act of oblation for which he is destined. They make much of his vulnerability, of the mean circumstances of his birth, and they insist upon these points until the reader must in the end respond by seeing in his imagination a divinity shivering in a shed like an unwanted brat :

> Child, it is a weping dale þat þu art comen inne,
> Þi pore clutes it prouen wel, þi bed mad in þe binne ;
> Cold & hunger þu must þolen as þu were geten in senne.[1]

In this vein the mother complains ; her son is king and made all things and now must lie on hay. Every detail of this kind these poets unashamedly exploit, and every time they have successfully awakened pathos they forecast the worse suffering to come. Poetically these *lullay* poems are only slightly above the average level of achievement in Middle English religious poetry. Their particular charm consists in a lightness and grace that suits their pathos, and probably originates in the tenderness of their authors for the subject. They are principally remarkable for their effective exploitation of the principles of selection and emphasis for religious ends.

Some such solicitation of the reader's emotion by insistence on selected features of the subject is found in all the surviving lyrics whose purpose was to induce devotional meditation by an objective treatment. Many of these lyrics have as subject some incident or situation of the passion or crucifixion ; many seem to derive, directly or remotely, from standard texts of meditation.[2] In all, the intention of the poets has evidently been to throw the arresting and spectacular features of their subjects into prominence in order to induce a lively spiritual state. This purpose was religious in the first place ; its execution could, however, if the poet were gifted enough, conform incidentally to artistic principles and thus produce good poetry.

---

[1] C.B. *XIV* no. 65 ll. 13–15.
[2] Among many references to these see, for instance, *Ib.* 241–3, 247 265, 266.

The basic principle of this treatment is then a particular use of emphasis ; the differences between the poems are determined by the means with which this emphasis is achieved, and the degree of actual poetic vision discernible in the general treatment. To illustrate these differences it is convenient to consider three poems on the same or a similar theme, the first, third and fourth works in Carleton Brown's *Religious Lyrics of the Fourteenth Century*. These are crucifixion poems, all apparently of a derivative nature. In *Think, Man, of my Hard Stundes* [1] and *Look to Me on the Cross* [2] the form of communication is an appeal from Christ on the cross ; they begin

> Man, þu haue þine þout one me,
> Þenc hou dere i bouthe the.

and

> Man and wyman, loket to me
> U michel pine ich þolede for þe.

The first and best of these lyrics, *Candet Nudatum Pectus*,[3] is introduced by no appeal but simply represents certain pictorial details of the crucifixion. All set out to harrow the reader, to rouse first his compassion and then a sense of his own personal guilt for which such suffering was the necessary atonement ; this purpose is most clearly evident in *Look to Me on the Cross* :

> Loke upone mi rig, u sore ich was ibiten ;
> Loke to mi side, wat Blode ich haue ileten.
> Mine uet an mine honden nailed beth to þe rode ;
> Of þe þornes prikung min hiued urnth a blode.
> Fram side to side, fro hiued to þe fot,
> Turn mi bodi abuten, oueral þu findest blod.
> Man, þin hurte, þin hurte, þu turne to me,
> For þe vif wndes þe ich tholede for þe.

Notwithstanding the similarity of purpose there is a considerable difference in the poetic effects of these lyrics. *Think, Man of my Hard Stundes* is quite inartistically obvious :

> Hardere deth ne mai non ben—
> Þenc, man, al hit was for the.

---

[1] C.B. *XIV* no. 3.   [2] *Ib*. no. 4.   [3] *Ib*. no. 1.

Instead of gripping the imagination and the emotions it oppresses with the tedium of an indifferent sermon. *Look to Me on the Cross* is marred by an evident lack of the power of selection in its poet, who seems to have relied simply upon an accumulation of detail for his effects, until his product reads like a catalogue of suffering :

> Bigin at his molde and loke to his to,
> ne saltu no wit vinde bute anguisse and wo.[1]

Only in the first and best of the three is there evidence of the operation of the process of selection and of a sense of the spectacular or the dramatic to guide it ; this poem demonstrates its importance to the success of a religious lyric. In the Latin original of *Candet Nudatum Pectus* the details of the description are recited in a prosy monotone ; in the Middle English lyric a number have been omitted and the remainder arranged so as to create a picture of which the form is poetically and emotionally significant :

> Wyth was hys nakede brest and red of blood hys syde,
> Bleye was his fair handled, his wund dop ant wide,
> And his arms ystreith hey up-hon þe rode ;
> On fif studes an his body þe stremes ran o blod.

The man who made this from the bald list in the *Liber Meditationum* did more than merely translate ; he set out to obtain a sensational effect and succeeded. The heavy emphasis of his opening, the brevity, the striking contrast of colours that ensures a bright visual impression, the admission of an irrelevant worldly concept of beauty into the picture in ' fair handled ', the romanticism of the designedly spectacular and evocative phrase ' hey up-hon þe rode ', the ably managed combination of sentence structure and prosody by which within four lines a transition is convincingly made from the stridency of indignation to the awful quiet of resolution, all contribute to making *Candet Nudatum Pectus* not only a better poem than the others of its kind but also, in consequence, a better persuader to meditation. In this connexion we should note that it contains no invitation to worship, that it

[1] C.B. *XIV* no 2 B. ll. 11–12.

does not employ a single ' soliciting ' adjective, and that its effect is not designed to mount by accumulation but is made both quieter and more intense by selection and arrangement. *Candet Nudatum Pectus* has been touched by the creative imagination ; it is more than merely religion in verse.

In this consideration of poems that present their subjects for devotion objectively we observed two varieties of treatment of the crucifixion theme, one a direct record of the poet's vision of the occasion, the other his conception of a speech by Christ from the cross. Examples of the second variety are numerous, and several are more successful than the specimen considered above.[1] Two at least [2] are directly derived from the *Improperia*, the Reproaches of Christ which to this day form part of the service of Good Friday in the Roman Church. Christ says to the Jews

> My volk, what habbe y do þe
> Oþer in what þyng toened þe ?
> Gyn nouþe and onswere þou me ;

then as if in anticipation of their answer He recites the instances of His care for them. There is little poetic effect in these two lyrics beyond that ensured by the actual religious occasion, and they are interesting principally as elementary examples of a type in which a fair creative success was possible. *Christ's Three Songs to Man* [3] is a more advanced specimen, and has an effect of some poignancy, but is marred by the faults common in this type, uncritical accumulation of detail and an insistence on the one point of all which would be obvious about the subject to any Christian :

> Mi herte is forsmite ato,
> Al, mankinde, for loue of þe.

Homo Vide quid pro Te Patior,[4] possibly by Rolle and certainly in his manner, is enthusiastically and inartistically fluent, but apparently for the author its emotional meaning was enhanced

---

[1] See, for example, C.B. *XIV* nos. 15, 72, 74, 76, 77 ; C.B. *XV* nos. 103, 104, 109.

[2] C.B. *XIV* nos. 15 and 72. See *Ib.* no. 247.

[3] *Ib.* no. 76.   [4] *Ib.* no. 77.

by special mystical suggestions that are at best imperfectly conveyed to earth-bound readers ; its effect is in consequence scarcely intense. *O vos omnes qui transitis per viam*,[1] however, is much nearer in both its effect and the method of obtaining this to *Candet Nudatum Pectus*. Either the immediate author or some unknown meditational source has expanded the allegorical interpretation of this verse from *Lamentations* in a fashion both poetic and intensely human :

> ȝe þat pasen be þe weyȝe,
> Abidet a litel stounde !
> Be-holdet, al mi felawes,
> ȝef ani me lik is founde.
> To þe tre with nailes þre
> Wol fast i hange bounde,
> With a spere al þoru mi side
> To min herte is mad a wounde.

This lyric gains in concentrated effect by its brevity, and in significance by the weight of suggestion in its omissions. At the same time its appeal is homely and direct. The second verse is designedly wistful ; ' al mi felawes ' is meant by its intimacy to make it hard to turn away with an excuse. Then there is restraint in the account of the suffering made not circumstantially and at length but almost symbolically by references to the nails and the spear. This is, within the limits of its intention as a religious lyric, a good poem. *Aspice Mitissime Conditor*,[2] an appeal from the cross to God the Father for mercy for mankind, originates from another version of the actual Bernardine meditation *Candet Nudatum Pectus*. It has few merits, but is valuable to us because it confirms the opinion that the success of the lyric *Candet Nudatum Pectus* was not inevitable, or determined for the poet by his original.

The most successful variations of the basic treatment depend upon the introduction of a second personality, the mother of Christ, and the presentation of her reaction to the

---

[1] C.B. *XIV* no. 74. Brown notes (*ib.* no. 268) that in the MS. there is 'an express reference to the Scriptural source', *Lamentations* i, 12.

[2] C.B. *XIII* no. 33. See also notes, 193–4.

suffering of her Son, either as an outburst of grief from her, or in dialogue form. In the surviving specimens the dialogue treatment is the less successful;[1] it tends to diffuseness and clumsy handling or else, by the obviousness of its standard answers to the customary rhetorical questions of her lamentations, distracts attention from what seems the most striking feature of the situation, namely Mary's emotion as a human mother face to face with her suffering Son. The dialogue treatment is the easy way of showing how an incarnate God and His mother are victims of the conflict between divine and human purposes. By dialogue the reasons for this conflict can be not only made explicit but also developed beyond any possibility of misconception, or else Christ can offer consolation to His mother within which doctrinal instruction for the hearers is contained. Poetry, however, does not necessarily thrive on the obvious; the effect of these dialogues is weak and diluted compared with that of poems which concentrate upon her bewildered grief,[2] and leave to the reader some of the effort of understanding. *Lamentacio Dolorosa*, in which Mary prays her Son either to break out of His bonds or let her die, is good enough to illustrate the superiority of this method, although in this poem too there is unnecessary explicitness. *The Blessed Virgin's Appeal to the Jews* is the best poem of this kind. Here Mary speaks with the voice of any disconsolate mother to her son's torturers.

> Wy haue ȝe no reuthe on my child?
> Haue reuthe on me ful of murning,
> Taket doun on rode my derworþi child,
> Or prek me on rode with my derling.
>
> More pine ne may me ben don
> Þan laten me liuen in sorwe & schame;
> Als loue me bindet to my sone,
> So lat vs deyȝen boþen isame.

---

[1] See, for instance, *op. cit.* no. 49, *Dialogue between Our Lady and Jesus on the Cross*; C.B. *XIV* no. 67, *Dialogue between Jesus and the Blessed Virgin at the Cross*; no. 128, *The Blessed Virgin to her Son on the Cross*.

[2] For example, *op. cit.* no 60., *The Blessed Virgin's Appeal to the Jews*; no. 64, *Lamentacio Dolorosa*.

No detailed description of the crucifixion, and no suggestion of the enormity of the sacrifice made there, could convey Mary's grief as completely as this desperate plea. Moreover, no specifically religious treatment exists with such a powerful effect of inducing first sympathy and then devotion in the reader. He knows the identity of ' my derling ', and will the more readily make the transference from the particular instance to the general plan which necessitated the suffering and occasioned the unhappiness because, as this imaginative experience is presented, it could be the grief of all mothers.

The artistic value of making a religious subject human and immediate in this way is further illustrated by two poems which treat not of the actual passion and crucifixion but of moments before and after, namely, *Christ's Prayer in Gethsemane* [1] and *Christ Triumphant*.[2] The first extracts the pathetic emotion from the very human prayer of Christ in the garden by elaborating in human terms the words ascribed to him in the gospels. The effect in the first stanza is finely dramatic, but the figure in which the poet apprehends his subject cannot be extended to the final resignation, and so the effect is not sustained. *Christ Triumphant* I take to be a purely fanciful conception of the mind of Christ after His death :

> I haue laborede sore and suffered dey3th,
> And now I Rest and draw my breyght ;
> But I schall come and call Ryght sone
> Heuene and erght and hell to dome ;
> And thane schall know both devyll and mane,
> What I was and what I ame.

The resting and drawing breath are a human figure applied to a circumstance not human ; the expression of almost gloating triumph put into Christ's mouth is not Christian. But the poem is effective, for again in human terms it represents a subject and an experience otherwise barely conceivable.

The devotional and meditative poetry which presents the subject for meditation objectively depends for its effect, then, upon the skill of the poet's selection of his material

[1] C.B. *XIV* no. 62.　　　　[2] C.B. *XV* no. III.

and the emphasis that he applies to it for the purpose of communicating his apprehension of it.   There is, finally, a kind of devotional poetry in which this process of selection and emphasis is highly intensified, and is accompanied by an artistic transformation of the subject through the successful operation of the poet's fancy or his creative imagination. It has this nature probably because in the conception and creation of the lyrics concerned the religious and artistic intentions were equated ; the composition of poetry was not merely incidental to the religious function of communicating a subject for contemplation but was of equal importance with it.   The authors of this kind of religious lyric were not merely devotees who sought to employ the most effective means of representation for their subjects, but also artists, whom these subjects inspired to a more or less successful creative effort.

The transformation of their material, whereby this was endowed with significant form, appears to have taken place by the three usual means.   It might be the result of a ' literary ' treatment involving the use of rhetorical, stylistic adornment, particularly of the special poetic vocabulary which began to be developed during the later fourteenth century.   It might be brought about by the play of the poet's fancy upon his material with results which we would call either ' metaphysical ' or ' romantic ' depending on the mixture of intellectual and emotional elements in the transformation.   Or it might—as actually seems to have happened very rarely indeed—result from a pure poetic conception of the subject in which the creative imagination of the author apprehended it, selected its striking features, and arranged these in such a way that its permanent qualities were communicated by his representation of it.

By no means all of the lyrics in which this poetic treatment is discernible are poetically successful.   Even more than in any other kind of Middle English religious poetry, poetic excellence here is a question of delicate adjustment between the matter and the manner of a poem, as well as of a correspondence between the effect that its poet intended and the limits of his artistic powers.   In the less highly developed religious poetry it would sometimes be possible to make shift with adequacy, with a tolerably successful plodding effort. The evident sincerity of a poet's religious emotion could compensate in some degree for his shortcomings of conception or expression. But in this last kind we are inclined, perhaps unfairly, to require more of the poet because he has essayed more. What he is attempting to create is less robust and finer, and may the more easily be spoiled. A number of conditions, therefore, become particularly important : whether the poem appears to be artistically sincere, whether it is poetic as the result of an evidently calculated enlistment of the fancy, whether the poet appears to have been transported either by the excitement of exercising his creative talent or by the subject of his poetic vision, and after all these, whether he was equipped with the talent and the literary experience necessary to obtain the effect he set out to achieve.

If the surviving Middle English lyrics are any indication, the purely literary treatment of devotional and meditative subjects seems a relatively late development which reached its height only in the fifteenth century after the Chaucerian school had popularized its master's style and exaggerated, among other things, its tendency to aureate language. In a sense every fifteenth-century religious poem from which poetic inspiration is evidently absent, but which is competently expressed, might be described as having been subjected to such literary embellishment. There are, however, poems in which the manner or style is refined or exaggerated to such a degree that we can safely assume it to have been the writers' main preoccupation, and conclude that if these men were carried away at all it was by the enthusiasm of success in their verbal *jeux d'esprit*.

To us moderns the least attractive of such works are the ingenious poems, acrostics, macaronic verses, and inflations of Latin originals.[1] The least developed from an artistic point of view are those numerous devotional and meditative poems which open with a conventional literary gambit, or are directed by a conventional poetic motive arbitrarily imposed upon their content and often actually quite incongruous with it [2] The most advanced, in the strictly literary sense, are the

[1] E.g. C.B. *XIV* nos. 131, 135 ; C.B. *XV* nos. 26, 28, 31
[2] E.g. C.B. *XV* nos. 2, 10, 105.

lyrics in which the embellishment applied is the aureate style. In such poems the Virgin at the foot of the cross will say not ' Look upon me ' but *Cast py respeccyoun one my mortall countenance*,[1] the poet who addresses her will say not ' Hail Mary full of grace ' but

> All haile ! whose solempne glorious concepcioun
> fful of glorie and hye ioye tryumphaunte,
> Bothe celestyall & terrestriall gif laude with Iubilacioun
> Of new ioy & gladnesse with solace incessaunte.[2]

Undoubtedly this treatment invests the subject with an entirely new quality of elegance which it lacked in the bare, rough-seeming thirteenth-century language, or in the sober dress of fourteenth-century religious vocabulary as we see it, for instance, in the ' Vernon Series '. The question is, however, whether the poets who accomplished this transformation were artistically sincere, and whether the verses they wrote were primarily devotional and meditative poetry or merely excuses for striking these fine literary attitudes. Certainly it is correct to observe that the higher the style the less the devotional effect, at least in these instances. By contrast it is even agreeable to encounter a naïve and undiscriminating versifier like the author of *Filius Regis Mortuus Est*[3] who, apparently deficient in a sense of harmony, fluently and avidly used a combination of verbal and prosodic tricks from the alliterative tradition, the special, tenderly playful vocabulary of the *lullay* poems, a macaronic refrain, some superficial features of the frenchified, courtly poetry, and the commoner turns of rhetoric. The incongruity between his matter and manner is no more offensive than that in the aureate poems, and there seems less doubt of his sincerity and enthusiasm.

It is its isolation from other poetic qualities that throws the merely literary transformation of a subject into disagreeable prominence and conveys the sense of incongruity from which we infer that an author was lacking in taste. When it

---

[1] C.B. *XV* no. 8 line 2.
[2] *Ib.* no. 12 ll. 8–12. Cf. among many similar instances, also nos. 13, 112.
[3] *Ib.* no. 6.

accompanies what we might call other creative elements in the composition of a poem, it readily takes its due ancillary place as no more than a condition of the medium of expression. When the operation of intellectual or emotional forces determines the arrangement, presentation and effect of a religious subject designed to be communicated as poetry, style properly becomes a feature of secondary importance.

This subordination is well illustrated in those devotional and meditative lyrics where the poet's intellect accomplished the transformation of doctrine into poetry. In *The Divine Paradox*, a lyric that raises the question of the mysteries of Christianity and resolves them by faith, the importance of the intellectual element to the form and quality of the lyric is well apparent :

> A God and yet a man ?
> A mayde and yet a mother ?
> Witt wonders what witt Can
> Conceave this or the other.
>
> A god, and Can he die ?
> A dead man, can he live ?
> What witt can well replie ?
> What reason reason give ?
>
> God, truth itselfe, doth teach it ;
> Mans witt senckis too farr vnder
> By reasons power to reach it.
> Beleeve and leave to wonder ! [1]

The poet's mind had first to reach the essential nature of these four great impossibilities, next to compress them into a verbal structure of the required pattern, then somehow to convey their effect upon the human mind which tries to comprehend them, and finally to communicate an impression of the faith by which he would resolve them. The discipline to which these obligations subjected him inevitably extended to his language which is accordingly not only close-knit but austerely free of ornament. The lyric is, in consequence, tense with the spiritual excitement which grows out of the act of subjection of reason to faith.

[1] C.B. *XV* no. 120.

Two quite different instances of an intellectual transformation of the poet's material occur in *Christ's Love-Song to Man*[1]
and *Christ's 'Love-Aunter'*.[2]   Both are concerned with
making accessible in simple concepts the divine Charity which
expressed itself in the redemption.   The author of *Christ's
'Love-Aunter'* explains his subject by the figure of Christ as
a lover of man's soul who is to be her champion at the crucifixion.   He does not, however, as one might expect, develop
this figure romantically but instead expresses it gnomically,
by extracting from the subject and casting as generalizations
such of its features as seem to him striking.   His concept is
original but not poetically successful, for the generalizations
are only loosely strung together so that the effect of the poem
is of a number of unrelated parts.   *Christ's Love-Song to Man*
is equally original and a better poem.   While it is an intensely
serious consideration of its subject, the sufferings of Christ
during His life and crucifixion, the poet has given it a light,
almost flippant turn by the effect he creates with his prosody
and play of conceits.   The emphasis is made to fall not on
the suffering of the passion, but on the fact that it is past and
was successful and can now be cheerfully viewed:

> Loue is my pes,
> For loue i ches,
> Man to byȝen dere.
>
> Ne dred þe nouth,
> I haue þe south,
> Boþen day & nith,
>   To hauen þe,
>   Wel is me,
> I haue þe wonnen in fith.

The effect of this lyric is good, but it is also interesting because
of the manner in which the poet's intellectual apprehension
of his subject as a swift, inevitable and necessarily painful
process now past and so to be happily regarded influences and
indeed informs his treatment.

As might, however, be expected of times as romantic as the
Middle Ages, more specimens survive of lyrics in which the

---

[1] C.B. *XIV* no. 66.   [2] *Ib.* no. 73.

religious material is transformed by the emotion or fancy of the poet than of those in which the intellect is the main agent of the change. This second kind of transformation can, in its simplest form, be accomplished by a joyous emotion which excites the poet's creative powers and through them colours the poem. Such joy brightens and brings to life two lyrics which translate Latin hymns, *Aurora lucis rutilat* [1] and *Crux fidelis*.[2] In the first the content is not much more than the commonplace of doctrine, but with it the poet has conveyed a great, and in the good sense, simple-minded happiness :

> An Ernemorwe þe dayliȝt spryngeþ,
> Þe angles in heuene Murye syngeþ,
> Þe world is bliþe & ek glad—

The second, almost as uncomplicated, develops the common figure of the cross as a tree bearing precious fruit. The poet knows no other such in the woods. But that unoriginal concept comes to life with his feeling which is again most simple and most appropriately conveyed :

> Swete be þe nalys
> And swete be þe tre
> And sweter be þe birdyn þat hangis vppon the !

Less simple but no less effective is the transformation of material brought about by a combination of the emotion of the poet with his fancy. Here his feeling not only awakens his creative powers to the point of choosing an appropriate but unadorned expression, but goes further by uttering itself in a poetic figure designed to make its communication the more complete. A good instance of the process operating without notable success. and therefore the more accessible for observation, is the lyric *Ecce sto ad hostium et pulso* [3] where the poet, seemingly deeply moved by the figure of Christ as a lover knocking for admission, attempts to make this govern his poem.

> Vndo þi dore, my spuse dere,
> Allas ! wy stond i loken out here ?
> Fre am i þi make.

---

[1] C.B. *XIV* no. 37.   [2] *Ib.* no. 40.   [3] *Ib.* no. 68.

The creative excitement which his emotion awakens is not,
however, sufficiently great to maintain this figure, and
dissipates itself first in an inharmonious description of Christ
not as a lover but as He might have come from the cross,
and then in an act of contrition which, however commendable,
is hardly poetry in any sense.   Feeling and fancy appear to
have been unable to supply the author's deficiency in a sense
of form and congruity.

   In *Christ pleads with His Sweet Leman* [1] a similar kind of
transformation is more successful.   This time the figure is of a
message from a dead knight to the mistress in whose cause he
was killed.   This lyric, although marred by the admission of a
moral precept which in no way contributes to its effect, is
the product of a genuine and sustained inspiration :

> Take myne armes pryuely
> & do þam in þi tresory,
> In what stede sa þou dwelles,
> And, swete lemman, forget þow noght
> Þat I þi lufe sa dere haue boght,
> And I aske þe noght elles.

The well-worn moral lesson has been transformed into good,
if not exceptional poetry.   A much subtler change and a
more interesting one produced the lyric *Quis est iste qui
venit de Edom ?* [2]   Technically this is a poor performance,
ill-defined and indeed perhaps also fragmentary, which may
have been designed to resemble the strophic arrangement
of its Old Testament original.[3]   Nevertheless, the poet's
transformation of his material is a real one, achieved by the
suggestion of two sets of associations absent from his original,
that of the knight champion returning from battle, and that
of Christ triumphant after the crucifixion.   He writes not
simply *Quis est iste qui venit de Edom* but ' What ys he, þys
lordling þat cometh vrom þe vyht ', not *formosus in stola
sua, gradiens in multitudine fortitudinis suae* but

> So vayre ycoyntised, so semlich in syht,
> So styflyche ȝongeþ, so douhti a knyht,

---

[1] C.B. *XIV* no. 78.   [2] *Ib.* no. 25.
[3] Isaiah lxiii 6 ff.   See C.B.   *XIV* no. 254.

not *ego qui loquor justitiam, et propugnator sum ad salvandum* but

> Ich hyt am, Ich hyt am, þat ne speke bote ryht,
> Chaunpyoun to helen monkunde in vyht,

and for the rest of the poem this *is* a knight. But not only a knight ; the *tinctis vestibus de Bosra* becomes ' blode-rede wede so grysliche ydyht ', the question *quare ergo rubrum est indumentum tuum* is turned into ' Why þoenne ys þy schroud red wyth blod al ymeind ', and the knight has become Christ crucified as well. This second meaning is probably a common mediæval interpretation of Isaiah's prophetic symbolism, but the first is purely fanciful, and upon it the transformation of the vision into poetry depends. This poem as a whole is, however, more interesting than successful, both because of the shortcomings of its form and because when the poet came to the figure of the winepress in his original he encountered material which he either found intractable or else valued too much for its own sake. He does not seem to have tried to adapt it to his two other themes and so it remains as it was in the original, a powerful but unrelated metaphor. The effect of this lyric is, in consequence, mixed and bewildering, and its various parts obscure and weaken one another. The lyric *How Christ shall Come* [1] has similar characteristics ; in conception and effect it is highly imaginative and shows unmistakable marks of originating in a violent movement of both emotion and fancy, but it is again ill-formed to the extent of hardly being a poem at all.

It is in this connexion most important not to underestimate the evocative power of scriptural antiquity for such mediæval poets ; in these two lyrics it was evidently so great as to inflame the poetic imaginations of the authors to a point beyond their technical capabilities. Probably on such occasions a strong imaginative response would blind a man to serious formal shortcomings, or he might presume that a similarly strong response in his readers would excuse his faults as an artist. The lyric *Marye, mayde mylde and fre* [2] in which is reflected the symbolism of the litany to Mary with its accumulation of associations from Hebrew, Greek

[1] C.B. *XIV* no. 36. [2] *Ib.* no. 32.

6*

and Latin religious imagery also develops emotional association at the expense of form in this way. The effect of the
single stanzas of this lyric is very good ; some of them contain images of singular beauty. But for all its riches of
association a litany is hardly a poem, and this fourteenth-
century imitation is denied fulfilment as poetry by its inter-
rupted progression.

The most successful of these emotional and fanciful trans-
formations of devotional and meditative subjects are those
in which the poets make a full and ready surrender to contemporary romanticism. Obviously such a surrender cannot
take place unless the artistic intention of an author is at
least as well established as his religious purpose. As long as
the former is in any sense subordinated the operation of the
creative imagination will be in some way hindered. If they
are of equal importance, the processes of selection and arrangement by which the subjects are presented are intensified ;
almost inevitably the imagination of the poet brings about
alterations which, since the subjects are religious and sacrosanct, leave the doctrine intact, but certainly affect the
artistic quality of its expression.

Success and failure in the process of transformation are
conveniently illustrated at the outset by two of the *quia amore
langueo* poems, *In a tabernacle of a toure* [1] and *In a valey of
this restles minde.* [2] The first of these is made of the same
elements as the second but stops short of transforming them
into poetry, for its author, while he consciously adopts and
uses the special mode of courtly vision poetry, makes only
formal concessions to its spirit. His poem remains an instrument of religious teaching to the end, with such artistic
intentions as he may have entertained evidently subordinated
to the purpose of instruction. The result is clever, flat and
unmoving. The author of the second lyric, however, far
from keeping himself detached from the romanticism of
his poetic form, surrenders to it completely and allows his
fancy such a liberty that a number of remarkable changes
of motive within the poem result. The theme of *In a valey*

[1] C.B. *XIV* no. 132.
[2] E. K. Chambers and F. Sidgwick, *Early English Lyrics* (London
1937) lxxxiv.

of this restles minde is Christ's pursuit of the evasive soul of man. The poet, in the circumstances he indicates by his opening line, finds beneath a tree a knight of royal presence who bleeds from grievous wounds. He asks the reason for this knight's distress, and the reply he gets is already the second motive of the poem :

> I am true love that fals was nevere ;
> My sister, mannes soule, I loved her thus ;
> Because we wolde in no wise discevere,
> I lefte my kingdom glorious.
> I purveide for her a paleis precious ;
> Sche fleith, I folowe, I soughte her so ;
> I suffrede this peine piteuous,
> *Quia amore langueo.*

Like the Hound of Heaven the Knight has pursued her. He is constant, forbearing, forgiving, solicitous, he says, *quia amore langueo.* Next, with a change of motive he addresses her like any ardent lover :

> Fair love, lete us go pleye !
> Apples ben ripe in my gardaine.
> I schal thee clothe in a newe aray ;
> Thy mete schall be milk, hony, and win.
> Fair love, lete us go digne !
> Thy sustenaunce is in my crippe, lo !
> Tarie thou not, my faire spouse mine,
> *Quia amore langueo.*

After two stanzas of this lyrical wooing with its reminiscence of *Iam dulcis amica venito* a third, epithalamic motive is introduced,

> Her bed is made, her bolster is bliss,
> Her chaumber is chosen ;

but only for an instant. That fancy passes, and now the soul is a child asleep and he guards her with a mother's emotion ; now she is his wife whom he begs to come back to him. The knight wounded by love, the relentless hunter, the eager suitor, the bridegroom, the parent, the husband follow hard

upon one another in the poet's fancy, and one concept slips
into the next with an ease made possible only by the high
excitement of his creative faculty. There are elements in his
poem which as modern readers we may find distasteful, but
this circumstance does nothing to alter the genuinely poetic
conception of this lyric or the romanticism of its treatment.
After we have taken into account all the shortcomings of
construction which these changes of motive might suggest,
and admitted the differences of taste between our age and
that of the author, this lyric remains a product of the creative
imagination, with an effect that would not have been achieved
had the artistic purpose been subordinate to the religious.

One of the most successful surviving examples of such a
transformation is *The Spring under a Thorn*,[1] a much shorter
and simpler lyric, with a more unified conception of the subject,
and consequently an unbrokenly good effect :

> At a sprynge wel vnder a þorn
> Þer was bote of bale, a lytel here a-forn ;
> Þer by-syde stant a mayde,
> Fulle of loue ybounde.
> Ho-so wol seche trwe loue,
> Yn hyr hyt schal be founde.

In this lyric the transportation into the world of fancy is
immediate and complete. We can, of course, relate the
figures to their religious originals, the spring to Christ's
pierced and bleeding heart, the thorn to His crown. But in
the poem the spring is first and pictorially a spring of water
welling up beneath a tree, fully as romantic and magical as
the emerald-stone upon which Ywain poured water as a
challenge ; the maid in the bonds of love is not a complaining
Mary whose lamentations have so often been badly expressed
that they have acquired associations of tedium, but a type of
devoted love of any kind ; the two concluding lines are not
cast as a predicatory moral injunction but as an invitation to
the quest of romance. Out of this imaginative transformation
of religion arises a treatment not particular but general and
absolute, qualified to illustrate, even perhaps to enlarge, the
reader's conception of a religious truth. It is miniature,

[1] C.B. *XIV* no. 130.

limited, but within the limitations entirely successful not only as poetry but also as religion, for such a poetic conception of the doctrine of the redemption might well restore its freshness and its meaning, and thus bring the more forcefully home what from long custom and the human weakness of taking for granted could easily lose part of its significance.[1] But that is not important to us in the first instance ; we for our part must admire the manner in which a noble doctrinal abstraction is made into an imaginative picture compelling and full of meaning.

The Spring under a Thorn is good poetry, beautiful, moving and romantic, but hardly great. That epithet is to be applied, in my opinion, to one only of the surviving religious and devotional lyrics, *The Maiden Makeles*,[2] a poem of the purest poetic conception, in which the author's creative imagination has discerned and ordered the artistically permanent qualities of his subject and presented them in a form that transcends differences of time and background. The effect of this poem is to communicate a delicately and deeply beautiful sense of devotion, of a more than religious attachment to the subject. The emotional content of the poem is soft and tender, but the poem is in no sense weak ; indeed, nothing could be stronger than its perfect felicity of utterance from which both appeals to the audience to share the poet's experience and open expressions of his own attachment to his theme are excluded.

We are lucky to have both evidence of the probable source of this poet's inspiration and an illustration of his artistic intention and of his method of achieving this in the form of a thirteenth-century lyric, *I Sing of One That is Matchless*.[3] The relation between the two treatments affords an interesting demonstration of the operation of the later poet's creative faculties. The earlier lyric is a relatively mechanical and explicit account of the annunciation of which two stanzas, the first and the fifth, seem to contain both the inspiration

---

[1] Conceivably the man responsible for the survival of the lyric had this in mind. See *Ib.* no. 285.

[2] C.B. *XV* no. 81 : EEL liv.

[3] C.B. *XIII* no. 31. The resemblance between the two poems was first noted by Sir W. W. Greg, *Modern Philology* vii (1909–10) 166.

and the material of the second and greater poem. The thirteenth-century lyric opens

> Nu þis fules singet hand maket hure blisse
> And þat gres up þringet and leued þe ris ;
> Of on ic wille singen þat is makeles.
> Þe king of halle kinges to moder he hire ches.

She is sinless,. immaculate, royally descended, and bore the Lord of Mankind to redeem us. Gabriel came to her, addressed to her the angelic salutation, and without knowledge of man she became God's virgin mother :

> Mayden heo was uid childe & Maiden her biforen
> & maiden ar sothent hire chid was iboren ;
> Maiden and moder nas neuer non wimon boten he—
> Wel mitte he berigge of godes sune be.

Blessed be the child, the mother that suckled it, and the time of its birth when we were released from pain.

I would not have this lyric thought too bad ; it has the charm of the archaic, but its author is over-explicit and will not assume knowledge or readiness to co-operate in the reader. His elaborate demonstrations of the obvious detract from the quality of the poem. Moreover, his attitude to the subject is mainly religious, and little affected by the operation of the creative imagination.

The Maiden Makeles differs from the earlier lyric in every one of these points. The author respects the intelligence of his readers and their knowledge of the subject, suggests rather than demonstrates its striking qualities, regards it artistically while maintaining his devoutness, communicates his own attachment to it fully, and evidently works with a profound movement of the creative faculty. The process of transformation of the subject is most interesting to observe. First must have come the inspiration, the recognition, whether intellectual or intuitive, of artistic possibilities in the doctrine. Next, perhaps, the conception of the manner in which it ought to be treated anew, and then the apprehension of those features in the old poem which were artistically the most effective, and the retention and alteration or development of them to fit the new conception.

Throughout this process the poet's instinct as an artist was unfailingly sure. He rejected all the explicit doctrinal material, of which the repetition in the earlier work amounts to homily. He retained the spring setting but discarded the conventional expression, ' Nu þis fules singet and maket hure blisse ', in favour of a suggestion more strongly allusive, more explicit and shorter, contained in the repeated line ' as dew in aprylle '.[1] The grace by which Mary conceived came upon her as silently, imperceptibly, almost magically, as the dew which is not seen to fall ; it came, too, not in the conventionally set springtime of well-worn poetic usage, at best now a faintly evocative source of reverie, but in the very April when spring does break. From the second verse of the old poem, ' þat gres up þringet and leued þe ris ' he may have got the idea for the lovely sequence of the dew falling successively upon grass and flower and spray. Principally, however, by his selection and exclusion of material he directed the emphasis of his poem upon the three features of his subject that he wished to communicate : first, the matchlessness of the lady which he makes a theme of his first and last stanzas; second, the importance of her acquiescence, which the earlier poet omits to mention but which the later man designedly emphasizes by changing ' þe king of halle kinges to moder he hire ches ' to ' kyng of alle kynges to here sone che ches' so that the *ecce ancilla domini, fiat mihi secundum verbum tuum* of Luke is preserved in ' che ches'; and third, the essentially mysterious nature of the incarnation, which he suggests in the repeated ' stylle ' and the beautiful simile of the mysteriously appearing dew.

The form of his poem is highly developed, not upon any French model but according to the logic of the subject as he

---

[1] Chambers, EEL 349, seems to suggest that figuring the conception in the falling of dew from heaven may be traced to four lines from Jacques de Cambrai, which he quotes :

> Ensi com sor la verdure
> Descent rosee des ciels,
> Vint en vos cors, Virge pure,
> De paradis vos dous Fiels.

But it seems more likely that the common source of this figure was some illustration originally devised for doctrinal instruction.

apprehended it. The beginning and end of the poem contain
two of its three themes, more briefly presented than the one
developed in its body, but properly so, for they can be
intellectually, not imaginatively grasped. The manner of
the opening is direct and unadorned :

> I syng of a myden
> Þat is makeles ;
> Kyng of alle kynges
> To here sone che ches.

The themes of the lady's peerlessness, and of her acquiescence
in the incarnation are stated simply indeed. But the tone
is faultless ; the superlatives are acceptable without sense
of hyperbole or strain. With the first stanza of the body of
the poem, however, the quality changes somewhat ; now
not the intellect but the imagination is invoked, required
to comprehend the magnitude of the contrast between the
greatness of the ' kyng of alle kynges ' and the silence of his
arrival in ' his moderes bowr ', in which magnitude, it is
implied, lies the mystery :

> He cam also stylle
> Þer his moder was
> As dew in aprille,
> Þat fallyt on þe gras.

All pomp, ceremony and passion, and to symbolize them,
all sound are absent. The hush is one of reverence and awe.
Three times, with mounting effect, this pattern is repeated
and varied ; his coming is like dew upon the grass, upon the
single flower, and finally upon the blossoming bough which
most perfectly symbolizes the height of spring. Meanwhile
a great restraint is imposed in this part of the poem ; there
are no superlatives, no expressions of the poet's own emotion,
no intrusions of his personality. The emphatic statement
is reserved for the last stanza, which returns to the theme of
the first, the maiden's matchlessness and the reason for it.
Out of this assertion the plain words of that last stanza,
tremendous in their implications, create a climax that is
intensified not only by the theology of the doctrine and the

faith that enlivens it, but also by the emotions, æsthetic and
personal, which the imaginative portion of the poem have
excited :

> Moder & mayden
> Was neuer non but che—
> Wel may swych a lady
> Godes moder be.

The Maiden Makeles is, in my opinion, an instance of the
ideal religious lyric, that farthest removed from the expression
of homily or doctrine or devotion with tags and tricks of
poetry attached to it. Artistically it is one of the most finely
conceived and delicately executed poems of the Middle
English period. In its conception and creation the movement
of religion and of the artistic faculty must have kept perfect
pace. The religious impulse was probably the original one,
but it must have entered almost at the moment of its coming
into existence into a co-operation with the creative imagination,
the result of which is very beautiful, exquisitely ordered, and
deeply moving. The poem is miniature, to be sure, and
might conceivably for that reason be held to be not truly
great. But its size does not affect the consideration of its
perfect taste, by no means to be taken for granted, its
absolute clarity, and the simple logic of the structure from
which it derives its lovely and moving grace.

Beyond this peak of achievement the surviving Middle
English religious lyrics do not rise. If we view them chrono-
logically, as far as that is possible, no steady improvement
in quality is discernible in them such as would have led one
to expect a poem as good as this ; the only respect in which
they seem to develop is that of the prosody, and even there
the development will probably have been made in secular
verse and its results adopted by the religious writers. The
same patterns of failure and success, originating in the
attitudes of the poets to their subjects, and in their conceptions of their own function, are discernible from the
earliest recorded examples till those composed at the end
of the Middle Ages.

Just as those patterns recur in the Middle English religious
lyrics as a whole, so they show themselves particularly in the

case of the mediæval religious carol, the only one of the forms
used by the religious poets which was at the same time so
well defined, so widely used and so characteristic that its
specimens constitute a special case and must be separately
considered. The individual character of this body of verse,
of which a very considerable number of specimens has been
preserved,[1] is quite unmistakable, and can, in my opinion,
best be explained in terms of the effects which its authors
intended, and the influence of the form and use of the carol
upon these effects. When a carol is poetically successful,
its success is likely to be of the same kind as that of a correspondingly good non-carol lyric of a similar devotional type ;
when, however, its success is only limited, or when indeed it
cannot be regarded as poetry proper, it shows the same
patterns of failure, intensified, however, by characteristic
faults and shortcomings not especially common in the other
sorts of Middle English religious lyric. Since of the many
religious carols that survive only a very few are genuinely
successful as poetry it is important to consider these
characteristic faults and shortcomings.

Considered as poetry and not merely as words to be sung
to music, many of the religious carols have a commonplace
quality expressed most often in the absence from them of any
strong feeling for the subject or any deep understanding of
it, and in a corresponding triteness and even triviality of
expression. In many cases they have a bustling, domestic
air, as if they had been hastily and perfunctorily made up.
Prosodically they give an impression of eagerness to get
through the necessary but oppressive business of the stanza
to the more stimulating, rousing and violent burden. They
seldom seem to have had leisure for the due development of
their material. In consequence transitions are often baldly
or otherwise badly made, and the content, itself often of an
elementary nature, is sometimes too simply and crudely
presented. As the texts stand without music many look
dull and uninspired, entirely commonplace in expression ;
apparently superior instances are decked out in conventional

---

[1] R. L. Greene in *The Early English Carols* (Oxford 1935) records
474 distinct carols, many of which survive in several versions, as well
as a number of fragments.

religious imagery, or headed by a promise of romantic treatment subsequently often unfulfilled. To read many of them sympathetically requires a considerable effort ; it is necessary to imagine them being sung, to supply the music upon which most of the authors of carols seem to have relied for a great part of their emotional effect.

For these shortcomings there are corresponding compensations. Almost all the carols impress one with great liveliness and vitality. When it is appropriate to the subject the simplicity of their treatment can be felicitous. Sometimes, although not quite as often as one might hope, they set and maintain, even without the music from which most of them should never have been separated, the lovely singing note that is one of the rarest and most delicate effects of any poetry. This singing note probably occurs most often in nativity and other festal carols where the subject itself carries associations of joyous emotion that predispose to this effect. Such carols are very lively, remarkably fluent, generally direct and simple ; the religious excitement infuses itself into the expression, especially of the burdens. Their literary quality is seldom very high, and their strictly poetic felicities are unpredictable and fortuitous, but they must have made wonderful songs. The least musical carols, although these are generally the most fluent and prosodically accomplished, are the moral carols which, whether they preach directly or indirectly are almost all so heavy and sombre in content and tone that one wonders to what sort of music they were sung.

Indeed, the indispensability of music to the text of a carol is only the beginning of the explanation of its quality. A variety of factors may have contributed to produce the special effect peculiar to the carols as a class of verse. Of these, the close connexion with music is certainly one of the most important for the way in which it could affect the author's intention and his attitude to his subject. It would be very easy for him to consider his verse as merely the complement of the music, and to rely upon the aid of the music, from outside his work as poetry proper, to supply the emotional transport necessary to its success. The possibility of this reliance upon external aid would introduce a second factor by dispensing with the sense of need for inspiration in the composition of a carol designed to be simply adequate for singing. Anyone, then, with the necessary fluency and understanding of the technicalities of versifying, could string together a set of smoothly moving commonplaces, believing meanwhile that nothing seriously poetic was expected of him. Conceivably, too, the nature of the effect of the majority of carols was determined partly by their being the occasion of communal activity. This would tend to debase their quality by reducing them, as symbols of emotion, to the lowest common denominator of the group for which they were designed. A poet proper indeed intends that his compositions should perform the function of communication, but he will not exclude all private and individual subjectivity from them because of this intention. Such subjectivity, and such a personal vision or record of a personal experience are extremely rare in the surviving carols. *We* and *you* are commoner pronouns there than *I*, and the emotions which most carols convey, or more often enjoin, are in the great majority of cases of a general and public kind with little of the special vision of the characteristically poetic mind about them.

All these factors seem to have operated in varying preponderance to determine the nature and quality of the majority of the carols, and to set limits to their general success. There are, however, notable if not numerous cases which pass these limits and show what an artist could do with a popular form of this kind. For that matter it is possible even within the characteristic limitations to detect and admire successful treatments where, for instance, the text of a carol was evidently entirely appropriate for singing, where sound and movement supplied the want of arresting sense or deep emotion,[1] or where the lightness which is the carol's most felicitous quality was developed in terms of the emotion implicit in the subject, and the subject itself not so much vulgarized as simplified.[2] A hint of greater possibilities is sometimes given from within the carol by suggestions that

---

[1] Greene no. 36 : EEL lxii; Greene no. 40 : EEL lxi; Greene no. 188 : EEL lv.

[2] Greene no. 35A : EEL lxx; Greene no. 79A : EEL lxvi; Greene no. 143 : EEL lxix; Greene no. 150 : EEL lxiv; Greene no. 175C : EEL li.

a poetic fancy attended its conception [1] or by signs that the author wished to elaborate and deepen his treatment.[2] It is in fact possible to illustrate a number of degrees and kinds of success in the carol, from the undeveloped but nevertheless entirely joyous kind of which *That Lord that lay in asse stalle* [3] is a good instance to the mysterious and lovely *Corpus Christi Carol, He bare hym vp, he bare hym down,*[4] which, although it preserves the singing note, otherwise quite transcends the form to which it technically belongs.

Except for the line by which this carol is named, *That Lord that lay in asse stalle* contains no poetry, and that one line, without music, is not enough to make the whole poetic. Even the burden of this carol is unexciting. Nevertheless the appropriateness of its treatment *qua* carol can easily be seen. There is not one halting or stumbling moment in its four stanzas, which, in the simplest possible terms, develop the elementary theme,

> Wel mowe we glad and mery bee,
> Sith we were thralle and nowe be free ;
> The fende oure foo he made to flee
> *Qui natus fuit hodie.*

The treatment is light, swift and energetic ; with music these qualities would combine to create a sense of spirit and significance and would make a good song of indifferent verse.

It might seem mistaken to expect more than this success from the carol kind or to remark on the limitations of that success if there were not, implicit in some carols, the suggestion that the actual composers of these songs did in fact aspire to something more than simply the production of singable verses. There are a number of carols into which a running symbolism was introduced, evidently designed for imaginative and emotional effect rather than to increase the *significatio*. Poetically this practice generally remained on the most elementary level; one of John Audelay's carols [5] is a good index of the common degree of success which

[1] Greene no. 145 : EEL lxxvii ; Greene no. 323 : C.B. *XV* no. 116.
[2] Greene no. 44 : EEL lxxiii.   [3] Greene no. 34 : C.B. *XV* no. 80.
[4] Greene no. 322A : EEL lxxxi.   [5] Greene no. 172 : EEL lvii.

attended the use of this device. Audelay was a fluent and
facile versifier, but without inspiration, and his development
of the figure of the flower sprung from the root of Jesse is
mechanical rather than imaginative. There is a more
successful use of the figure of the rose in another carol to the
Virgin ; [1] the effect is still limited and in no way profound
or intense, but the calculated prettiness of the burden,

> Of a rose, a louely rose,
> Of a rose is al myn song

will have appealed to the imagination, if indeed again on
an elementary level, and may have shed glamour upon the
carol as a whole.

One can only guess at the exact intention of these authors,
but it seems to have been more than the mere arrangement
of words for singing. Enthusiasm, exhilaration and like
emotions these men could and did often communicate, but
was it design or accident when they achieved a fitful illumination of the imagination as in the two specimens just considered, or, on occasion, bold and sweeping effects that
Blake might have admired and sought ?

> Now man is brighter than the sonne ;
> Now man in heuen an hye shal wone,
> Blessyd be God this game is begonne
> And his moder emperesse of helle.
>
> That euer was thralle, now ys he fre ;
> That euer was smalle, now grete is she ;
> Now shal God deme both the and me
> Vnto his blysse yf we do wel.[2]

To me it seems that such successes are the result of deliberate
effort, and that the men who achieved them, despite the
easy-going tradition of the form in which they wrote, were
seeking, as best they could, a fuller, deeper and more moving
effect in the carol than that readily won facility which anyone
sufficiently fluent and clever with rhymes could obtain.

[1] Greene no. 175 : EEL li   [2] Greene no. 30 : EEL lix.

The bounds of their success might be set by the deficiencies of their own talent, by the weight of the tradition of the adequacy of the slight, the commonplace, and the elementary in the carol form, or by the exhaustion of the religious subjects which, by the fifteenth century, had been so often exploited in verse that to achieve only freshness, to say nothing of originality, must have taxed severely the minds of the men who wrote of them. The really exceptional authors, however, overcame all these handicaps, and it is probable that even these limited successes were not accidental.

The effect of the few carols which are distinctly poetic is indeed so different from that of the majority of surviving specimens as to make an accompanying difference of intention and also of attitude to the subject in their authors practically certain. The composer of a carol poetically undistinguished, whatever its value as words to be sung might be, would probably have no more than an imperfect conception of the importance of any imaginative and emotional development of his subject. In addition he might be distracted by his technical commitments from any awareness of the need for such a development, or else he might be encouraged to stifle his sense of it with the comfortable assurance that the music would 'carry' what he composed. The poet proper who wrote in the carol form would, on the other hand, very likely be in the first place a versifier capable enough to match and master his rhymes without too much attention to them ; he would have a sufficient gift of words to write with a style at least distinguished from the commonplace, and he would have a clear notion both of the effect that he intended to produce, and of the means by which, in this medium, it could be obtained. In addition to his other qualifications he might even, conceivably, be inspired, that is, have himself undergone an emotional and imaginative experience which he wished to communicate by the effect of his poem. In any case what he wrote would be distinctive, and set apart from the ordinary run of carols.

The first distinguishing quality in these genuinely poetic carols is the presence of emotion which can be directly attributed to the author's personality. This relation is variously revealed ; it may be admitted openly as in the burden of the carol *Bowght and sold full traytorsly* : [1]

> To see the maydyn wepe her Sones passion,
> It entrid my hart full depe with grete compassion ;

it may be revealed by a treatment so successful dramatically that, to produce it, the poet must personally have entered into the character of his subject as in *Whan that my swete Son was thirti wynter old*,[2] or else it may express itself in the actual participation of the author in the action he describes, as in *With fauoure in hir face ferr passyng my reason*.[3] In each case the feeling originates from and belongs to a single individual and not to a group ; it is, therefore, incidentally both more intense and of a less average kind. While, indeed, it can generally be matched with effects in other Middle English religious lyrics it is not, like the elementary if strong feeling that sometimes informs the carols, kept down on the community level.

The second distinguishing feature is a creative transformation of the subject, with all that this process implies. Under this head the few carols which are set apart by the presence of these two characteristics in them may profitably be studied. *Bowght and sold full traytorsly* is in this respect the least-developed of the examples under consideration. Its author has indeed responded imaginatively to his subject, but his eye moves too rapidly among its features and incidents, and the intensity of his effect is diminished by the consequent dispersal of interest. Nevertheless this effect as a whole is reasonably good ; each stanza creates a pictorial impression clear and well-defined, with its emphasis directed to displaying the pathetic emotion that moved the poet. In *Whan that my swete Son was thirti wynter old* the conception is dramatic ; not only does Mary speak her sorrow with her own voice, but her protestations of grief carry conviction, and the effect of the carol mounts steadily to the last stanza :

> Thowgh I were sorowfull, no man haue at yt wonder,
> For howge was the erthquak, horyble was the thonder.
> I loked on my swet Son on the crosse that I stode vnder ;
> Than cam Lungeus with a spere and clift his hart in sonder.

---

[1] Greene no. 162.   [2] *Ib.* no. 163 : EEL lxxviii.
[3] Greene no. 161 : C.B. *XV* no. 9.

All the responsibility for communicating emotion is thrown upon the speaker ; at no point does the poet in his own person intrude description like

> There sat a lady with sory chere
> That sore dyd sygh and grone.

Within the stanzas she does not over-emphasize her grief with protestations ; the two occasions when she openly expresses it are directly related to the incidents she describes. Her lamentation proper is confined to the burden, and by this means the poet avails himself of the greatest advantage of the carol form, the intensification of effect brought about by the repetition, possibly fortified by a larger number of voices.

With fauoure in hir face ferr passyng my reason is technically one of the most remarkable of the carols, in both form and treatment quite unlike the majority of those which survive. It has the characteristic burden and relatively uniform stanza which class it with this kind, but the stanza, instead of being a four-stress quatrain, is composed of nine lines, the first four longer than is usual in the carols and running upon one rhyme, the next three a kind of wheel composed of the same elements variously used in the four stanzas, and the last two a couplet of lines conforming in length to those in the first element, varied so lightly that they resemble a refrain before the burden. Parallelisms of sense and emotion have been developed between the corresponding parts of the respective stanzas. There appears to be no music preserved for this carol ; [1] if it was ever sung, the musical setting with its four divisions must have been interesting and complicated. The treatment of the subject is as elaborate as its structure. It introduces in the burden a vision fiction, relatively uncommon in the carols, and by this means the poet becomes the interlocutor of the lamenting woman. Thereafter her sorrow is elaborately developed in a conceited, almost metaphysical vein, with the tone set by lines like *Yif wepyng myght ripe bee, it seemyd than in season.* One cannot call this carol a poetic success ; it is artificial, elaborate and curious rather than intensely moving, but neither is it an artistic failure.

[1] See Greene nos. 345 and 386, and C.B. *XV* no. 298.

Only one of the surviving carols, the famous *Corpus Christi Carol*,[1] can be called completely successful. This carol is unique, not because of its form but for its quality as poetry of the imagination, for its haunting beauty, its great evocative power, its profound romanticism, and its exceptional delicacy. The other carols mentioned in this study can be matched with similar if less successful treatments, but nothing like the *Corpus Christi Carol* exists among all those which survive. Technically it conforms to the definition of the *genre*; in conception and quality it is far beyond the other carols and ranks with the best of the surviving Middle English lyrics of all kinds.

Whatever the truth about its origin,[2] this poem as it has been preserved has the perfect unity of a set of symbols all designed to indicate a deep, if incompletely defined significance. These symbols have been variously interpreted,[3] but surely the point of mediæval symbolism was less to give a single exact and unmistakable meaning to various interpreters than to enrich, by the variety of possible senses that it afforded, the effect of significance and of the profundity and moment of the subject. So at least it operates here. None of the possible meanings excludes the others. At the same time the mere recognition of correspondences between words and ideas which these words do not literally express gives pleasure both intellectual and emotional; the effect of remoteness, solemnity and beauty, the depth of poignancy stirred by this set of pictures delicately drawn and tenderly unfolded, all are intensified by the very awareness of a *significatio*, whether it be understood as referring to the entombment of Christ or—as seems rather more probable—with a double sense, to the motive of the Grail and to the sacrifice of Christ at the

---

[1] Greene no. 322A : EEL lxxxi.

[2] Greene (liv–lvi and xciv) suggests that it may originally not have been cast in the carol form, and (412) guesses that the version from Balliol College, Oxford, MS 354 quoted above ' is probably the work of a religious who followed and adapted a secular song '.

[3] E.g. by Miss Annie G. Gilchrist and others, *Journal of the Folk-Song Society* iv (1910–13) 52–6, and by Dr. Edith C. Batho, ' The Life of Christ in the Ballads ', *Essays and Studies by Members of the English Association* ix (1924) 93–4. See Greene 411–12 for a consideration of these opinions.

Mass.[1] At the same time the pictures themselves are exquisitely suggestive. They create an effect of awe and wonder like that found in *The Spring under a Thorn*; they draw upon the treasury of allusions of mediæval romance not only to illustrate and enhance a religious point, but also for the very pleasure that accompanies association with the remote, the mysterious and the more beautiful than life. Each of them adds more mystery and meaning to those that have preceded it; all are in harmony, and the effect of the whole set is intensely suggestive and moving:

> Lully, lulley; lully lulley;
> The fawcon hath born my mak away.
>
> He bare hym vp, he bare hym down;
> He bare hym into an orchard brown.
>
> In that orchard ther was an hall,
> That was hangid with purpill and pall.
>
> And in that hall ther was a bede;
> Hit was hangid with gold so rede.
>
> And yn that bed ther lythe a knyght,
> His wowndes bledyng day and nyght.
>
> By that bedes side ther kneleth a may,
> And she wepeth both nyght and day.
>
> And by that beddes side ther stondith a ston,
> ' Corpus Christi ' wretyn theron.

That modern critics cannot agree upon an interpretation of what this poem signifies need not impair its effect. The poetic experience, in the poet or in his public, is not yet subject to scientific measurement. For all the disagreement about its *significatio* this carol is nevertheless a rare and wonderful poem.

[1] It seems to me that the correspondences introduced by the mediæval man's *that bemeneth* were, except in ' text book ' cases like, for instance, that illustrated in H. O. Taylor's account of Hugo of St. Victor (*The Medieval Mind* II (New York 1919) chapters xxviii–xxx 67–130), usually simpler, less recondite and less exactly correlated than the interpretations suggested by modern academic persons attempting to think according to the mentality of the Middle Ages.

It is, however, quite alone among the surviving religious carols in its high artistic quality. For whatever reason, the great majority of these fail to rise above the level of light and fluent verse, apt for singing, but commonplace or trivial or slight without the support of the music for which they were designed. Whether they moralize, or whether they worship in the direct and elementary way of communities, or whether, as less commonly occurs, they reflect inspiration and creative activity that enable the poet to take his product beyond the usual limits of achievement in the form, none of them is even nearly as good as this one in any way. Indeed, it almost seems that there was in the carol form as it was used during the Middle English period yet one more factor to add to those which operated against the success of Middle English religious verse as poetry.

For, looking back over the body of surviving Middle English lyrics, one is led to form the opinions, first, that this poetry, taken as a whole, does not achieve a very high standard of quality; then, that its failure to satisfy modern expectation may be caused by a difference in kind between many of the surviving Middle English religious poems and poetry as we profess to recognize it by our modern *idea*; and finally, that this difference in kind suggests the existence of a fundamental difference between the conception of the function of religious poetry evidently held by some of the authors of the surviving lyrics and that by which today we attempt to define poetry both religious and secular.

By an examination of the religious lyrics according to the types of moral or devotional activity that they reflect, it has been possible to obtain some insight into the attitudes of the authors of the Middle English religious lyrics to their subjects and their medium, as well as to account for these attitudes in terms of those same subjects and of their effects upon the authors' intentions. We observed in particular that many of the Middle English religious poets seem to have believed that their subject conferred upon them a dispensation from artistic obligations and that this subject was itself sufficiently substantial and important to succeed by its intrinsic appeal without the aid of imaginative transformation. Such an attitude, in the religious circumstances of the times, was indeed natural and even obviously logical to a certain type of mind, and it is not the concern of this study to discuss its validity. It also appeared, however, that this attitude was not universally held among the authors of the surviving religious lyrics, but that there were exceptions in the shape of poets who either set about enhancing their religious topics, great and sacred though they were, by means of external poetic embellishment, or else experienced them emotionally to such an extent that the fervent sincerity of their treatments, combined generally with a simple and honest utterance, made their communication particularly effective, or who, less often, conceived their subjects with a creative imagination able to transform them into poetry that not only was successful as a communication of religion but also had a permanent appeal. We observed also an approximate correspondence between the kinds of religious function reflected in these lyrics and the type or degree of their success as poetry. This correspondence seemed to be related to the kinds of emotion which attend the exercise of the various functions of religion, to the extent of the poet's personal apprehension of his subject, and to the intensity of the imaginative and creative activity involved and the relative preponderance of religious and artistic purpose in this activity.

Not even the most sympathetic consideration of the Middle English religious lyrics can, however, fail to take into account two remarkable phenomena which seem to reflect unfavourably upon this poetry. Whereas, considered singly or read in anthologies among various other kinds of poetry, the Middle English religious lyric seems relatively good, if it is studied with other specimens of its own kind it seems, as it were, to recede into a common sameness of theme and effect from which only a very few specimens distinguish themselves. The Middle English religious lyrics are in fact monotonous in this sense that they treat of a very limited number of themes, that the variations of their treatments are often minute, and that in all but the most successful the degrees of poetic transport are neither very great nor very widely separated. The second phenomenon, conceivably delusive in the light of the circumstances of preservation but unmistakable as things are, is that there are few signs of an artistic technique developing steadily in the treatment of religious subjects in verse in any other respects than those that reflect the progress of secular poetry.   The rarity of really good specimens only confirms this observation.   If the surviving religious lyrics accurately reflect the quality of the whole output, then this phenomenon is important in the light of the first one, for it confirms a suggestion there implicit of the static nature of this particular combination of medium and subject which the few exceptions fail to dismiss.   The inference based on this suggestion receives confirmation from other considerations. The religion which provided the themes for this body of poetry did not change between 1200 and 1500.   The themes themselves, and the attitudes of the devout to them, were as fully implicit in it, and most of them were as widely developed in sermon, devotion and liturgy at the beginning as at the close of these three centuries.   Moreover, the themes themselves were sacrosanct and could be varied only within narrow limits.   Even the romantic treatment of them is as fully suggested in *Sunset on Calvary* or *On God Vreisun of Vre Lefdi* from the thirteenth century as in *The Spring under a Thorn* from the fourteenth, or *The Corpus Christi Carol* from the fifteenth.   Its expressions differ in externals corresponding to the development of secular poetry, and in the terms of apprehension which reflect inevitable personal differences in the poets, but the impression of a fundamentally similar attitude maintained for three centuries remains.   It seems probable then that the effect of its subject upon this poetry was restrictive, and that in many individual cases it might have confined an original vision which, in other, easier circumstances, might have achieved more and greater poetry, but which was not strong enough, or indeed may not have wished, to break out from the bounds that its religion imposed upon it.

A comparison of English mediæval religious poetry with its Latin counterpart appears to test but does not, I think, seriously disturb this conclusion ; [1] the greatness achieved by

[1] Pictorial, sculptural and musical religious art must not be invoked for similar comparisons, for they are not truly analogous.   The relation between religion and poetry is unlike the relation between religion and the other arts, for poetry has language as its medium, and by

some of the Latin religious poets of the Middle Ages fails to set it aside. Indeed, if we did not allow that the religious subject as a whole had a restrictive effect upon its poets, we would be obliged to conclude that the majority of those whose Middle English treatments of it have survived were singularly insensitive and incompetent, which seems improbable. The important thing, however, is to carry the comparison between English and Latin mediæval religious verse through to the full. Middle English religious verse, in all probability originating in a religious and not a poetic purpose, is the product of some three centuries of effort, during which the vernacular lyric poetry as a whole was struggling to establish itself, to determine the kind of its expression, to confirm its native character and to overcome a variety of circumstances which, if they did not actually threaten its survival, tended to cause it to be regarded as the plaything of the young, the frivolous, and those unschooled in the fashionable French culture which, until at least the middle of the fourteenth century, over-shadowed it. While this went on the writers of religious lyrics imitated secular verse, itself derivative and unassured, and in this imitation had to come to terms with their models by establishing a relationship in which the sacred quality of their subject would be preserved while the greatest advantage was extracted from the employment of the profane convention. Despite these obstacles to success there were produced in Middle English a number of good religious lyrics and a few great ones.

Mediæval Latin religious verse, on the other hand, is represented by nearly a thousand years of composition, more generally preserved, carried on with canonical approval, practised with complete assurance of propriety by some of the most brilliant members of an organization which drew upon the best European talent, authoritarian, in the sense that no national culture could vie with it, beyond danger of being made to seem provincial and rustic and unpolished as English was for centuries by the vogue of French in court.

---

means of language two types of representation are possible, that with and that without artistic intention. It is around the possibility of a choice between these, and the circumstances which attend such a choice, that the problem of religious poetry centres.

Moreover, Latin religious poetry was the pioneer and the leader ; it created and established its own forms, which were aped by the secular poets in both Latin and the vernaculars, upon whom, in this case, it fell to establish the legitimacy of their practice. It is hardly surprising that with all these circumstances in its favour mediæval Latin religious poetry attained to the greatness of the specimens by which we best know it.

If, however, we take the circumstances that governed the production of Middle English and mediæval Latin religious poetry fully into account, the differences in their respective success are shown to be of degree, and similarities are thrown into prominence of which the important one in this connexion is that for every good or great Latin religious lyric composed during the Middle Ages there is probably as large a proportion of uninspired versification buried away in the collections as is to be found for each good or great Middle English religious lyric. *Altus Prosator* and *Crux Fidelis* and *Vexilla Regis* and *Dies Irae* are as distinct in their quality from the great mass of mediæval Latin religious verse as are *The Maiden Makeles* and *The Corpus Christi Carol* from the few hundred Middle English religious poems which have survived. The comparison shows how every advantage was on the side of the Latin poetry ; in view of the size of the output, the possibilities of free technical development over many centuries, its undisputed eminence in the literary field and the recruitment of artists from all over the western world, it is not surprising that Latin religious poetry achieved greatness more often than did a despised vernacular with a derivative poetic tradition. The wonder is that the Middle English religious poets had any kind of success at all.

These circumstances, however, by no means authorize the modern student of English literature to dismiss the Middle English religious lyrics as trifling or unimportant. They are the products of a situation which must be both interesting and enlightening to the lover of poetry ; if we are prepared to make the effort necessary to understand this situation our appreciation of the lyrics cannot fail to increase. At the same time, to observe the conduct of their authors and the individual successes that some of these obtained must be valuable critical experience. For the mediævalist who pursues this study the constant vigilance and making of allowance are strenuous and exacting, but the reward comes in those moments of contact with the poetic illumination which occasionally not only breaks out in the darkness but also enables him to understand this.

7

PART III

'THE VISION OF PIERS PLOWMAN'

' THE VISION OF PIERS PLOWMAN ' [1] is undoubtedly one of the most puzzling and, probably for that reason, most controversial works that the Middle Ages have produced. Its importance has never been denied, but the precise nature of its meaning and, therefore, of that importance as well has frequently been in question. It has satirical elements but could hardly be called a satire ; because it is full of the life of its times it is of the utmost importance to the historian, but it was never intended to be a historical document, and is in no way a ' complete picture ' of a ' cross section ' of fourteenth-century life ; it is packed with both allegory and symbolism but the allegory is not radical or thoroughgoing and the symbolism constantly changes both shape and meaning with the movement of the author's thoughts ; it treats of a well-worn theme in the language and idiom of its age, but the expression of this theme is never trite and seldom obvious. Felicities of the highest order stand side by side in its great bulk with dull, apparently careless or obscure passages, and the occasional clumsiness of both thought and expression which mars it has led scholars of great repute to find inconsistencies in it incompatible with single authorship. Almost every opinion expressed about it has been contradicted ; the only ones that pass unchallenged are very general, that it is important, and great, and ' significant '.

[1] In this study I have used Skeat's editions , Text A, EETS 28 (London 1867) ; Text B, EETS 38 (London 1869) ; Text C, EETS 54 (London 1873). I quote from any of the three versions as my illustrations require ; where any one of them will do equally well I use the B-version because it is already apparent that the new text of this version, now in preparation, will resemble Skeat's edition in dialect and therefore in appearance more closely than will A or C, of which the new editions are being prepared on basic MSS. other than those adopted by Skeat.

Since the study of our ancient literature was begun in this country *Piers Plowman* has been variously interpreted. In the sixteenth century it was held to be a sort of precursor of the Reformation and printed four times in eleven years [1]— a remarkable distinction for any work so full of mediæval Catholicism. In the eighteenth century its satirical features attracted notice ; to the nineteenth it seemed a historical and social manifesto.[2] None of these descriptions excludes the others, and conceivably all might fit the poem. But in fact they simply illustrate how successive ages have seen *Piers Plowman* according to their own pattern. No fourteenth-century writer speaks out more plainly than its author against religious abuses, but that does not make him a Protestant. He was merciless in his attacks on both vice and folly, but if that lack of mercy alone qualifies him for the name of satirist then another term must be found for Juvenal and Swift. Nor was he a social revolutionary ; on the contrary he vigorously supported the social structure of his youth, lamented its decay, and showed as plainly as any diehard his dislike of all departures from it. These errors in emphasis of our predecessors are indeed natural and pardonable, and we make the same mistake in the same natural way when we find him a man disappointed in and disillusioned of his faith in human nature, or when, because we do not understand his mentality, we try to make him into several men.

Our popular misconceptions of this kind are too essentially simple to be permanently dangerous. Indeed those to which I have just referred have all enough of the truth in them to have done the poem some service. But the two most important modern approaches to it, both made with the aid of great

[1] Robert Crowley published three separate impressions in the year 1550 ; in 1561 Owen Rogers reprinted the third of these. Both were staunch Protestants.

[2] Cf. e.g. George Hickes, *Linguarum Vett. Septentrionalium Thesaurus* etc. (Oxford 1705) esp. m. 196 ; Joseph Ritson, *Bibliographica Poetica, A Catalogue of Engleish Poets* (London 1802) 26, 27 ; Thomas Whitaker *Uisio Willi de Petro Plouhman* (London 1813) ii–iv ; Thomas Warton, *A History of English Poetry* II, ed. by W. Carew Hazlitt (London 1871) 250 ; W. J. Courthope, *A History of English Poetry* I (London 1895) 226 ff.

learning and fine scholarship, are potentially more misleading, for out of them the popular notions of the future will develop. They consist in studying two isolated features of *Piers Plowman*, its plan, and the unfolding of its symbolism.[1] The danger inherent in them is twofold. First, it is impossible to separate either feature from the other, for they develop together ; second, they are so complex that to concentrate upon either leads to ignoring the obvious and consequently easily forgotten principle that neither is as fine or important as the poem in which it is expressed. Both are best understood in terms of an analysis not of themselves but of the highly individual art and personality of the author, the proper understanding of which must include considerations of every single feature of his work and temperament. In any case the exclusive study of the plan, content or symbolism of *Piers Plowman* involves enormous difficulties for the modern student. For instance, however conversant he may be with the doctrine of fourteenth-century Catholicism, unless he knows the personality of the author of this poem he cannot hope to reconstruct his attitude to the religion of his time, even in the relatively small matter of knowing what doctrines he took for granted (these often represent unexpressed but important steps in his arguments) or why certain points which seem either quite trivial or perfectly logical to us should have troubled him considerably. No single feature of *Piers Plowman* can safely be treated in isolation. To begin one's study of this poem with the plan or the content is at least as dangerous as to start with any one of the preconceptions that it is simply a document of moral reform, or a satire, or a specimen of characteristic allegorical and symbolical thinking, or a record of personal spiritual development. What is true within limits is not of necessity true if taken into account as a first principle, and may as such dangerously influence subsequent judgements. Thus discussions of plan and authorship have hand in hand danced a vicious and dizzy circle, and studies of the symbolism of the poem have

---

[1] Outstanding as well as typical instances of these approaches are H. W. Wells, ' The Construction of *Piers Plowman* ', *P.M.L.A.* xliv (1929) ; Nevill K. Coghill, ' The Character of *Piers Plowman* ', *Medium Ævum* ii (1933).

become so concentrically obscure as to defeat their own purpose.

Yet we have sure ground to set out from. It has always been acknowledged that in artistic greatness and magnitude of conception *Piers Plowman* vies with the noblest works of the Middle Ages. Upon examination it proves to be a remarkable mixture of diffuseness and felicities, of flatness and the sublime. One of its theological expositions rivals Dante's account of the spots on the moon for sheer deliberate dullness.[1] Yet the effect of the whole is tremendous, and there is no sublimity in the other literature of mediæval England to rival that of some passages. Surely the starting-point is this paradox of total greatness and local failures. *Piers Plowman* must be studied first of all as a poem with the mark of genius upon it, belonging with the *Divine Comedy* and *Paradise Lost* and *The Pilgrim's Progress* and *The Marriage of Heaven and Hell*, like them to be understood best in terms of the qualities of its author as a man and an artist and of the light thrown by these upon the poem itself as a work of art. At once the vexed questions of its plan and content assume their properly subordinate places, and indeed are considerably simplified by a consideration of the author's poetic genius as it shows itself in his treatment of his subject. The nature of the plan becomes apparent when the reasons for its limitations are made evident ; and by studying the sources of the symbolism in the poem we are enabled to understand and indeed to feel that symbolism again with an immediacy and completeness that no narrow analysis of it could hope to bring about. A study of *Piers Plowman* in this broad sense will afford pleasure to the lover of poetry who cares to understand what he enjoys, interest to the collector of poetic personalities, who will find its author as rare and remarkable an individualist as England has produced, and a safeguard to the specialist anxious to lose himself in the *minutiæ* of mediæval studies. To consider *Piers Plowman* as a poem is not only the safest but also the most fruitful means of studying it, and should precede the detailed consideration of its single features and qualities.

The first and most difficult point to settle on approaching *Piers Plowman* as poetry is the relationship of the three

[1] C iv ll. 292 ff.

versions.[1]   This   problem   has   already   occasioned   much
speculation from which no clear agreement has emerged ;
what is, however, abundantly clear, is that to students of
poetry all three versions are valid, for as poetry none of the
three is distinctly inferior to the others. The earliest version,
the A-text, is certainly not the work of a beginner ; in fact it
shows great poetic assurance in its author, as well as a freedom
from the sense of moral constraint which occasionally hinders
him in the B- and C-texts. It is, however, plainly inconclusive,
and the probability is that precisely the creative freedom which
its author appears to have allowed himself in his first attempt
is partly responsible for his failure to complete it. In his
eagerness he probably failed to visualize the whole, and his
creative impetus carried him forward only until the complications of the subject pulled him up sharp. The B-text
follows both the plan and the expression of A pretty closely
for the first nine passus, tackles the difficulties which held up
A in a new way, and then, from the look of the arrangement
of its remaining contents, works out its course in opportunist
fashion as it goes along. The plan of the C-text differs in
detail from that of B, but the reasons for the changes that
were made are generally apparent : these changes expand
explanations and make them clearer, increase the explicitness
of attacks upon abuses, meet new topical circumstances, or
redistribute the emphasis of a passage. The effect of the
changes upon the poetry of the C-text is decidedly mixed.
When the motive of revision seems to have been didactic the
C-version is likely to be more diffuse, or more elaborately
explanatory than B. But not all the changes in the C-revision
make for prosiness ; often a passage in C is tidier and knit
closer than the corresponding lines in B, and some of the new
material is as original and characteristic poetically as anything

---

[1] Since the present study was made a most illuminating treatment of
part of this problem has been published in E. Talbot Donaldson's
Piers Plowman. The C-Text and Its Poet (London 1949). The views of
the reviewer of this book in *The Times Literary Supplement* (London
10 February and 17 March 1950) that the classification of MSS. into the
A, B, and C versions is an artificial one, and of H. L. Meroney, ' The
Life and Death of Long Wille ', *English Literary History* xvii (1950),
that the A-version is a compendium of B, have not been supported by
serious evidence.

to be found in the earlier versions. In the C-version we can observe the working of the author's poetic fancy side by side with that of the intellectual faculty which directed the content of his work. Occasionally the two parts of his creative genius work together ; then the product in the revised version is finer and more forceful than its prototype in B, if not always more imaginative. At other times he introduces into the revision new lines or passages full of that unmistakable mixture of sternness and tenderness which emerges as the most remarkable single characteristic common to all three versions of *Piers Plowman*, and which is scarcely to be found elsewhere in Middle English poetry. Thus the transforming fancy of the revising poet both acts upon the original B-material and adds newly created elements which enrich the whole. The impression which the revisions in the C-text give is that they are the work not of an unauthorized person meddling with a finished product, and inevitably spoiling much of it, but of a man trying after an interval, with very fair success, to improve upon the same effects for which he strove before. To balance the occasions when, in pouring out more hatred of an abuse, he blurs the edges of his poetry, there are other rehandlings which harden and sharpen his attacks. When he is concerned with doctrinal points he never fails to make them clearer by his revising, although they may seem to become unduly long ; when his purpose is artistic he almost always improves on the earlier work.

The comparison of the three versions of *Piers Plowman* is not made any easier by the state of preservation of the poem. Because it was composed in the alliterative long line it was more subject to scribal corruption than a poem in syllabic and rhyming verse would be, for not only did the apparent syllabic freedom of the alliterative long line give scribes endless opportunities for improvisation and interpolation, but also (it seems likely) some of them understood only imperfectly or even not at all the measure of the poem which they were copying, and paid little heed to its prosodic requirements. In consequence the texture of the poem, in any of the three versions, is often rough. Even when the texts have been fixed it will not always be possible to decide with full certainty whether the metrical shortcomings of a particular line are to be ascribed to the poet or to a scribe. The scribe seems on general grounds to be the more probable culprit, for it is possible to argue that if I can supply a word to improve the prosody of a line while leaving its sense intact, the poet could very likely have set down such a word in the first instance, whereas some of the men who copied his poem may well have been ' Southren ' men unable to ' geste *rum ram ruf* by lettre '. But such reasoning is not conclusive, and the present need for leaving the question open forbids any precise comparison of the prosody of the three versions.

It is, then, at present difficult to assess exactly the place of *Piers Plowman* in the alliterative tradition or to state with any conviction the precise manner in which the author treated and modified this tradition.   Certain broad probabilities can, however, be established which will afford valuable indications of both his originality and the quality of his poetic genius.

To begin with, *Piers Plowman* seems to have been written for a much wider public than were most of the alliterative poems.   It is unmistakably a product of the alliterative tradition ; the author must have been steeped in this tradition in his formative youth and must already have had behind him a considerable amount of poetic composition by the time he wrote the opening lines of the A-text, for he works there like a man completely at ease with his medium and completely in command of it.   Such mastery of a remote, archaic and provincial measure could scarcely have been achieved by a man taking it up by arbitrary choice in maturity.   Nevertheless, although he was most probably born and bred to this kind of poetry, he did, in one sense, break away from its tradition.   Most of the alliterative poems give the impression that their authors gloried in the strangeness and remoteness of their kind of writing, in the difficulties with which it confronted both poet and public, and in the virtuosity needed for any successful use of it.   They seem to have flaunted their apartness and to have accentuated it by the adoption of Northernisms that they might not have used in ordinary speech, by overburdening it with the particularly artificial rhetoric of the mode, and by general devotion to the prosody at the expense of the material.   In consequence, much fourteenth-century alliterative poetry is less good than clever.

It becomes too ingeniously nervous, cramped and condensed, too elaborately artificial for the taste of any but the contemporary amateur. Indeed in some of the most ingenious and least attractive works, where the display of virtuosity is most remarkable, the prosody seems to take complete control of its user and to force upon him, as the price of his show of talent, artificiality of expression, obscurity of meaning, and a deadly monotony of effect.[1] The author of *Piers Plowman* allowed himself to be turned aside from his purpose by none of these distractions. What he had to say was for everyone to read and he took care, whilst using the alliterative long line with complete mastery as long as it served his purpose, to avoid the obscurity, the stiffness and the deliberate difference which often characterize its use by other fourteenth-century poets. He seems to have used as little of the poetic vocabulary of the tradition as was possible for a man obliged constantly to match initial sounds, to have discarded almost entirely the involuted or elliptical syntax which even the author of *Sir Gawain and the Green Knight* affected, and to have conformed to the natural word-order of the English of his generation wherever the exigencies of his metre at all allowed him to do so.

Nevertheless he was far from destroying the value or the essential nature of the alliterative long line, for as he used it he retained the exceptional power of emphasis which is given to it by the repetition of sounds in conjunction with stress, and at the same time he developed to the very fullest extent the great possibilities for rhythmic variation implicit in the syllabic freedom of the measure. By these means he came near to transforming the alliterative long line, for he made it generally intelligible, used it with unfailing variety, vastly increased the range of its effects, and overcame its tendency to claim too much of the reader's attention.

His poetry is unquestionably in and of the tradition, but it is at the same time entirely personal and original, and always exceptionally sensitive. *Piers Plowman* stands apart from the stylistic groupings of the surviving alliterative poetry; two works only from this body of composition resemble it both in the nature of its use of the alliterative long

[1] Cf. e.g. above, 52–3.

7*

line and in the ability with which this appears to have been used, namely, *William of Palerne* and *The Alliterative Alexander Fragments*. *Mum and Sothsegger* and *Pierce the Plowman's Creed* are similar to *Piers Plowman* in the kind of their prosody but nothing like it in the skill in verse-making that they display, and the four poems ascribed to the *Gawain* poet, or *The Alliterative Morte Arthur*, for all their fine quality, differ from *Piers Plowman* in the use of the alliterative measure almost as much as is possible within the limits of a single poetic convention. Yet it must be reasserted that the author of *Piers Plowman* belongs to the tradition, and achieves within it striking emotional and artistic effects sometimes not unrelated to the quality of strangeness and remoteness that was at the disposal of even the least successful users of the alliterative long line.

Such effects, when their success depends upon the emotion with which any passage of poetry is charged, are usually a part of the poem's larger artistic pattern, and as such are to a great extent both generated and maintained by the impetus of its development. The author's successes with such effects, while they demonstrate the extent to which the alliterative long line could be used for the expression of intense emotional force, are actually less remarkable than his further achievement in adapting his prosody to a use for which its common diffuseness and exuberance, its libertarian nature in fact, would have seemed to make it quite unsuited, namely, the pointed, epigrammatic statement. When he turns it to this task the result is as self-contained and forceful, even as polished as an Augustan couplet, a closed, concise statement remarkably memorable out of context. Consider these instances, only a few among many. Of men's equality after death he writes with terrible point that

> In charnel atte chirche   cherles ben yuel to knowe,
> Or a kniȝte fram a knaue þere   knowe þis in þin herte,
> (B vi ll. 50–1)

of the rich spendthrift that

> He is worse þan Iudas   þat ȝiueth a iaper siluer
> And biddeth þe begger go   for his broke clothes,
> (B ix ll. 90–1)

and on the awful theme of *memento mori* a single, ringing line the equal of which has not survived from his times,

> We haue no lettre of owre lyf   how longe it shaldure,
> (B x line 89)

as terrifying in its way as the cry of Syr Wanhope, Despair, who will not heed it,

> Go ich to helle, go ich to heuene   ich shal nouht [go] myn one.
> (C xii line 200)

There are many other instances of this striking use of a prosody which, whatever its advantages, has from its earliest recorded instances tended to induce its users to ramble. They are the measure of his mastery over this medium and his transformation of it. When we take this rare gift of being able to find the most apt expression for an idea in conjunction with the author's poetic powers of other kinds we may well be moved to regret that his subject was, by his own avowal, so much more important to him than the form in which he expressed it, and to imagine, if no more, at least the technical contribution he might have made to Middle English poetry had his art and not his religion come first in his scale of values.

But such speculation is idle. *The Vision of Piers Plowman* is the work of the man as he was, and we must be thankful that it is poetry at all and not simply homily as it might well have been if his nature had been anything but the particular compound of contradictions that the poem shows it to have been. There, sometimes deliberately, sometimes unconsciously, he reveals himself to us ; if we are prepared to turn his revelations into an understanding of his temperament and character we are enabled to interpret qualities in his poetry which may otherwise look like anomalies or contradictions. The relation of a man's personality to his poetry is seldom as strikingly revealed as in *Piers Plowman*. The imprint is there to see, for all who will recognize it, of a roaming and discursive mind driven by a yearning religion made stern by disappointment, by indignation at greed, injustice, selfishness and uncharity, and of a vast, sweeping and at the same time

intense imagination equalled by few divine poets other than
Dante and Milton. That to these qualities of his mind
should have been added a passionate if guilty love for poetry
is the good fortune of posterity, even if, as it seems, the poet
himself suffered from the contradiction which its presence
implied.

Piers Plowman the poem is in the fullest sense the product
of these contradictions and the outward sign of their resolution ; both in the evidence that it affords of contrary tendencies
within the author and in the complex intensity of its more
emotional moments it shows the signs of strain. No simple,
uncomplicated character brought it into being, for its content
and quality, and even more the diversity of temper which it
displays, bear witness that the overriding purpose of the poet,
directed by an agency which had its beginnings outside him,
had to force unity not only upon his matter and his expression
of this but indeed upon his very character.

To study this character it is necessary to isolate the main
features of his personality by inferring them from his poem.
Inevitably in the course of the analysis by which this is done
there will be over-simplification, but that should not affect
the accuracy of our identification of these features, for the
artificial simplicity in which they will be caused to appear
will be only a temporary impression. The obvious fact that
they were never free from interaction in the man will be re-
established when, having first separated them out, we study
the manner in which they worked upon each other to create,
to determine, and to stamp with an unmistakable private
mark the poetry that he composed.

Our beginning must be the simplest elements, physical and
mental, in his composition. He himself apprises us of the
first. By his own account he was tall to the point of deformity,
and conscious of his abnormality. Such a condition is not
likely to be without effect upon a man's temperament,
especially if, as he again tells us, he is a pauper, disappointed
of the expectations of his youth, who nevertheless knows that
despite his failure in the eyes of the world he is a better man
than many who enjoy place and power. Sensitive on the
one score, bitter on the other, this poet comforted himself

with a pride which, as he recalls half ruefully, half in confession, made him conspicuous for refusing to pay the outward
shows of respect where they were due. Within his long
frame which was too weak, he tells us, to work, there were
strong passions pent up, both of the body and of the mind.
Probably, like many religious reformers before and after his
time, he had found it necessary to suppress these passions
by strenuous self-discipline, and to direct their energy into
channels that would not run counter to the ethics of his religion.
He certainly writes as if he had experience of such self-
discipline. He did not, however, suppress one related quality
of his proud and passionate nature, a violence which shows
itself in both thought and expression. Like Dante he was
quickly ready to be angry, and he had no sense of compromise.
Having once mastered himself he was inclined to forget the
difficulty of the struggle and to remember only the victory
and the value of self-discipline.

He was consequently a stern man, fiercely outspoken,
quite unrelenting in his fight against anything that threatened
the cause in which he believed, rough in his condemnation of
it, and unable to see any good in what his principles directed
him to condemn. His sternness is abundantly illustrated in
Piers Plowman, but I introduce three instances of it, each
with a particular point. The first is a passage describing a
worldly monk, probably no worse a man than Chaucer's
Monk of the Prologue. In the description of the latter there
is ironic affection, almost as if Chaucer had understood, like
Browning, how hard the monastic life could be for a full-
blooded man without a vocation. In *Piers Plowman*, however,
there is no sympathy, no affection, no tolerance, no willingness
to understand the fraility of the flesh. The disapproval there
is so uncompromising that the passage glows cold, not hot:

Now is religioun a ryder   a rowmer by stretes,
A leder of louedayes   and a londe bugger,
A priker on a palfray   fro manere to manere,
An heep of houndes at his ers   as he a lorde were.
And but if his knaue knele   þat shal his cuppe brynge,
He loureth on hym and axeth hym   who tauȝte hym curteisye.

(B x ll. 306–11)

Both our poet and Chaucer recall the same text to reprove
such conduct, namely,

> That a monk, whan he is recchelees
> Is likned til a fissh that is waterlees—
> This is to seyn a monk out of his cloystre.
>
> *(Canterbury Tales* I (A) ll. 179–81)

But there is a world of difference in the attitude to the abuse.
Chaucer's disapproval, in these lines and those that follow,
is veiled and inactive ; he will even agree with the Monk's
' how shall the world be served '.   ' Let him stew in his
worldliness ' he may have thought as he wrote ' And I seyde
his opinion was good '.   In *Piers Plowman* the *sicut piscis
sine aqua caret vita, ita sine monasterio monachus* is no more
than the gentle beginning of a crescendo of stern reproof
which moves through the passage quoted, and through a
representation of the folly of endowing religious orders that
' haue no reuthe þough it reyne on here auteres ' to a
prediction that rang like a bell through two centuries until
it found a fulfilment more terrible than ever its author
anticipated :

> Þere shal come a kyng   and confesse ȝow religiouses
> And bete ȝow as þe bible telleth   for brekynge of ȝowre
>   reule. . . .

and again

> Þanne shal þe abbot of Abyndoun   and alle his issu for euere
> Haue a knokke of a kynge   and incurable þe wounde.
>
> (B x ll. 317–18, 326–7)

The same sternness which packs these verses with their
explosive rebuke is evident in another passage where the poet
attacks a related abuse, this time, however, by no prophecy
but by one of the most direct and outspoken criticisms of
ecclesiastical possession to be found in the writing of any
orthodox critic of the Church in the Middle Ages.   He uses
here the legend of the angel who, at Rome, when Constantine,

as the story went, conferred the temporalities upon Pope Sylvester, was heard to cry out

> ' *Dos ecclesie* þis day   hath ydronke venym
> And þo þat han petres powere   arn apoysoned alle.'

The angel's ominous pronouncement is explicit enough, but the poet adds a mightily inflammatory injunction to it.

> A medecyne mote þerto   þat may amende prelates,
> Þat sholden preye for þe pees   possessioun hem letteth.
> Take her landes, ȝe lordes   and let hem lyue by dymes.
> If possessioun be poysoun   & inparfit hem make,
> Good were to dischargen hem   for holicherche sake,
> And purgen hem of poysoun   or more perile falle.
>
> (B xv ll. 524–9)

His complete conviction, made fearless by righteous anger, has led the poet here to urge men to an action the consequences of which, when it was finally taken, he would have been the first to deplore.

A comparable outspokenness is not always to be found in his criticisms, but whether he uses the bludgeon or the sharp edge, the temper is always one of inflexible sternness. That sternness can express itself in every shade of subtlety from the merely sarcastic to the profoundly ironic, and his indirect condemnations are no less damning than the direct. Take the case where Lady Meed teaches the friars to be comfortable confessors to those lords and ladies who have been over-liberal in their loving. Her glib argument fairly rolls off the tongue. Lechery, she says,

> Is a frelete of flesche   ȝe fynde it in bokes,
> And a course of kynde   wherof we komen alle ;
> Who may scape þe sklaundre   þe skaþe is sone amended ;
> It is synne of þe seuene   sonnest relessed.
>
> (B iii ll. 55–8)

No outright condemnation could be more effective than this liberal and persuasive speech, for the poet's actual hatred of the sin that it pretends to excuse sharpens his art to the point where he can make the diabolical sophistry of the argument defeat its own purpose.

Sternness, however, is one of the first qualities we look for in religious reformers, from whose temperament its absence would be more remarkable than its presence is. Taken by itself the indignation of the author of *Piers Plowman* was rather to be expected than otherwise. The striking thing was to find that in his mind there existed side by side with the sternness a deep and gentle tenderness embracing the whole of nature and even erring mankind, so long as misfortune, or the will to amend, or even ignorance excused its unregenerate state. The sternness was that of the moralist for men who refuse to take the right way when they know it, the tenderness an instinctive response. The two did not conflict because a third quality in the poet directed them to move together.

The tenderness of this poet is the source of some of his most moving poetry. He loved life and all living creatures so much that his affection could infuse poetry into the most elementary symbols of expression. Thus one of his descriptions, of a vision seen in the ' mirour of myddel-erde ', is made of elements that derive from the cold and artificial vogue begun by Alanus de Insulis, but he has brought it to life and endowed it with a warm existence of its own :

> [Ich] seih þe sonne and þe see   and þe sand after,
> Wher þat briddes and bestes   by here makes ʒeden,
> Wilde wormes in wodes   and wonderful foules
> With fleckede fetheres   and of fele colours ;
> Man and hus make   ich myghte see boþe,
> Pouerte and plente   bothe pees and werre,
> Blisse and biter bale   bothe ich seih at ones.
>
> (C xiv ll. 135–41)

Affection and the deepest sympathy show plainly in the whole of the passage from which these lines come ; these qualities between them foster the tenderness that is always uppermost in his nature when the moralist in him has not been aroused. For instance, he hates the professional beggars, the unemployables ; once he says of them ' Reccheþ neuere, ȝe ryche, þauh suche lorelles steruen ',[1] yet he writes far more sympathetically than any of his contemporaries of the very poor, how

> Beggeres aboute Midsomer   bredlees þei soupe,
> And ȝit is wynter for hem worse   for wete-shodde þei gange,
> Afyrst sore and afyngred   and foule yrebuked,
> And arated of riche men   þat reuthe is to here.
>
> (B xiv ll. 160–3)

He knows the wretched life of the man

> Þat hath meny children,
> And hath no catel bote hus crafte   to cloþy hem and to fede,
> And fele to fonge þer to   and fewe pans takeþ,
>
> (C x ll. 89–91)

how he works from dawn far into the night at carding or spinning to pay his rapacious landlord, starves himself for his family, and tries meanwhile ' to turne þe fayre out-warde '. ' God's prisoners in the pit of misfortune ' he calls such people, and prays movingly for them :

> Conforte þo creatures   þat moche care suffren
> Þorw derth, þorw drouth   alle her dayes here,
> Wo in wynter tymes   for wantyng of clothes
> And in somer tyme selde   soupen to þe fulle ;
> Conforte þi careful   cryst, in þi ryche.
>
> (B xiv ll. 175–9)

In this mood of tenderness he writes with a sensitive and delicate touch ; the evident kindness of his nature is here uppermost, gentle, subdued, and vastly different from his harshly energetic moralistic side.

A third quality in the poet's temperament is responsible for preventing either his sternness or his tender kindness from gaining the ascendency and suppressing or ousting the other quality, namely his religion, the most important single element in his make-up. It is easy to give this religion a label and hard to describe it. It was a spiritual appetite, originating in his nature and formed by his times, which

---

[1] See, for instance, B vi *passim* or C x ll. 101–4 from which this line is quoted.

demanded both emotional and intellectual satisfaction. It was an orthodox Christianity that cared nothing for the letter of the observance unless the spirit was there to give this life. It was a discipline, embracing, confining and restraining his character, and by the compression of great mental energy both determining the form in which this energy must express itself and giving strength to that expression. It was the source, in the man, of a profound humility towards creation as a whole, which by abolishing in him all condescension towards his material, gave his poetry a rare quality of intimacy. It was the only flux which could have enabled the diverse elements of his character to be welded together.

At this point the last is its important function. A logic whereby the extreme degrees of sternness and tenderness that he evinces can co-exist in the same man can be constructed only in Christian terms, for Christianity condemns the sin while it tries to raise the sinner, teaches the equality of man before God, and affords by the doctrine of divine Grace a means of avoiding the too rigorous punitive application of an ethical code. Thus upon our poet as a devout Christian his religion imposed a law of great strictness while at the same time it admitted the possibility of special mercy. By this means an accord between the two qualities of sternness and tenderness was dramatically achieved : no evil must be spared, yet the worst sinner may be saved :

> Þanne Marye Magdaleyne   what womman dede worse ?
> Or who worse þan dauid   þat vries deth conspired ?
> Or Poule þe apostle   þat no pitee hadde,
> Moche crystene kynde   to kylle to deth ?
> And [now] ben þise as souereynes   wyth seyntes in heuene,
> Þo þat wrouȝte wikkedlokest   in worlde þo þei were.
>
> (B x ll. 422–7)

Indeed the prayer of such a sinner, of the thief on the cross, or of Robert the Robber, his ' brother ', is the strongest of emotional symbols for the poet :

> For þi mykel mercy   mitigacioun I biseche,
> Ne dampne me nouȝte at domesday   for þat I did so ille.
>
> (B v ll. 477–8)

In such a pattern the sternness and the tenderness can exist side by side without conflict, the first encouraged by the religion and strengthened or mitigated in any particular case, the other a natural instinct that found correspondences in the religion and was most happily expressed in the dramatic act of forgiveness. The importance of this relation in the author of *Piers Plowman* is shown by the manner in which the themes of repentance and grace unfailingly awaken his creative powers.

At the same time as it accounts for this apparent dualism in his temperament the poet's religion has various important effects upon his writing. Obvious relations like its affording him a subject and forming his moral intention are no more important to the quality of his poetry than the fact that his religion provided him with a ready-made set of symbols of great evocative power, and thus determined almost detail by detail the texture of his poetry. That his art preserved its individuality while he used this ready-made material is evidence of his poetic originality. The advantage of these symbols consisted in their being not private or personal, but most widely current, and in the poet's being able to use them as a starting point of common ground from which to make his emotional flights. These symbols are so essential a part of all his poetry that their emotional effect survives even to-day to make his religious temper seem not a priggish *pietade acerba*, or a remote and icy superiority, but by turns a human and understandable anger, and a deeply tender sympathy.

On the other hand it also seems possible that the poet's experience of life threw into prominence the pattern of his temperament as I have sketched it. As far as can be guessed from the scanty information he vouchsafes, he was a man disappointed in his expectations. He seems, for instance, to imply that his father and the friends who paid for his schooling might have continued to advance him had they been able, but that for some reason he found himself left without prospects. This in itself might easily increase his severity with those more fortunate, especially if these failed to attain the standard of generous patronage by which he liked to measure the rich. Whether his hatred of lawyers, exceptionally strong even for the times in which he lived, bears any relation to some actual disappointment with which they had to do cannot be determined, but there is no doubt that his animus against them is so violent that it amounts nearly to an obsession. They are almost the only class of people of whom he finds nothing good to say ; he even denies that they have any right to payment from those who have the benefit of their counsel. Meanwhile their rapacity is undeniable :

Þow myȝtest better mete þe myste   on maluerne hulles
Þan gete a momme of here mouthe   but money were shewed.
(B Prol. ll. 214–15) [1]

His hatred for physicians and professional entertainers is comparable, but not quite so complete.[2] It is not worth guessing what the source of his violent feeling against these two classes of men might be ; the important fact is that all three of these prejudices can be relied upon to arouse him to harsh and righteously indignant explosions of anger which increase the impression of sternness in his poetry and possibly even by contrast that of its tenderness on other occasions. The importance of these obsessions to his character as a whole is not as great as it may seem ; as idiosyncracies unreasonable or excessively indulged they simply correspond to the prejudices of any man in any age. If, however, it were correct to relate one or all of them to a hypothetical sense of grievance in the man, then such a feeling of having been wronged might well have found its compensation in an intensification of the turning to religion. But such a connexion could never be conclusively established.

This complicated interplay of great moral sternness intensified by prejudices, and of a compassionate tenderness, both within the framework of the poet's intense religion, takes place in a temperament of which the intellectual operations, while simple themselves, are by no means always so simple in their relationship to the man's whole character.

[1] Cf. also, among other instances, B VII ll. 39 ff.
[2] See e.g. B VI ll. 275 and X ll. 38–44. Such instances could be multiplied.

His outstanding mental quality is a consuming intellectual curiosity, of which his own description cannot be bettered:

> By so no man were greued,
> Alle þe sciences vnder sonne   and alle þe sotyle craftes
> I wolde I knewe and couth   kyndely in myne herte.
>
> (B xv ll. 47–9)

The whole of *Piers Plowman* supports the sincerity of this wish, for which, indeed, he is reproved as ' inparfit ' a moment later.   However, his religion fixes limits to his curiosity: he may try to understand, but even if his understanding fails he must never doubt.   This restriction is sacrosanct ; of a mystery of the faith he will stop short and say that

> Alle þe clerkes vnder cryst   ne couthe þis assoille
> But þus it bilongeth to bileue—   (B x ll. 245–6)

Nor is gratuitous speculation laudable ; those professors deserve only rebuke who

> Dryuele at her deyse   þe deite to knowe
> And gnawen god with þe gorge   whan her gutte is fulle.
>
> (B x ll. 56–7)

These limits indeed explain the condition expressed in his ' by so no man were greued '.   It is not an unctious and hypocritical display of self-depreciation but a careful and necessary qualification : ' so long as no scandal were given '.   These same limits and his respect for them explain also the violence of his outburst against any questioning of God's plan, hard words pointed by the confession of faith which follows them :

> For alle þat wilneth to wyte   þe weyes of god almi3ty
> I wolde his eye were in his ers   and his fynger after . . .
> Al was as þow wolde, lorde   yworschiped be þow,
> And al worth as þow wolte   what so we dispute.
>
> (B x ll. 122–3, 127–9)

It is conceivable that this outburst and others like it are topical, and that a sense of the imminence of danger to the

Church may have had something to do with their violence. For his own purposes he interprets the restrictions upon the spirit of enquiry as limited in their application to the dogmatic articles of faith, and outside them he freely indulges his questing curiosity. That curiosity was probably the most important single factor in determining the plan of the poem, which is that of a search,[1] and was responsible for at least one of the finest passages of poetry in the Lucretian tradition that the Middle Ages produced.

I hadde wonder at whom and where þe pye lerned
To legge þe stykkes in which she [leyeþ] and bredeth ;
Þere nys wriȝte as I wene shulde worche hir neste to paye ;
If any masoun made a molde þerto moche wonder it were.
And ȝet me merueilled more how many other briddes
Hudden and hileden her egges ful derne
In mareys and mores for men sholde hem nouȝt fynde. . . .
And sythen I loked vpon þe see and so forth vpon þe sterres
Many selcouthes I seygh ben nought to seye nouthe.
I seigh floures in þe fritthe and her faire coloures,
And how amonge þe grene grasse grewe so many hewes,
And somme soure and some swete selcouthe me þouȝte ;
Of her kynde and her coloure to carpe it were to longe.
Ac þat moste moeued me and my mode chaunged,
Þat resoun rewarded and reuled alle bestes,
Saue man and his make— (B xi ll. 338–62)

From this enquiring observation of nature and man the author of *Piers Plowman* drew a conclusion which was indeed obvious, but of which his personal apprehension had much to do with the temper of his poetry, namely that mankind, and he himself with it, fell far short of the standards of conduct to which they might have attained. His particular awareness of this fact, indeed its dominance of his consciousness, both governed his judgements of human behaviour and developed in him a habit of irony which is the second important quality in his intellectual make-up. This habit of irony might have turned a man of a less instant religion into a cynic ; it

[1] As Robert Crowley, or the scribe of his MS. recognized. See his *incipit* to B viii : *et hic incipit inquisitio prima de dowell.* On the plan of *Piers Plowman*, see below 243 ff

taught the author of *Piers Plowman* to expect the disappointment of his ideals, but did not lead him to discard them.

His irony afforded him a most important outlet for the
expression of his disappointment with mankind. That aspect
of human misbehaviour which seems to have struck him most
was the excessive self-indulgence in which man alone, among
all living creatures, offended, the same weakness upon which
Swift insisted in his comparison of Houyhnhnm and Yahoo.
It is upon this kind of human brutishness that he draws for
the lurid characteristics of the unpleasant characters in his
poem, especially the Deadly Sins. Had the whole force of his
bitter experience in this respect been allowed to turn inward
and accumulate there, the loathing suggested in his occasional
outbursts [1] might have hardened into a permanent condition
that could easily have affected the balance of his mind. But
the practice of irony gave him relief and enabled him to
remember that while all flesh is grass, it is yet God's creation
and therefore good if made to serve the ends that He determined for it. He was able, by relieving the pressure of
his distaste on a literary level, to protect himself against
the growth of any cancer of misanthropy, and at the same
time to turn his experience to the great advantage of
his art.

His first and simplest use of irony rests upon an implied
contrast : ' Here is a thing as I find it, but indeed you know
how it ought to be.' On such an understanding between
author and public is based the success of his use of the
grotesque, for instance in the account of Glutton's drinking
bout, in the emphatic answer Avarice makes to Repentance's
question whether he has ever made restitution,

' ȝus, ones I was herberwed ' quod he ' with an hep of chapmen,
   I roos whan þei were arest and yrifled here males,'

(B v ll. 233–4)

and in the fluent insolence of the Dreamer's leave-taking
from the friars,[2] the sting of which becomes apparent only
when it is remembered that he who was leaving these
' Maistres of þe Menoures, men of grete witte ' with a prayer

---

[1] E.g. B xx ll. 182–97.   [2] B viii ll. 59–61.

that they might have God's grace to live a good life, had himself come to them begging to be taught that very thing.

Instances of this practice of using ironic contrast for moral purposes are almost innumerable in *Piers Plowman*. They have much to do with the impression it can convey of having for its subject a distorted world of abnormally evil people.

To serve his moral purpose the author uses another kind of irony as well, based not simply upon implied contrast, but upon the assumption that he is addressing two audiences, one of which has more knowledge than the other. Instances of this more sophisticated form of irony are also numerous, but not quite as common as those of the simpler kind. They can be classified according to the identity of the initiated, second audience. This might consist of those readers or hearers capable of following his allusions, as in the remarkable passage of rebuke against the bishops, which could pass, with those ignorant of scripture, for merely clever macaronic verse, but which gains enormously in strength if it is recognized to contain in fact a quotation from Mark, a mixed allusion to Simon called Peter and Simon Magus, and quotations from Isaiah, Zechariah and Luke,[1] to say nothing of more that may not have been recognized. Alternately he might himself constitute the second audience as he seems to have done in one case where with no conscience whatever he recruits authority in praise of honesty :

> Meny prouerbis ich myghte haue   of meny holy seyntes
> To testifie for treuthe   þe tale þat ich shewe,
> And poetes to preouen hit   porfirie and plato,
> Aristotle, ouidius   and elleuene hundred,
> Tullius, tholomeus   ich can nat telle here names.
>   (C xiii ll. 171–5 ; cf. C xv line 190 or B xi line 36)

This might simply be the not uncommon mediæval trick of citing a non-existent or inapplicable authority with intent to deceive, if the extravagant ' and elleuene hundred ' did not show that the poet was saying in effect, ' Anyone who is taken in by this show of names deserves to be duped—and yet what I say is true '.

[1] C x ll. 257–74. See also Skeat, *Piers Plowman* iv, EETS 67, 195–6.

The range of the poet's irony will then be observed to include extreme instances, those in which it performs the function of a safety valve, and those like this last where it is actually playful, a symptom of the wry humour of which a few traces are to be remarked in *Piers Plowman* but which, one conjectures, the moralistic strain in its author caused him generally to stifle. But one kind of manifestation of his irony at least is quite unconnected with any moral purpose and quite original in its nature. This is a poetic, and more specifically a stylistic kind, which may conceivably have originated in a deliberate cultivation of the startling, or even apparently indecorous poetic figure. Nowhere in fourteenth-century poetry except *Piers Plowman* does this characteristic appear with any frequency; in all three versions of our poem it is one of the most important single stylistic features.

In using these ironic figures the poet seems to have been his own second audience, and to have satisfied his ironic impulse by displaying to himself the manner in which he was able to harmonize discordances. Just how he himself viewed the process we can only guess; it may well have become with use an unconscious trick of style, but his artistic pleasure in it is always evident. As a poetic device it is entirely successful, for the variety ensured by each separate combination of sense, emotion and the spirit of the context prevents it from seeming either tediously repetitive, or mannered. In fact the only common element in the majority of these ironic figures is the principle of incongruity. Thus it is incongruous to learn of the mouse who talked such good sense in the fable of belling the cat, that when he went up to the platform to speak, he 'stroke forth sternly', (B Prol. line 183), to hear the Great Commandment described as a charm against the devil (B XVII line 17), or the faculty of speech called a 'spire of grace' and 'God's gleeman' and a 'game of heaven' (B IX ll. 98–103). Such unsustained expressions of irony in style are common throughout the three versions. Indeed, taken by themselves, they might be evidence of nothing more than a straining after singularity by the poet. There are, however, enough sustained examples to show that they are not merely signs of an idiosyncracy of expression but spring from an attitude of mind to both matter and language that lies far beneath the surface of expression and style.

These sustained instances most commonly occur when there is a specific moral purpose in the poet's mind. Thus, pleading for charitable kindness to poor mad creatures he writes of them that

> Hit aren murye-mouthede men　mynstrales of heuene,
> And godes boyes, bordiours　as þe bok telleþ,
>
> (C x ll. 126–7)

and in the same vein he writes

> —I rede ʒow riche　reueles whan ʒe maketh
> For to solace ʒoure soules　suche ministrales to haue :
> Þe pore, for a fol sage　syttynge at þe heyʒ table,
> And a lered man to lere þe　what oure lorde suffred . . .
> And fithel þe, without flaterynge　of gode friday þe storye,
> And a blynd man for a bourdeoure　or a bedrede womman.
> To crie a largesse byfor oure lorde　ʒoure gode loos to schewe ;
> Þise thre maner ministrales　maketh a man to lawhe
> And in his deth-deyinge　þei don him grete conforte.
>
> (B xiii ll. 442–51)

He is not striving for singularity in expressions like *godes boyes*, ' God's rascals ', or ' fiddling the story of Good Friday '. The first purpose of these tropes is to illustrate in a little space both the similarities and the differences, in this instance, between the company the rich man ought to keep and his actual hangers on, and to emphasize the degree of the difference by the surprise in the discovery of the similarities. Their success in fulfilling this moral purpose, however, confers upon them importance as literary devices. They become then those instances of his irony farthest removed from the point of origin of this state of mind in the poet, for they serve no personal end, but are maintained on an entirely artistic level. In them the ironic mood has no grimness, no undue moralist's importance. Created in anger, used upon occasion as a means of expressing bitterness and disillusionment, the irony of the *Piers Plowman* poet could become, while the wrath of the moralist in him was lulled, a delicate poetic instrument.

This transformation is in keeping with the presence in his temperament of an element of which he himself was suspicious on religious grounds, namely his own artistic impulse. To survive in the fiercely logical religiosity of his temperament this impulse must have been enormously strong. Meanwhile its nature seems to have been conventional, in so far as any poet's urge to poetry can be so described. It involved his need to create; so much is quite obvious. Probably it also involved a need to establish his identity by publishing his opinions,[1] and to satisfy a vanity, dependent upon literary achievement, of whose existence he was probably not aware. These are customary elements in the nature of the poet. But in the author of *Piers Plowman* there was present a complication in the shape of a religious single-mindedness that seems to have afflicted him with a nagging doubt about the propriety of his literary activity.[2] It may be hard for a modern student to imagine what possible exception could be taken to the composition of poetry when the result was as devout as *Piers Plowman*; he must remember first the enormous vitality of the Gregorian objection to literary vanities, and second that on the one occasion in the poem when the objection is raised, it is meant to imply that verse-making is a less meritorious occupation than praying, and to suggest that the sinful man should find time for little else but prayer. This objection, as the existence of the three versions of the poem demonstrates, never got the upper hand, and indeed, judging from the quality of the A-text, the author must have been at poetry too long to give it up even at the time when he began this first version. It is, however, probable that his doubts destroyed his wholeness of heart, and made him emphasize, at the expense of his poetry, the moralistic side of his writing. Fortunately such emphasis was not carried to extremes;

[1] For a consideration of this point, see B xi ll. 86 ff. or C xiii ll. 28 ff.
[2] He describes how, in his middle age, Imagynatyf, that is his reflective faculty, suggested to him that instead of atoning for the frivolities of his youth he is wasting his time with versifying, and using his religious theme as an excuse for this lack of seriousness.

'þow medlest þe with makynges and myȝtest go sey þi sauter
And bidde for hem þat ȝiueth þe bred for þer ar bokes ynowe
To telle men what dowel is dobet and dobest bothe.'
(B xii ll. 16–18)

his poetic impulse was strong enough to win its turn at predominance in his poem often enough to display its fine
quality, as well as to give life and strength to a piece of
writing that without it might have been, like contemporary
works of its kind, sprawling and inert.

Indeed it may be that the effect of this very doubt was not
a bad one ; it may have prevented any but the strongest
creative impulses from achieving poetic expression in the
poem.   Equally it is perhaps a consequence of such restriction
that *Piers Plowman* is a mixture of extremes of good and bad,
with relatively little work of middle quality in it.   A passage
is either raised to the highest level by a genuine poetic inspiration, or else it remains simply ordinary religious verse, with
religious emotion possibly supplying the lack of poetic feeling.
Evidence of the poet's having deliberately cultivated an
established poetic manner, or resorted to literary elegance to
conceal a want of inspiration, are not to be found in this poem.
Its quality is a mixture of extremes, of the flatness of simple
communication and the most felicitous poetry.   Thus in the
suppression and occasional breaking out of this poet's artistic
impulse we must seek explanation not only of the impression of
strength that it conveys, but also perhaps of its uneven quality.

However, his suggestion of doubt in the wisdom of his own
preoccupation with verse-making is only one more element of
contradiction in the composition of his temperament, which
can do no more than intensify the possibilities of conflict
already inherent in him.   We must be prepared for constant
changes of temper in this violently passionate nature, brought
back to balance from its extremes of sternness and tenderness
by its deep religion, while its restlessly inquiring intellect
veers between attitudes of ironic detachment and the passionate attachment of poetic creation.

Compounded of such contradictions a man will be either
very weak or very strong, weak if he lets the various tendencies
within him pull him this way and that, strong if by any
means a single purpose is imposed upon them, whether from
within or without.   His religion provided the author of
Piers Plowman with such an overriding purpose in its end
of salvation, able to turn the conflicting elements of his
temperament to a single end, and able itself to derive strength

from the violent forces that it ruled. But this single religious
purpose could not destroy or abolish the originality of the
man. The particular combination of elements in him continued to be important from this point of view, for these
elements acted upon and modified one another to give each
its touch of difference, to make the poet's very religion as
personal as his satire or his poetry, and to transform the
essentially commonplace material that he used into a strange
new substance from which derives much of the pleasure that
the poem seldom fails to give.

Out of the combination of elements in the poet's temperament four main impulses seem to have taken shape, to have
expressed themselves in terms of his religion, and to have
found satisfaction in the poem. The recognition of them is
the first stage in the synthesis of those qualities which were
identified in the poet by analysis ; at the same time it is the
best means of discovering his intention whether as moralist
or as artist. The process of synthesis begins with the observation that each of three of these four impulses is the product of
a combination of the poet's religion with another of his
characteristics. Thus *Piers Plowman* variously expresses and
satisfies a religious and moral, a religious and emotional, a
religious and intellectual impulse, and an artistic impulse.
Separating the first three of these out is not gratuitous ;
any one of them could conceivably be absent, for none of the
three elements, moral, intellectual or emotional is indispensable to the religious experience. Moreover, it is not possible
to maintain that any one of the three impulses predominates
in the man's character ; they come to the fore together or
severally as the circumstances of any context determine.
At the most it is possible to deduce that the intellectual
impulse is the first to be sacrificed if there is any question of
predominance, as that one which is not only without merit
in itself but can actually diminish merit ; the poet himself,
notwithstanding his inquiring habit of mind, properly admits
this and quotes from Gregory *fides non habet meritum ubi
humana racio prebet experimentum,* and elsewhere the Pauline
non plus sapere quam oportet.[1] As for the artistic or poetic

[1] B x line 248 and B x line 116. Much of the content of this passus
has to do with the relation of knowledge to salvation.

impulse, this too was potentially at odds with strict religion and may for that reason in fact never have held a primary place under its own name in the poet's consciousness. It could, however, by the simple circumstances, first, that it did survive and, second, that *Piers Plowman* is written in verse, find incidental satisfaction and fulfilment in company with any of the others. Such satisfaction would be no less complete or profound because the poet's first intention was other than artistic; conversely, however, the artistic impulse in him could at any time be dormant, to the detriment of the passage in question.

Illustrations of the operation of the author's poetic impulse in a theoretically conceived pure form would be hard indeed to collect, for this impulse is by its nature unlikely to show itself in isolation from the matter. It will, however, be manifested in many particular ways. It may be seen, for instance, in a sudden glorification of the language, as when Christ, harrowing hell, calls to the parliament of demons

> Dukes of þis dim place   anon vndo þis ȝates,
>
> (B xviii line 317)

in the unartificial expansion of a simile for the simple poetic joy of doing so,

> Riht as þe Rose, þat Red is and swote,
> Out of a Ragged Roote   and of Rouwe Breres
> Springeþ and spredeþ   þat spicers desyreþ,
> Or as whete out of a weod   waxeþ vppon eorþe
> So Dobest out of Dowel   and Dobet doþ springe,
>
> (A x ll. 119–23)

in the frolic play of the fancy, as in Dame Study's long speech,

> Plato þe poete   I put hym fyrste to boke,
> Aristotle and other moo   to argue I tauȝte,
> Grammer for gerles   I garte first wryte
> And bette hem with a baleis   but if þei wolde lerne,
>
> (B x ll. 173–6)

in the expression of a deeply emotional recollection,

> If heuen be on þis erthe   and ese to any soule
> It is in cloistere or in scole   be many skilles I fynde,
>
> (B x ll. 300–1)

in a line at least as apt as *eheu fugaces*,

> How fele fern3eres are faren   and so fewe to come,
> (B xii line 5)

in the playful perfection of allegory, as when his Soul says
to the Dreamer

> Is noyther peter þe porter   ne poule with his fauchoune
> þa[t] wil defende me þe dore   dynge ich neuer so late,
> (B xv ll. 18–19)

or in a description of the nature of charity that rivals Paul's
own rhapsody,

> Charyte is goddis champioun   and às A good chylde hende,
> And þe meryest of mouth   at mete where he sitteth.
> Þe loue þat lith in his herte   maketh hym ly3te of speche,
> And is [companable] and confortatyf   as cryst bit hymselue.
> (B xv ll. 210–13)

Such examples of this impulse, and of the variety of ways
in which it manifests itself could be multiplied. The quality
of the above instances will, however, be enough to demonstrate
that the creative urge of the author of *Piers Plowman* could
not be put down by any amount of stern religion, but that it
demanded a positive satisfaction which, indeed, it wrested
from its material wherever this was possible, and that the
poet's anxieties about its propriety were not serious enough
to make him suppress it.

The intellectual impulse in the poet achieved its satisfaction
in the face of a similar objection. The precept *fides non habet
meritum* was real enough to him in theory, and a genuine
part of his belief, but in practice it became a counsel of
perfection because, although he could accept the higher
dogmas, he was too readily able, on lesser, controversial
points, to call to mind quotations and authorities on either
side of a question.[1] Thus he was given to occupying himself
with problems which, in an ideal state of faith, would not have
exercised him at all. But this habit of matching authority

[1] This trick of his mind is illustrated, e.g. at B vii ll. 148 ff, ix ll.
142 ff., x ll. 189 ff., x ll. 372 ff., xii ll. 156 ff. and xii ll. 277 ff.

with authority is only a symptom of the deeply questioning
impulse of his mind, which no dogma weaker than that of
the Church into which he was born could have contained and
repressed. As it was, within the limits of this dogma he
weighed and questioned and tested points not canonically
settled,[1] or else indulged in the most elaborately difficult
scholastic exercises in illustration of mysteries to which
fides non habet meritum would indeed most appropriately
have applied.[2] I have in classifying this impulse related it
directly to his religion, for under the circumstances the
connexion is inevitable ; within the terms of the subject of
his poem he could scarcely have exercised his mind upon
any but religious questions. Nevertheless, for him as for
many fathers and doctors far above him in theological attainment, *fides non habet meritum* was Dobest, as it were, a little
out of reach, and like them he preferred to make the act
of faith after some intellectual support could be adduced,
not indeed to strengthen faith, but as it were to give it heart
once the act of will of which it consists was made. There
was, however, another reason for his theological speculations,
one unnecessary by all the counsels of perfection. In the
intelligent man, however devout, the mind had an existence
independent of religion, and demanded satisfaction in the
fulfilment of its function ; for the pleasure, therefore, that
a man might take in speculation, he would close an eye to
the simple dogmatic answers to his questions, and worry out
new ones, or else rediscover the old ones himself.[3] It is not,
therefore, surprising to find a tolerably large portion of
Piers Plowman devoted to the satisfaction of the intellectual,
and for the moment only incidentally religious impulse
responsible for such exercises.

To observe the operation of this independent intellect is,
of course, not in any way to put the man's religion in doubt.
The deepest and simplest impulse in him is his emotional

---

[1] As, e.g. at B xi ll. 83 ff.   [2] As, e.g. at B xvi ll. 181 ff.

[3] A good example of such speculation occurs at B xi ll. 312 ff. ; the
Church answered the question why man alone of all created beings
fails to observe reason and moderation in conduct by the doctrine of
original sin, but the poet chose to pretend ignorance of that easy
solution.

religion, an urge which demanded the fullest spiritual fulfilment. This religious and emotional impulse is the easiest to illustrate, for its depth and strength are evident at countless points in the poem. In literary shape it stands the poem in good stead; it can enliven allegory (C XIX ll. 4-15), turn religious teaching into poetry by the strength of its outbursts (C XVII ll. 297-323) or create a poetic figure more apt for illustration than a dozen definitions (B I ll. 151-6). It loads with emotion the very commonest themes of Christianity, Charity, the Redemption, Grace, God's mercy to sinners and mean men; by the violence of its response to them it evokes, almost every time they occur, some fine explosion of poetry in which, for an instant, religious and poetic impulses are identified, the distinction between artistic and devotional fervour (the bane of Middle English religious poetry) disappears, and a new and noble experience is communicated. Probably the prayer of Robert the Robber is the best instance of such a transformation in *Piers Plowman*:

Cryst, þat on caluarye vppon þe crosse deydest,
Tho dismas my brother bisouȝte ȝow of grace,
And haddest mercy on þat man for *memento* sake,
So rewe on þis robbere þat *reddere* ne haue,
Ne neuere wene to wynne with crafte þat I owe,
But for þi mykel mercy mitigacioun I biseche,
Ne dampne me nouȝte at domesday for þat I did so ille.
(B v ll. 472-8)

Almost certainly, however, the evocative power of the act of repentance is also to be related to the fourth impulse which the poet's temperament set him to satisfy, namely the religious and moral one. In this case the religious half of the impulse is of fundamental importance, and no mere accident of time and culture; it had everything to do with determining the nature of the poet's attitude to moral problems. Without it he would have been a misanthropist as outright and absolute as Juvenal or Swift, or else a libertine, for he was not by nature given to half-measures. In several ways he resembles the satirists; he feels the *saeva indignatio*, he shares their nostalgia for the better days of the past,[1] is

[1] See, e.g. B x ll. 94-100; xv ll. 264-90, 347-77, 495-509.

8

convinced of the degeneracy of his own time,[1] and prepared
to let his imagination play with the notion of a golden age
to come.[2]   Moreover, he is never easy with evil, never
shows signs of being prepared to tolerate it for the sake of
sparing the effort of rebuke ; indeed he hates all forms of
spiritual degeneracy, especially when they involve the evasion
of responsibility or neglect of the cure of souls.   He could
never have gone on pilgrimage in the company of pardoner
and somnour, or have said of the monk, soberly or in jest,
that ' his opinioun was good '.   He was obliged to speak out
plain and direct, sometimes with loud violence, to satisfy
the moral impulse in his temperament.

Yet he was no more of a satirist than Dante, in the strict
sense of the term.   Unlike Juvenal he did not abandon
mankind ; his attitude toward even those whom he condemned was that of his religion, to hold out a forgiving
hand to the sinner while he denounced the sin.   He had the
sense of kinship with all men which the Church encouraged,
and which he himself expressed in phrases full of symbolical
meaning like ' pylgrymes ar we alle ' and ' bretheren as of
o blode, as wel beggares as erles ' and ' no beggere ne boye
amonges vs, but if it synne made '.[3]   Indeed, this last
quotation illustrates his attitude to perfection ; it is that of
the orthodox Christian moralist and not of the satirist.   He
writes, in the last analysis, not for the relief of his moral
indignation, or for the gratification he experiences in practis-
ing the art of satire, but with the hope of amending wrongs
which both his religion and his intellect teach him are
unnecessary.   Thus the religious nature of his moral impulse
determines the quality of his reforming spirit and saves it
from the corrosion of hopelessness.

These three great forms of the author's religion, emotional,
moral and intellectual, which his nature drove him to satisfy
in his poem, cannot have existed in his character distinct
and separate from one another.   Each will have been constantly to some degree mixed with or influenced by one or
both of the others, and any monopoly of the author's attention

[1] See, e.g. C xviii ll. 85–93.
[2] See, e.g. B iii ll. 297–322 ; iv ll. 114 ff.   B xi ll. 234, 193, 197.

that one of them may seem to have gained represents in reality only a momentary preponderance. Moreover, the success with which any or all of them would be expressed at any point in the poem depended wholly upon the simultaneous fulfilment of the fourth, the poetic impulse. The second stage in the synthesis designed to illustrate the nature of his poem consists in studying the effects upon his art of these four great sources of energy and action in their various combinations.

At the outset it must be observed that unless the satisfaction of these three religious impulses was accompanied by an appreciable fulfilment of the author's artistic impulse, their expression could have an adverse effect, local or general, upon the quality of the poem. The force of this observation will be readily evident. For instance, the expression of the religious and emotional impulse by itself without the aid of any transforming poetic element results simply in the production of unremarkable devotional verse in which the religious feeling, which might supply the want of poetic inspiration, is often itself inadequately conveyed. An instance of this occurs in the account of the dinner given for the learned Doctor, where the Dreamer and Patience, sitting at a lower table, are served by Scripture.

> He sette a soure lof tofor vs and seyde ' agite penetenciam ',
> And sith he drough vs drynke [diu]-perseverans . . .
> And þanne he brouȝt vs forth a mees of other mete   of
>   miserere-mei-deus
> And he brouȝte vs of Beati quorum of beatus-virres makynge,
> Et-quorum-tecta-sunt peccata in a disshe
> Of derne shrifte, dixi and confitebor tibi.
>
> (B XIII ll. 48–55)

These lines are artificial, cold and bad, not because the subject is religious or the treatment allegorical, but because the artist in the author had no part in their composition ; his fervent religion hid their artistic inadequacy from him. We know from other passages that these tags from the psalms and the theme of repentance to which they relate were charged with religious emotion in the man's mind. But apparently because this religious emotion did not here blend or join or merge with the excitement of creation, even the religious fervour from which the verses sprang fails to be communicated. In other instances the creative excitement can add a poetic magic which transforms similar material, as it does in lines like

> *Dominus pars hereditatis mee*   is a meri verset
> þat has take fro tybourne   twenti stronge þeues.
>
> (B xii ll. 189–90)

A similar want of poetic inspiration is evident at some of those points in *Piers Plowman* where the author indulges in theological exposition or speculation to satisfy the intellectual side of his religion. The passages which contain such material unrelieved by poetry are among the dullest and least effective parts of the poem. The lecture of the Friars on free will, the allegory of Anima, much of the consideration of the salvation of the righteous heathen [1] not only detract from the total emotional force of the poem, but also have the effect of obscuring the plan and hampering the free progress of the argument by the very weight of their dullness. In passages of this kind there appears least often the relief of those momentary flashes of poetry, happy phrases or lines such as, even at his least inspired, the poet can generally produce. As for those passages devoted to the satisfaction of the poet's moral impulse by itself, they seldom suffer from any lack of vehement feeling, whether that feeling is expressed poetically or not, but they too leave much to be desired, for as a rule, where the author's indignation is not moderated by the direction of some of its energy into the creative activity, his expression is uncomfortably harsh and loud, and by reason of this undue violence immeasurably less effective as a moral corrective than if the moral impulse had been joined in its satisfaction to the poetic.

It is these passages in which, without particular inspiration, the poet is responding to only a single one of his three great religious motives, that are immediately responsible for the impressions of patchwork, general unevenness of quality and lack of unity which *Piers Plowman* can convey. They reflect upon the ability of its author to sustain his effects ; indeed,

[1] B passus VIII, IX, XI.

in this respect, he is no better a man than most mediæval poets. It cannot be maintained that they are not a serious defect, but I believe that they should be understood in terms of his personality not so much as evidences of his want of poetic power, but as the products of moments in which his attention was, properly or improperly, concentrated upon non-artistic ends.   They allow us then conveniently to measure the degree of his absorption with religion by the falling off of literary quality.

They do not, however, fairly represent the common level of his work, for only a very little of his poem is totally barren of poetic inspiration. More usually not one but several of the impulses which governed his temperament express themselves at the same time, and generally such a combination seems to be attended by a poetic awakening as well. The loftiest poetry in *Piers Plowman* indeed results when the emotional, intellectual and moral impulses of his religion make themselves felt and find expression either in close proximity or together. The closer and more complete their trinity, the more imperiously do these impulses seem to call forth the poet in the author, or else, by working him up to a state of great excitement, they allow his art a liberty from religious restraint that it does not otherwise enjoy.

For example, in the notable passage after Conscience has preached his mission and the Seven Deadly Sins have confessed, the effect is successively tender, triumphant, sublime and satirical in a dozen lines ; the changes of effect occur directly without the intervention of any unformed transitional material, and the twelve lines taken together are a glorious, ringing climax to the passus. The passage begins with the concluding appeal of Conscience to Christ :

Þat art owre fader and owre brother   be merciable to vs
And haue reuthe on þise Ribaudes   þat repente hem here sore
Þat euere þei wratthed þe in þis worlde   in worde, þouȝte or
    dedes.

This is emotional religion afire with the blessed knowledge of Divine mercy, claiming it outright on the ground of Christ's Humanity, surrendering itself to the sacramental act of repentance with a still further intensification of feeling.

Then, while the emotion remains at the same pitch, the emphasis changes, and the poet's mind, in a play of allegory, seeks intellectual justification for the prayer :

Þanne hent hope an horne of *deus tu conuersus uiuificabis* [*nos*]
And blew it with *Beati quorum remisse sunt iniquitates*
Þat alle seyntes in heuene songen at ones
    Homines & iumenta saluabis, quemadmodum multiplicasti
    misericordiam tuam deus.

Now both mind and heart are aflame with the assurance of mercy ; with the poetic vision that shares their room in the man's character they see the impact of this grace upon mankind and set it forth in one of the sublimest pictures in the poem, one that represents with the perfection of utter simplicity the vision of man regenerate.

    A thousand of men þo thrungen togyderes ;
    Criede vpward to Cryst and to his clene moder
    To haue grace to go with hem treuthe to seke.

In these lines the poet expresses his highest conception of good, mankind united in submission to God's will and receptive of his grace ; no wonder then at the strength of feeling here, or the appropriateness of the expression. But this vision of mankind truly repentant is a vision of perfection which cannot be sustained ; the moralist in the poet, lulled for the moment by the enthusiasm of his high religion, reawakens to the old bitter knowledge that mankind will fail in its good intentions. With this consciousness the mood of the composition changes to the disheartened contemplation of man's incapacity to remain, unaided, in the state of grace :

    Ac þere was wyȝte non so wys þe wey þider couthe,
    But blustreden forth as bestes ouer bankes and hilles
    Til late was and longe—   (B v ll. 511–21)

Poetically these twelve lines are of the highest quality ; emotionally, and as an intellectual assertion of doctrine they are endowed with the full strength of Christianity ; technically, for the changes of mood and effect, they are a masterpiece of compression. They are also remarkable for the manner in which they gather up and contain the emotion and the sense of the five hundred lines preceding, and for the fluency of the transitions that they make. Incidentally they afford an excellent illustration of the manner in which the poet's four sources of energy can serve a single creative end. The yearning for union with God, the intellectual assurance of man's right to hope for grace, the jubilant pleasure in the picture of mankind submissive to God's will, and the sober realization that this picture bears little relation to actuality, all from their separate sources come together and share in the supreme fulfilment of his art.

Similar instances of internal unity of purpose finding expression in the highest poetry are to be found on a few other occasions in *Piers Plowman*. Once in a confession of faith that comes after a long discussion of the Trinity, the act of faith itself, and a feeling of relief at having followed the arduous discussion all the way, and even a kind of triumph at having come near to grasping a great spiritual concept, endow a pair of lines with a lofty liturgical solemnity ;

> Riȝte so þe fader and þe sone & seynt spirit þe þridde
> Halt al þe wyde worlde within hem thre ;
>
> (B xvii ll. 158–9)

and twice, at least, in descriptions of charity, all the impulses of the poet's religion unite with his power of poetry to achieve a similar personal resolution, and attain the same degree of success :

> I haue seyn hym in sylke and somme tyme in russet,
> Bothe in grey and in grys and in gulte herneys,
> And as gladliche he it gaf to gomes þat it neded. . . .
> I haue seyne charite also syngen and reden,
> Ryden and rennen in ragged wedes.
> Ac biddyng as beggeres bihelde I hym neuere.
> Ac in riche robes rathest he walketh
> Ycalled and ycrimiled and his crowne shaue . . .
> And in a freres frokke he was yfounde ones
> Ac it is ferre agoo in seynt Fraunceys tyme ;
> In þat secte sitthe to selde hath he be knowen—
>
> (B xv ll. 214–27) [1]

Here again the necessary combination of elements is to be

---

[1] Cf. also A xi ll. 185 ff. and C xvii ll. 297–323.

remarked, the emotional attachment to the subject everywhere evident, the activity of the intellect by which the
categories and distinctions are achieved, the moralistic strain
that cannot refrain from a thrust at the friars, the poetry
which creates the form for the thought, endows the expression
of the content with its individual character, mingles the
reproof against the friars with nostalgia for their lost sanctity,
and finally the embracing religion that informs and directs
the whole creative effort.

The importance for his poetry of such a co-operation of all
the elements in the author's temperament will be evident
in the final stage of our synthesis, where we observe the
action of the three kinds of religious impulse more or less
independently and separate from one another but in a
relatively successful union with the poetic impulse. It will
become apparent that whatever the merit of any particular
passage where only the emotional or intellectual or moral side
of the poet was the source of energy, such a passage is likely
to fall short of those rare and splendid occasions in the poem
when the author's personality worked as a whole in undivided
creative unity.

Of the three religious impulses, emotional, intellectual and
moral, the first was the most nearly related to the poetic
impulse in the author of *Piers Plowman*. The closeness of this
association is illustrated by the power of certain religious
subjects or motives to raise him to a state of exaltation, and
by means of this exaltation to bring into action his creative
powers. Without exception these themes belong to the gentle
and merciful side of Christianity, and are aspects of the poet's
concept of Divine goodness, a fact which itself might permit
one to make inferences about the nature of his poetic genius
and the kind of experience that inspired it. These themes
include the virtue of charity,[1] the redemption [2] in which
charity is most perfectly expressed,[3] the doctrine of God's
grace to sinners,[4] the poet's own symbol of Piers Plowman

---

[1] See, e.g. A xi ll. 185 ff. ; B i ll. 151–6, 161–9 ; B xiii ll. 120 ff. ;
B xv ll. 210 ff. ; C xvi ll. 137 ff. ; C xvii ll. 297–323 ; C xix ll. 4–15.

[2] See especially B v ll. 469 ff.

[3] See especially B i ll. 151–6 and C ii ll. 149–55.

[4] See especially B x ll. 414–29.

who comes to typify the operation of grace in mankind,[1] and the idea of a special grace for mean men and great sinners.[2] All these ideas seem to have moved him profoundly, and, when he entertained them not merely in their simple doctrinal form, but meditatively as parts of a larger concept, they seldom failed to stimulate his creative faculty. In them he had at his artistic disposal the whole emotional power of Christianity.

As might be expected the poetry composed by the author of *Piers Plowman* when he is moved simply by a religious emotion is fervent, highly coloured, always greatly enthusiastic, but sometimes unduly expanded or ill-disciplined, or uneven in quality. At times it verges on the simple unoriginality of prayer. It seems that although his religious emotion could arouse his creative faculty, there were times when it outstripped that faculty, and when the poet, possibly mistaking his religious fervour for a *furor poeticus*, was liable to write diffuse and prosy verse, as well as others when it roused him to such enthusiasm that he created sensationally violent figures. An instance of the latter occurs early in the B-text ; he calls charity the 'treacle' of heaven and the 'plant' of peace ; then his fancy leads his expression still farther from the commonplace into a rare and original conceit in which his overwhelming excitement is evident :

Heuene myȝte nouȝte holden it   it was so heuy of hym-self,
Tyl it hadde of þe erthe   yeten his fille.
And whan it haued of þis folde   flesshe & blode taken
Was neuere leef vpon lynde   liȝter þer-after,
And portatyf and persant   as þe poynt of a nedle,
That myȝte non armure it lette   ne none heiȝ walles.

(B i ll. 151–6)

The succession of images here is startling ; bold and novel as it is it might have been the better for a little more control.[3]

---

[1] See especially B xvi ll. 18–19 and below 241–3.

[2] See especially B x ll. 456–64 and 414–27.

[3] It is quite possible that the poet himself found this passage unsatisfactory and altered it in the C-version, or else that *yeten his fille* of Skeat's B-text is a wrong reading. In either case we might infer that the passage was already found to be difficult in its own time.

The paradox which, as the passage stands, seems to be the poetic point, checks the reader, whose next step will be an attempt to visualize the whole. This he will find difficult not because of the transitions, which are bridged by the poet's emotion, but because the separate images, especially the first, of the ' it ' which heaven could not contain, are not clear enough.

Another example of a similar emotion producing an equally violent but different kind of result is afforded by a later description of Charity on earth, this time in the person of Christ :

> God al his grete ioye   gostliche he left,
> And cam & toke mankynde   and bycam nedy.
> So nedy he was, as seyth þe boke   in many sondry places,
> Þat he seyde in his sorwe   on þe selue Rode,
> ' Bothe fox & foule   may fleighe to hole & crepe,
> And þe fisshe hath fyn   to flete with to reste ;
> Þere nede hath ynome me   þat I mote nede abyde,
> And suffre sorwes ful sowre   þat shal to ioye tourne'.
>
> (B xx ll. 39-46)

Here the poet has not striven for singularity of metaphor but has instead drawn close to his subject by adopting an expression of extreme simplicity perfectly appropriate to it, from which is evident the depth of devotion with which he approaches it. But again there is a check in the reader's response, for he recalls that Christ did not actually speak these words on the cross. The process of reasoning by which he excuses the poet's taking liberties with the known facts of his subject interferes, even if only a little, with the communication of emotion.[1]

I have remarked that there were occasions in his composition when the poet's religious emotion outran his creative and critical faculties. We may conversely observe how the creative activity could be aroused by religious emotion, but how nevertheless an excess of religious enthusiasm over

---

[1] Skeat (EETS 67, *Langland's Vision of Piers Plowman*, Part IV § 1, *Notes to Texts*, p. 441) describes this transfer of the speech as ' a singular mistake '. He may be right ; it is also possible that the poet wrote with an assumption of ignorance in his public.

creative awareness could produce a passage distinctly uneven in quality and, therefore, the less effective. One instance of such a process occurs in a summary of Christ's life on earth. The poet begins with the Annunciation (B XVI ll. 90–102) and at the outset, by straining for effect either to show his reverence for the subject or to avoid the commonplaces of treatment, falls into an uncomfortable singularity of manner. As he proceeds with his account he becomes a little more at ease, but there is no mark of particular inspiration in his treatment until he comes to the Last Supper when, unexpectedly, he puts into Christ's mouth a speech which expresses to perfection the bitterness of mediæval Christendom against that traitor, Judas:

> Falsenesse I fynde   in þi faire speche
> And gyle in þi gladde chere   and galle is in þi lawghynge.
> Þow shalt be myroure to manye   men to deceyue
> Ac þe wors and þi wikkednesse   shal worth vpon þi selue.
>
> (B XVI ll. 154–7)

We have had to wait long for this moment, and meanwhile, matter full of artistic possibilities has been less well handled than it deserved. Now, however, both enthusiasms, religious and poetic, are awake, the poet loses the sense of constraint because of which he was writing awkward and stilted verse, and finally sees the climax of Christ's life in a figure of a high poetic order which he thereafter uses to dominate much of the remainder of the poem—the concept of Christ the Knight jousting in Jerusalem against Death and the devil:

> On a thoresday in thesternesse   þus was he taken
> Þorw iudas and iewes   ihesus was his name
> Þat on þe fryday folwynge   for mankynde sake
> Iusted in ierusalem   a ioye to vs alle.
> On crosse vpon caluarye   cryst toke þe bataille
> Aȝeines deth and þe deuel   destruyed her botheres myȝtes,
> Deyde, and deth fordid   and day of nyȝte made.
>
> (B XVI ll. 160–6)

The sublimity of this splendid vision must not be allowed to draw our critical attention from the dullness which surrounds it, or the actual technical shortcomings of the passage itself.

However, even when these are admitted and taken into account, the reader's response to the passage remains as testimony that, whatever the faults of detail, the poet could transmit the main force of his emotional experience here.

Whether expressed in good poetry or bad, the sum of such religious emotion adds enormously to the strength of the impression of deep and sincere feeling conveyed by *Piers Plowman*. It manifests itself endlessly in little, affectionate touches of expression, unnecessary expansions and developments like the conventional one of writing not simply ' For Marie loue of heuene ', but adding also ' That bar þat blisful barne þat bouȝte vs on þe Rode '. Such activity can hardly be called creative; the poet seems to write in this way mainly for the pleasure of handling again, as it were, familiar thoughts and concepts, and re-affirming their familiarity. His deep affection for his religion, as well as confirming him in this habit of mind, conveys a general impression that there is between the poet and his subject an intimacy which makes nought of distinctions of time and place, renders the most artificial allegory more acceptable, and undertakes seemingly impossible transitions with complete ease.[1] The finest instance of this last function occurs at the end of the vision of the Four Daughters of God, from the sublimity of which the poem descends with ease to an everyday, personal level :

Tyl þe daye dawed   þis damaiseles daunced
That men rongen to þe resurexioun   & riȝt with þat I waked
And called kitte my wyf   and kalote my douȝter—
'Ariseth & reuerenceth   goddes resurrexioun
And crepeth to þe crosse on knees   & kisseth it for a iuwel !
For goddes blissed body   it bar for owre bote'.

(B xviii ll. 424-9)

The poet's religious emotion here takes the form of an affection strong enough to bridge any gulf that might have seemed to separate the stupendous creation of his imagination from the homely act of waking his family for church. At other times the strength of his religion manifests itself in a natural but elementary form of partisanship like that shown

[1] Conceivably the passage discussed above (221-2) is difficult for us because we do not share this intimacy.

in the terrible sternness with which Christ rebukes Satan in the harrowing of hell, or Faith the Jews at the crucifixion. Most commonly, however, it finds its outlet in emphasis, in complete conviction, in an unwavering assurance of man's purpose and his duty to fulfil this. However his religious emotion is revealed, and whether it is good or bad for the poetry of the moment, it never fails to strengthen the impression of the spiritual unity of the poem, and the force with which, by constantly repeated professions of enthusiastic belief, its earnest and urgent message is brought home to the reader. The virtue of the religious emotion for the poem consists then in that energy which, more than any other single quality, sustains *Piers Plowman*; it becomes dangerous when at times it seems to take the place of the creative impulse, and generally so because the ready and unlaboured response that any religious symbol can arouse in the poet can lull his critical faculty and deceive him into accepting as good poetry that which is merely fervently devout.

After having made these general observations about the possibly unfavourable effect of the religious and emotional impulse upon the poetry of *Piers Plowman* it is necessary to restore the balance by recalling that there are occasions on which this impulse can serve the very highest poetic ends. The truth of this statement can be shown by a pair of poetic examples that differ widely in character, in point of origin, and in the sensational and dramatic quality with which, like many of the religious symbols of the mediæval church, they were invested. The first is occasioned by the remote and theologically trivial patristic legends of the holy hermits of the Egyptian desert :

> It is reuth to rede how riȝtwis men lyued,
> How þei defouled her flessh, forsoke her owne wille,
> Fer fro kitth and fro kynne yuel yclothed ȝeden,
> Badly ybedded, no boke but conscience,
> Ne no richchesse but þe Rode to reioyse hem Inne.
>
> (B xv ll. 495–9)

Some alchemy of association has transformed this expression of pity for those men who denied the flesh so completely into a most moving assertion of the magnitude of their sacrifice. The

mechanics of these lines alone cannot explain their mounting
pathos; that must come from within the poet. The second
example is nearer the centre of his religion, but still the result
as poetry is vastly greater than its source, for from the simple
doctrine that poor, unlettered men who know only the bare
essentials of their faith are less exposed to doubt, and, therefore, more readily saved than the most learned doctors, the
poet, by no means qualified for this grace himself, has made
a text of hope in the magnitude of God's mercy that is
moving out of all proportion to his uneasy material:

> Aren none rather yrauysshed   fro þe riȝte byleue
> Þan ar þis cunnynge clerkes   þat conne many bokes;
> Ne none sonner saued   ne sadder of bileue
> Þan plowmen and pastoures   & pore comune laboreres.
> Souteres and shepherdes   suche lewed iottes
> Percen with a *pater noster*   þe paleys of heuene
> And passen purgatorie penaunceles   at her hennes partynge,
> Into þe blisse of paradys   for her pure byleue
> Þat inparfitly here   knewe and eke lyued.
>
> (B x ll. 456–64)

The mounting pathetic emotion of the former, culminating in
a figure of the most felicitous irony, and the sublimely joyous
confidence in God's special favour of the latter with its fine
image, could scarcely be bettered. As a general rule, however,
when the emotional religion of any passage is not controlled
and upsets the balance of the elements, that passage will be
imperfect at any rate poetically. With the warmth and the
tenderness of the religious impulse we must accept its faults
of uncritical enthusiasm, diffuseness, mixed figures and
occasionally banal or commonplace or even affected expression.

The relation of the poet's religious and intellectual impulse
to his poetic art is quite another matter. It was observed
that his religious emotion could readily generate a warmth
which might pass for poetic emotion, or take the place of
such, but which did not always lead to the production of
poetry of a high quality. The poet's intellectual impulse
by itself is naturally less fervid and inspired. It is liable to
produce a detached and contemplative poetry, almost ' metaphysical ' in character, with signs of a cultivation of remote
or singular analogies. Meanwhile, this impulse does not

easily or readily kindle the poet's creative imagination.[1]
Much of that part of *Piers Plowman* which is governed by
his intellect is hardly more than versifying. Except for the
best of the allegory in the poem,[2] for occasional solemn and
lofty utterances on doctrinal subjects,[3] speculations 'on the
perversity of human behaviour,[4] or straightforward expositions
of theological relations,[5] the activity of the intellectual side of
the poet's religion is seldom even distinguished by beauty
of expression, and only very rarely shows signs of an attendant
creative excitement.

Cases do, however, occur in which intellectual concepts pure
and simple become sources of poetic emotion in the author and
awaken his creative faculty. When this faculty is sufficiently
awake, and when at the same time the idea or concept in
question is aptly expressed, then the product is very fine
indeed, for it is generally free from the indiscipline of the more
emotional writing. Often the matter itself imposes compact-
ness and careful logic upon the passage, which indeed does
not necessarily make it poetry, but at least keeps the verse
from sprawling. The idea or concept itself usually generates
the poetic excitement, often because the contemplation of it is
attended by a sense of achievement or discovery. The poetic
expression of an idea thus enjoyably entertained adds for the
poet the pleasure of creation to that of contemplation. The
two between them move him to a sober, quiet poetry :

Lente neuere was lyf   but lyflode was shapen
Wherof or wherfore   or whereby to lybbe.
First þe wylde worme   vnder weet erthe,
Fissche to lyue in þe flode   and in þe fyre þe crykat,
Þe corlue by kynde of þe eyre   moste clennest flesch of bryddes,
And bestes by grasse and by greyne   and by grene rotis
In menynge þat alle men   myȝte þe same
Lyue þorw lele byleue   and loue, as god witnesseth.

(B xiv ll. 39–46)

---

[1] In this he seems to differ from the metaphysical poets of the
seventeenth century.

[2] C xix ll. 4–15 is one of the happiest instances of this, but cf. also
B xv ll. 16–21 and 210 ff.

[3] E.g. B ix ll. 26–58

[4] E.g. C xiv ll. 188–96.   [5] E.g. B i ll. 161–9.

Reduced to prose, the idea contained in this passage is colour-less and unimpressive ; yet it must have been exciting to the poet, for his choice of instances for the analogy he illus-trates is so felicitous that it can have been determined only by his poetic instincts. A passage similar in kind but some-what livelier is begotten by the discovery of an analogy as startling as many of the conceits of the metaphysical poets, in which the poet compares Christ's life on earth to that of a pretender to a throne :

> Sum tyme he suffred & sum tyme he hydde hym;
> And sum tyme he fauȝte faste & fleigh otherwhile ;
> And some tyme he gaf good & graunted hele bothe;
> Lyf & lyme as hym lyste he wrought.
> As kynde is of a conquerour so comsed ihesu
> Tyl he had alle hem þat he fore bledde.
>
> (B xix ll. 98–103)

The poet is evidently delighted with the notion that the hardships and the hiding, the secrecy and flight and fighting, and finally the conferment of benefits upon loyal friends, occur in both cases. The singularity in the comparison may be taken to have added a little to the excitement of express-ing it.

Such singularity is not, however, a necessary feature of the poet's happy expression of his intellectual impulse. Once at least he satisfies it successfully in poetic form simply by assembling a number of plain and indeed obvious figures which in combination become extraordinarily effective ; together they constitute a definition of Holy Church :

> Charite . . .
> Lyf, and loue, and leaute in o byleue and lawe,
> [A loue-knotte] of leaute and of leel byleyue,
> Alle kynne cristene cleuynge on o wyl,
> Withoute gyle and gabbynge gyue and selle and lene.
>
> (C xviii ll. 125–9)

The simplicity of this passage is deceptive ; each element in the cumulative definition, taken by itself, is to be sure plain and easy, but the meaning expands with each addition, and with it the impression of poetic value in what is said.

In a similar multiplication of instances, perhaps a trifle more spontaneous, lies the success of a beautiful description of the invulnerability of charity :

> Bi hym þat me made miȝte neuere pouerte,
> Miseise, ne myschief ne man with his tonge,
> Colde, ne care ne compaignye of theues
> Ne noither hete, ne haille ne non helle pouke
> Ne noither fuire ne flode ne fere of þine enemy
> Tene þe eny tyme and þow take it with þe.
>   *Caritas nichil timet.*   (B XIII ll. 158–63)

Here the poet's enthusiasm for his subject and his pleasure in the identification and enumeration of its qualities has become so intense that it carries him well over the borders of simple thought into a kind of inspired imaginative perception, by means of which he is able to express a meaning lovelier, richer, and more striking almost than the lofty one with which he began. But such a transformation is rare indeed ; as a general rule, where the intellectual impulse of this poet's religion is dominant, his work, if poetic at all, is quiet, controlled and, more than any of his other writing, serene.

None of these adjectives applies to that part of his poem which is directed by his moral impulse. The qualities of the indignation which drove this impulse have already been considered ; [1] it remains only to study its expression in poetry, and to compare its marks with those made by the other expressions of the poet's religion. The moral impulse itself is not easy to isolate by definition, for it is both most intimately connected with the intellect which recognizes and condemns the wrongdoing, and is itself actually a special kind of religious emotion. Nevertheless there can be no mistaking those passages in *Piers Plowman* which it dominates, for wherever it is present there is a likelihood that it will subordinate both emotional and intellectual religion to its own ends of rebuke, while it has upon the poetry where it gains the ascendancy a number of pronounced and entirely individual effects.

The common quality of all the moral poetry in *Piers Plowman* is violence. Yet not all this poetry is untutored,

[1] See above 193–6 and 213–14.

9*

over-impulsive or simply rough, as the strength of the author's feeling might have made it ; more often than one would expect this powerful emotion shapes its expression in form and figure well matched to the content. As long as we recognize that forceful correction was the author's first purpose, and that literary elegances were of secondary importance to him as a moralist, we may profitably, from this beginning of violence, study his effects.

It would, for instance, be hard to increase the force of the author's open reproof of professional beggars (C x ll. 98–104), or of the entertainers who called themselves minstrels but lived by destroying both their own dignity as God's creatures and the good names of their fellow men (B x ll. 38–50). Open rebuke of this kind reveals the strength of the poet's *saeva indignatio*. Colder and therefore perhaps more frightening is another trick he has, of exposing an abuse baldly and methodically, explaining how it comes to be and to persist, and letting its uncovered ugliness work its own condemnation, as he does with false religious (C x ll. 188–280), with the great lords who fail in their obligation to support as large a household as they can afford (B x ll. 58–65 and 87–100), or with the men in high places who question the Divine wisdom and ' lay faults upon the Father that formed us all ' :

> Whi shulde we þat now ben   for þe werkes of Adam
> Roten and torende ?   resoun wolde it neuere—
>
> (B x ll. 111–12)

However, the most effective kind of direct rebuke to which he has recourse is the aphorism, which he has developed into the most remarkable example of disciplined writing to be found in the Middle English alliterative long line. In the aphorism as he employs it, the logic of his argument, its point, and often a contrast spoken or implied are made to fit the verse perfectly so that there is neither any answer to his contention nor any possibility of sharpening its expression. What, for instance, can be said about this comment on the practice of religion except that it is true ?

> God is moche in þe gorge   of þise grete maystres,
> Ac amonges mene men   his mercy and his werkis.
>
> (B x ll. 66–7)

Or what is to be added to the disillusioned understanding of poverty displayed in these lines ?

> Þe pore is ay prest to plese þe riche
> And buxome at his byddyng for his broke loues.
>
> (B xiv ll. 220–1)

Or of the rich in these ?

> Þe more he wynneth and welt welthes & ricchesse,
> And lordeth in londes þe lasse good he deleth.
>
> (B x ll. 83–4)

The gnomic strain has always been strong in English reforming poetry, but seldom before the Augustan age did it find a more perfect expression than here.

The poet's indirect attacks are both varied and interesting in their methods. He will sometimes deliberately appear to support the preposterous, as in the marriage settlement of Lady Meed (B ii ll. 73 ff.) or put all his skill into an argument that he abhors in order to expose both its sophistry and the nature of those who use it (B iii ll. 55–8. See above 195–6), or he will with one small sardonic touch bring the abuse of the moment into the highlight, and by the wit of his contrast show how far removed it is from the right practice that it has ousted :

> Bothe riche and religious þat Rode þei honoure
> Þat in grotes is ygraue and in golde nobles.
>
> (B xv ll. 506–7)

At other times by sheer concentration of effects of ugliness and filth he creates a terrifying impression of the unhealthily grotesque (B xx ll. 79–104) ; or else he uses this effect of ugliness to drive home the lesson of the miserable condition of unregenerate man. The names of his allegorical characters stink of evil : Favel, Lyer, Gyle, Falsenesse, the Erle of Enuye, Waryn Wysdom, Wastour, Lecchour, Bakbitinge, Wratthe and Coueytise ; they are no less effectively unsavoury than the flesh and blood creatures with which he peoples his sordid underworld, Piers the Pardoner, Rainald the Reue, Godefrey of Garlickhithe, Rose the Regratere, Clarice of Cokkeslane and Peronel of Flaunders, Denote the Baude, Sir Piers o

Pridie the dissolute priest, and many more, a pack of some fifty in all who skulk about his poem adding the weight of their offences to the mass of evil under which he wishes us to see the world bowed.

There are, however, persons in high places whom sometimes his discretion prevents him from rebuking as freely as he does these mean creatures, and who could be dangerous to him if he provoked them. If he chooses to speak against such men he must veil his reproof in allusions,[1] or in a show of courtesy,[2] or put it into the mouths of characters with whom he does not openly side.[3]   Here motives not literary but of self-protection made him adopt an indirect method ; but there are other cases where for an instant the poetic side of his temperament gets the better of him, and where he writes, indeed still conscious of the evil condition of the world, but for a brief interval carried away by a dream of a happy society from which all violence and rapacity are absent, a vision of a Golden Age almost Lucretian in its fervour.[4]   Similarly it is a dramatic and not a moral insight which reveals to him the state of mind of Sir Wanhope, the despairing sinner,[5] or the sudden stab of regret for the splendid figures of the past who came to bad ends, the great men and the lovely women, none of whom, Sir Wanhope consoled himself, would sit in God's seat or see Him in His bliss :

> Catel and kynde witte   was combraunce to hem alle.
> Felyce hir fayrnesse   fel hir al to sklaundre ;
> And Rosamounde riȝt so   reufully bysette,
> Þe bewte of hir body   in badnesse she dispended.
>
> (B xii ll. 46–9)

Although the poet does not for an instant cease to be the moralist, yet in the composition of these lines he is moved by a romantic regret for this greatness and beauty that comes to naught.

---

[1] C x ll. 257–74 ; see also above, 204.   [2] E.g. C xi ll. 187–201.
[3] Like the ' lewed vicory ' who attacks the Pope and the college of cardinals, B xix ll. 407–55. Cf. B Prol. ll. 123 ff.
[4] B iii ll. 297–310.   For another, somewhat less poetic instance, see B iv ll. 114 ff.
[5] C xii ll. 198–203.

Such softness in his moralistic writing is at least uncommon,
and requires some very special circumstance to call it forth.
Once, most strikingly, this occurs when the poet's reproach
is turned upon himself, and Ymagynatyf, reflection, says
to him

I haue folwed þe in feithe þis fyue and fourty wyntre
And many tymes haue moeued þe to þinke on þine ende,
And how fele fernȝeres are faren and so fewe to come ;
And of þi wyld wantounesse þo þow ȝonge were,
To amende it in þi myddelage lest miȝte þe faylled
In þyne olde elde þat yuel can suffre
Pouerte or penaunce or preyeres bidde.   (B xii ll. 3–9)

The sense is that of the moralist : do not put off repentance,
for you may wait too long.   But there are overtones of
regret, and in addition there is in these lines a suggestion of
that general sorrow which men feel over the passage of time
and the decay of life.

To take this attitude, however, is not his custom.   Most
of his moral poetry is stiffened by the iron of his stern
righteousness.   In quality it varies enormously.   Poetically
the few instances that I have quoted are probably the best ;
the writing that is open reproof as a rule contains the least
poetic merit, for there violence and the desire to make a point
often rule out the possibility of any art by requiring all his
interest and energy.   Nevertheless some of the plain
preaching, with no pretentious frills or elegance, is good,
hard writing with occasional moments of felicitous expression.

It will now be evident that each of the three impulses of
the poet's religion manifests itself poetically in a quite
distinctive manner.   Although those rare parts of *Piers
Plowman* where all the elements of the author's temperament
worked in fine harmony are beyond comparison the greatest,
nevertheless the fact that this balance was not always preserved was by no means entirely harmful to the poem.   The
emotional, the intellectual, and the moral sides of the poet's
religious temperament not only assured variety in his
creation by their separate influences, but each in its own
right made an essential contribution to the total effect of
the poem.

Piers Plowman cannot have anything but a cumulative effect ; it is too large, and changes pace and even apparent plan too often to be taken in or remembered at one grasp. A work of this size makes itself felt not as one whole but by a succession of impressions each of which, as it withdraws into the past, loses its precise identity and merges with others before it and to come. Under such circumstances the clarity of one's experience of the separate passages of the poem fades as the moments of reading pass, and the intensely righteous anger of the moralist and the tender pathos of the poet of crucifixions and conversions lose some of their identity to one another in a subtle way, and are further transmuted by added recollections of a speculative and digressive habit of mind which finds the manner of the peacock's mating and the possibility of a pagan emperor being saved and the nature of the Trinity all of equal interest. Moreover, the fact that one poetic style is the vehicle for all these kinds of poetry, devotional, moral and speculative, does much to give them and our recollection of them a semblance of uniformity, and to make their several impressions a part of the mounting effect of the whole poem.

It goes without saying that all these elements in the man's art depend finally for the quality of their expression upon his actual gift of poetic composition. The question of his technique, his use of that gift, is intensely complicated. The emotional sources of his creative impulse and the character which determined the plan and the purpose of his work both have a bearing upon his exercise of his art. That his religion both questioned the validity of poetry as an occupation and justified it by itself providing him with a sacred subject is another important point in relation to his style and craftsmanship. That the three forms of the religious impulse in him, emotional, intellectual and moral, kept him perpetually restless and dissatisfied has also much to do with the form of his poem and his uneasy questing. That in his moralistic writing he was prone to the particular weakness of the satirist, the disgression, affects this form even more.

This situation is finally complicated by what appears to have been his method of working. As far as can be deduced from his poem he was a man of immense natural talent who practised poetry not as a painstaking and conscious process of construction upon models, as did for instance Chaucer in the course of learning his craft, but by ear, as it wère, or as a man engages in an art in which, from long familiarity and association he has become extremely fluent, but with no apparent care for the *minutiæ* of craftsmanship. In consequence his work, with its unpredictable progress from one poetic association to another, its seeming lack of plan, and its considerable contempt for many of the conventions of its medium shows not only this amazing fluency, but also all the faults of haste and carelessness that are the defects of fluency.[1] Such faults are irritating, but not serious enough to affect our judgement of his poetry ; in fact his complete mastery of his medium is only confirmed by this readiness to do violence to it. His range is vast, and he seldom fails in his effects, whether they are of simple exposition, denunciatory, descriptive, lyrical, or pathetic.

The artless fluency of his composition displays in yet another way the nature and the temperament of the man himself. His style is almost violently direct in address and manner, never ornate or artificial ; it contains no formal rhetoric in the accepted sense of the term, and no literary tricks of expression that could not conceivably have been acquired by a man with a good ear and a retentive memory from acquaintance with liturgy and stage and sermon or developed from his attitude to life and mode of thinking. Moreover, his fluency has an air of distinction ; however slovenly he may seem in the manner of his writing, and however careless about alliteration, or overloading his lines with unstressed syllables, his verse is never quite ordinary, or trivial, or as lifeless as corresponding work in other contemporary literary dialects can be, for its shortcomings never suggest incapacity, but only neglect, and, good or bad, it is always charged with his emotion. His fluency endows him still further with several extremely useful special gifts, skill at composing dialogue, the art of giving rapid accounts of action so vivid

---

[1] It is, however, possible that a good deal of what seems to be hasty or slipshod writing in *Piers Plowman* is scribal in origin and will disappear when the three texts have been re-edited.

that one regrets the little scope his subject allowed him in this direction, and a knack of making even the most far-fetched allegory come to life. Whatever its origin, whether it was developed and trained in a literary apprenticeship the early results of which are lost or hidden in the anonymity of the fourteenth century, or whether it was an unschooled natural talent, his fluency is of the utmost importance to the style in which his poem was written.

After this fluency the next important quality in the author's character as an artist is an unusually powerful visual imagination. This quality in him has not been sufficiently remarked ; it is stronger and clearer even than Chaucer's, and functions with unbroken ease even when he is dealing with allegorical characters.[1] In consequence *Piers Plowman* has a most graphic style and a more completely pictorial effect than most Middle English poetry, despite the abstract nature of a good deal of its subject. The poet's visual imagination makes itself felt in a trick of selection of concrete material that may have been unconscious but is certainly effective : ' Ye lovely ladies *with your long fingers* ', ' Religious who have no ruth *though it rain on their altars* ', ' I am not lured with love *but there lie aught under the thumb* ', ' *As common as a cartway* to every knave that walks '. This ability to visualize could be made to produce descriptions uncommonly effective not for the amount of detail they include, or for the elegance of their language, but because they can make the reader see the subject with extraordinary clarity. With the fluency that enabled the poet to commit his thoughts to language, this gift of seeing them as pictures is an important element in the formation of his style.

I have mentioned in connexion with the poet's irony a habit which constitutes his third and probably most individual stylistic feature : the practice of the striking or startling metaphor or figure in which, whatever other quality it may have, the element of incongruity is prominent.[2] It seems as if this practice was related to, and developed together with the tendency to irony in his character, and that it may have begun as an outlet for emotion, or even as a somewhat

[1] See, e.g. B viii line 70, or xv ll. 12–13 or xviii line 228.
[2] See above, 205.

perverse means of leaving his mark upon what he wrote.
Probably it did not long remain deliberate, but became a habit,
an attitude of mind toward literary material and a tendency
to develop it in a certain way. With this change would go a
change in the nature of the gratification he derived from the
practice. The importance of the ironic element as such would
diminish, and all the wryness of mind, the tension, would
be replaced, to the advantage of the man's poetry, by a special
freedom, personally won, for the discovery of remote analogies,
and a kind of privilege of disregarding the ordinary rules and
conventions for the use of the metaphor in poetry. The results
of the exercise of this privilege are widely distributed in the
three versions of *Piers Plowman*; a very few illustrations
will suffice to be added to the many already incidentally
quoted. By this process a soul, for instance becomes

> A sotyl þinge withal,
> One withouten tonge and teeth;   (B xv ll. 12–13)

Holy Church is 'Duchess of Heaven' (C iii line 33); in thirty
winters St. Mary of Egypt ate but three little loaves ' and love
was her relish ' (C xviii line. 23–4); Adam and Eve deprived
themselves of paradise by eating ' apples unroasted ' (B v
611–12); when the golden age comes to the world men will see

> Prestes and parsones with *placebo* to hunte
> And dyngen vpon dauid eche a day til eue.
>   (B iii ll. 309–10)

Other instances will be remembered, the figure of Christ as a
kind of Young Pretender, charity as the ' treacle of heaven '
and the ' plenitude of peace ' (In the C-text this will read,
even more violently, ' plant of peace '), the poor as ' minstrals
of heaven ', ' God's rascals ', a learned clerk who is to ' fiddle
the story of Good Friday ' to the rich. No formula can be
set up to fit all the uses of this poetic figure; two conditions
only seem to have been necessary to produce it: first that
the comparison or analogy involved should be apt, and second
that its illuminating quality should be perceived only after
a first shock caused by its apparent incongruity.

We can only guess at the precise nature of the æsthetic
gratification that the poet evidently did obtain from the use

of this particular kind of poetic figure. It appears, however, that it could be used as a personal poetic symbol, a means by which he could record for his own satisfaction the importance of a theme or subject to himself. Naturally this discovery of resemblances in remote or improbable objects or ideas is not the monopoly of the author of *Piers Plowman* ; it is, however, justifiable to detect in his frequent use of it an individual, personal quality which makes it a highly character-istic single feature of the style of the poem as a whole, and to observe that it was most unusual in the fourteenth century.

The utmost fluency, an exceptionally keen visual imagina-tion, and this personal trick of expression are the main formative elements of this style. They are, however, only the external instruments which shaped it ; the subject they express and the manner of its expression were determined by the author's temperament and character, for it was his thoughts and emotions that created the need for the expres-sion, and awakened both his poetic imagination and the faculty of expression itself. A study of his style must, therefore, also attempt to explore the more problematic question of his temperament, of the never-ending commerce between the state of the poet's mind that causes creation to take place, and the language that records this state for the purpose, primary or not, of communicating it to others.

Much of this question we have already studied in the case of our poet by analysing the effect of the impulses that governed his writing upon his actual poetry. On the level of style there remains to be considered one very important item, namely his use of symbolism. Unlike the allegory in *Piers Plowman*, which seems generally to have been used deliber-ately, however habitual and familiar such a use might become,[1]

---

[1] On the whole the use of allegory in *Piers Plowman* is fairly conventional, but it is a little livelier as a rule than the normal performances of the fourteenth century in this kind. It is worth distinguishing three degrees of effectiveness in the author's use of allegory, and probably three corresponding intentions. There is first the simple, generally didactic use, as in the description of the high way to Truth (B v ll. 570-626), the Seven Sisters who serve Truth (B v ll. 627-32), Pier's family (B vi ll. 80-4), the five sons of Sir Inwitte (B ix ll. 20-2) or the road to learning (B x ll. 157-67) ; then the equally didactic but more dramatic allegory of character and situation in

the symbolism in the poem, except when designedly employed
to illustrate theological meanings, as at the beginning of
B Passus xvi, is generally the product not of a conscious
intellectual effort but of an imagination excited by the religious
experience of the moment to the extent of being able to
comprehénd more easily and embrace more widely the
significances and resemblances with which it deals, and to
express these by means of symbols at the same time both
poetic and religious.

The highly emotional nature of the symbolism in *Piers
Plowman* makes it imprudent to attempt an unbroken analysis
of its meaning on the several levels of sense that the mediæval
exegetist could find in a work of literature. It does not seem
probable that the author of our poem kept any sort of continuous tally in his mind of any three or four kinds of meaning
in his writing as the composition of his poem progressed. Such
a mechanical process is more necessary to the modern student
not trained to be aware of the potential existence of a plurality
of senses than it would be to a mediæval artist, who would be
more likely to be half-conscious of the possibility of several
meanings, than at all times aware of them all. In any case,
the cold exercise of intellect implied by composition with a
constant eye on several kinds of significance would hardly
accord with the high degree of poetic emotion to be found in
Piers Plowman.[1] The probability is that its author was
not continuously conscious of the several trains of significance
to be detected in his poem, but rather that he could rely upon
having a rich store of meaning at his disposal whenever he

---

which the names of the allegorical personages might readily be replaced
by the names of actual flesh-and-blood people, as in the litigation
between Peace and Wrong (B iv ll. 47–142), the confessions of the
Seven Deadly Sins (B v ll. 63–468) or the lament of Despair (C xii
ll. 198–203) ; and finally the personification of mental faculties, or of
great abstractions as in the splendid conception of the meeting of the
Four Daughters of God (B xviii ll. 112–269).

[1] Nevill Coghill quite rightly makes a statement to this general
effect at the end of his illuminating article, ' The Character of " Piers
Plowman " ', *Medium Ævum* ii (1933), although occasionally in the body
of the article he seems to write with the assumption that there are
in fact several sets of precise intellectual correspondences running
through the poem.

chose to avail himself of it. It is better to think of the system
of multiple meanings in relation to *Piers Plowman* not as a
number of continuous threads traceable from beginning to
end of the poem, but as a succession of flowerings or enrich-
ments of meaning at salient points.

By this means we may justly appreciate the manner in
which the symbolism in *Piers Plowman* constantly increases
both the meaning and the emotional force of the poem, not only
through the multiplication of senses at any given point, but
also through the steady accumulation of significant associations around each symbol. A symbol may change its meaning,
but in so doing it does not discard its earlier sense ; it simply
adds a new one to this, and although the new meaning is
uppermost for the moment, it soon merges with the previous
senses to the enrichment of the symbol. Thus as poetic
images and religious symbols occur time and again throughout
the poem, at each appearance they gain in force until at length
they carry great loads of both poetic and emotional associations accumulated in the various circumstances of their
earlier appearances.[1]

The close connexion between the poet's imaginative and
symbolical perception and the more dispassionate movement
of his intellect has a most important bearing upon the meaning
of the poem, one which can be ignored only at the risk of
losing much of that meaning. Just as the emotional value of
the poet's imagery and the significances of his symbols increase
with the progress of the poem, so also the meaning of the
poem as a whole grows, not changes, with each reconsideration
of a problem. The classic example of this process is the
definition of the Three Lives, Do Well, Do Better and Do
Best, which the Dreamer seeks. These Three Lives are
defined at least seven times, but it would be a mistake to
conclude from the frequency of these attempts [2] that each new
definition casts out the one that has preceded it. Quite to

[1] This point is admirably made by Nevill Coghill in ' The Pardon
of Piers Plowman ', *Proceedings of the British Academy* xxxi (London
1945). His sympathetic understanding of the poetic methods of the
author of *Piers Plowman* cannot be too highly praised.

[2] See B viii ll. 80–106 ; ix ll. 11–16 and 199–206 ; x ll. 230–59 ;
xi ll. 399 ff. ; xiii ll. 104 and 115–17 ; xiii ll. 136–47 ; C xv ll. 5–16.

the contrary, each new definition is to be taken to enlarge the meaning of the Three Lives as this has been previously developed, and thus augments, not replaces, the earlier definitions. Even the explanation given by the gluttonous friar at the dinner (B xiii ll. 104,115–17) must be taken into the account of the definition, which is finally completed only by means of illustrations from the several states of Christ's life on earth and by the symbolical representations of the Three Lives in the person of Piers Plowman.

The character of Piers himself is the most fascinating as well as the most difficult instance of such an accumulation of meaning. It is almost impossible to define briefly unless one resorts to too general assertions like stating that Piers symbolizes whatever aspect of Christianity the Dreamer is seeking most anxiously at any particular moment. The bewildering succession of identities which Piers assumes as this *desideratum* is worth reviewing.

On his first appearance in the poem Piers seems to figure successively as guidance in the righteous way of living, then the righteous life itself, and then the spirit of religion as opposed to the letter (B v line 544–vii line 138). He embodies a knowledge of the law of God as well as the victory of man enlightened by grace over original sin. Only for the first moments of this first appearance is he the simple ploughman ; his authority quickly becomes great, for grace has operated fully in him, and in a world of sinners he is regenerate and sanctified.[1] Then for a long interval he does not appear in the poem, but we gather from references to him that he is active as the champion of Charity (B xiii ll. 123–9), Truth's closest familiar and Christ's authoritative spokesman upon earth, *petrus id est christus* (B xv ll. 205–6), whose very name and the thought of whose nearness call forth transports of joy.[2] But in his next appearance, the mere hint of which was enough to set the Dreamer to swooning, the identity of Piers quickly proves to have undergone a radical change.

[1] See B v ll. 556 :

þou3e I seye it myself I serue hym to paye.

[2] B xvi ll. 18–20. The conception of the character of Piers in the B and C versions seems to differ at this point. Either text would serve equally well for purposes of illustration.

Now he is or symbolizes perfect understanding ʼof the deepest mysteries of religion, the Humanity of Christ (B xvi 1 ff. and xviii 10 ff.), His Divinity (B xvi 103 ff. ; but at C xix 138 *liberum arbitrium* is substituted), God's vicar upon earth (B xix line 255), the sacramental office of the priesthood (B xix ll. 384–5), and God's grace to all men good and evil alike (B xix ll. 432–6 and xx ll. 380–4).

Clearly these considerable changes themselves argue that the meaning of the symbol of Piers cannot possibly be confined to any one of the simplified senses by which one is obliged to express the impression it creates. No one of these senses, even at the moment when it is newest, can be isolated from those that have preceded it any more than the sum of the verbal expressions of its meaning given above can do more than merely approximate to the author's conception. Each time it appears the meaning of this symbol of Piers Plowman grows both in *significatio* and in the power of evoking emotion ; its force in the second respect mounts steadily towards the end of the poem until it can scarcely be confined within a definition at all, but has become a sort of signal for outbursts of emotion both poetic and religious, the last and most intense of which is the Dreamer's turning at the close of the poem from the disappointment of actuality to the source of his only hope.

The symbol of Piers then represents a succession of stages in the attitude of the poet to his subject, the focal point of an increasing emotional and religious attachment, and an important clue to the meaning of the poem. In a similar way the study of the growth of this symbol affords an insight into the much-discussed plan of the poem. The symbol of Piers was developed in part by imaginative association, in part by the exercise of the poet's invention, and in part by becoming a kind of point where the emotional and moral impulses found common ground, where the former was satisfied and the latter could find no fault. The intensification of all three kinds of growth was complementary : as the author came steadily nearer to the unhappy conviction which ends his poem, so his emotion fixed itself the more firmly upon this symbol and his moralism became increasingly overwhelmed by the sense of contrast between actuality as he saw it and the ideal state that in his fantasy he associated with Piers.

The plan of *Piers Plowman* is to be explained in terms of a similar set of imaginative associations, the direction and expression of which were determined by the emotional and moral impulses in the poet's religion. It seems improbable that any careful, detailed planning, any meticulously prepared and executed design played any part in the creation of this poem. It is much more likely that the nature of its genesis and its composition both were, like the character of its author, impulsive and even violent, governed more by imagination than by intellect. His impulsiveness, his readiness to digress for certain purposes, especially satirical, to follow up chance associations, or to stay with an absorbing topic a disproportionately long time are the best explanation of the absence from the poem of any external signs of a structure planned in detail. Instead of a well-ordered and beautifully proportioned whole the reader of *Piers Plowman* has to deal with a wild and luxuriant work which apparently outgrew and overgrew its original general plan, upon which the poet doubtless first embarked without knowing quite how it would end, which proceeds at a pace that varies continually as his indignation or his imagination respectively passes from the grip of one rage or enthusiasm to another, which follows no apparent direct line of progress, not all parts of which are developed in strict relation to their importance, and which will inevitably be unduly long.[1]

It should then be easy to understand why the plan of *Piers Plowman* is not readily intelligible to the modern reader. The actual material content of the poem is so peculiarly arranged that the mere task of familiarizing oneself with it is formidable, and yet a pattern and a plan are to be detected in the poem only after its imagery and symbolism become so familiar by constant association that they begin to fit into a relation from which a kind of order emerges. In this plan the most important motive is the search undertaken by the

---

[1] This is a purely literary judgement. Doubtless from a moral or didactic point of view many of these departures from conventional planning can be justified.

Dreamer,[1] which describes the poet's own attitude to his work and its arrangement, and illustrates his imaginative conception of it. Indeed the figure of a search affords an excellent analogy for the progress of the poem ; the false starts and changes of direction, frequent pauses, anxieties, hesitations and impatience which characterize it are thus excellently illustrated. Upon this literally tentative and enquiring process a certain logic is, however, forced by the nature of the object of the search. As this object is salvation, the search very naturally begins with a rejection of the vicious imperfections of ordinary living and develops through the stages of good counsel laid down by the Church to a last ideal which seems to the poet so high that he as much as acknowledges the impossibility of attaining it, and thus brings his search to an end.

Within this logic of the subject it is possible to observe the structure of *Piers Plowman*. It begins in the world, the earthly commonwealth, England, if one prefers. ' This is how things are ', the poet says, and shows us financial corruption destroying honest living throughout the realm. ' And this is how they ought to be ', he suggests, when Lady Meed, the source of this corruption, is arraigned in the King's Court and brought to order, and Conscience and Reason undertake to rule with the king.

The next stage in the poem is directed by the question, ' How are we to attain to this ideal state of affairs ? ' Reason, preaching a mission before the king and the commons, enjoins the keeping of the commandments, but once the Deadly Sins have confessed and Piers has come into the poem the more specific question, ' What must I do to be saved ? ' is raised. The first half of the answer to this question is Piers's direction of the way to St. Truth, the decalogue ; thereafter the poem proceeds inexorably to the second half of the reply : Christ's answer to the rich young man who asked this same question. There is a higher kind of life than simple righteousness. The remainder of the poem is to be a study of this higher kind of life ; the moment of division is Piers's renunciation of the world (B VII ll. 117). From this

[1] See, e.g. B II ll. 1–4 ; VII ll. 139–46 ; VIII ll. 1–2 ; XVI ll. 167–71 ; XVIII ll. 1–5 ; XX ll. 1–2.

point forward the external plan of the poem practically ceases to be discernible, and survives principally in the logic of the subject. In his pursuit of the Three Lives the poet establishes his motives with only the briefest intervals between them, when it might seem that the studies of Do Well, Do Better and Do Best ought to have been kept separate. It is not his carelessness, but his subject, the difficulty of which he appreciates,[1] that obliges him to adopt this complicated and unsatisfactory arrangement, for neither the second nor the third of the Three Lives can be defined without understanding the first, and the relative value of the first can be appreciated only by comparison with the other two. So then goes the plan of the poem. The treatment of the first and simplest counsel of virtue is quickly supplemented by that of the second and higher ; thenceforward the two are progressively studied side by side, and as the understanding of one increases, so does that of the other.

The Dreamer, whose experiences of these truths constitute the thread of the narrative, does not himself move easily to an understanding of the higher spirituality. Before long a third quest, that for the highest expression of spiritual perfection, is added to his task. This highest kind of spiritual life, again always taken together with the two preceding, is first defined, then adumbrated in the definition of the Trinity, described in the allegory of faith, hope and charity where charity is shown to follow after faith and hope as Do Best follows after Do Well and Do Better although it surpasses them, and finally symbolized in the account of Christ's life on earth, the Redemption and the Resurrection. One stage in the logic of the subject ends now ; the central questions of the poem have been answered ; charity, to which attention has been gradually shifting from the Three Lives, is exemplified in the activity of Christ upon earth, Do Best is shown to be the perfection of charity, the symbol of Piers attains its highest meaning as the indwelling of Christ in his Church, and the re-establishment of righteousness in that Church is allegorized

[1] ' Dowel and dobet aren two infinites,
Whiche infinites, with a feith fynden oute dobest,
Which shal saue mannes soule: þus seith piers þe ploughman.'
'I can nouȝt her-on ' quod conscience—   (B XIII ll. 127–30)

in the building of Unity Holychurch, the stronghold of virtue upon earth.

Exposed in this way, with all digressions rigidly excluded, and with its serious faults of disproportion concealed in the uniform brevity of a synopsis, the plan of *Piers Plowman* appears not too ill-constructed. Doubtless as the basis of a conception of the work this plan was adequate ; in its execution, however, the main body of the poem suffers from the manner in which the author will not discipline himself to stick to the logic of the subject, but neglects it for frequent and sometimes artistically unpardonable digressions, or distorts it by undue amplification, and from his omitting to show clearly, for the assistance of his readers, the stages in the development of his thought. Only at the conclusion of the poem does evidence of structural planning on his part once more become apparent ; the end of *Piers Plowman*, which consists of the attack on Unity Holychurch, designedly corresponds to the beginning.

The poem opened with a picture of the earthly commonwealth portrayed as it is and as it should be ; it ends with an allegory of the spiritual commonwealth as it should be and as it is. The poem finishes where it started, for it begins and ends in actuality. The detailed execution of this design appears in the re-emergence, in the last section of the poem, of many of the elements of the introduction, most of all that one which in the first and last instance comes nearest to undoing both church and state, Coueytise, the vice of cupidity. In the introduction this vice is figured in the lovely splendour of Lady Meed and in her power over men ; in the conclusion cupidity is still the villain, this time in the undisguised ugliness of his own person. At the end, too, h:s ravages are infinitely more damaging than they were at the beginning. However bravely the beleaguered forces of righteousness may rally, and however stoutly they may defend themselves, the attacks are unceasing. Cupidity corrupts the clergy until they sell absolution for silver : this wounds Contrition, and once he is out of the fight Holychurch falls.

There is, then, a pattern and a plan to be found in *Piers Plowman*, which will approximate to the one I have just sketched. It is, however, overlaid with detail to such an extent as to be seldom apparent, often obscured by digressions long or short, never developed for its own sake, and in fact surviving only because it is a necessary relation between the author's intention and his material. The complication of the situation is then apparent. The author's enthusiasms and excitements, his readiness to follow up chance associations, his impulsive and sometimes disproportionately long treatments of particular subjects, fail to destroy the plan of his poem only because that plan is laid down by the Christianity in terms of which the poet was making his search for salvation, and because the very fiction of the search which he adopted, although itself it implied a good part of the apparent indecision and inconclusiveness of treatment, meanwhile determined to a large extent the form of the detailed execution.

Pointing out these shortcomings is intended neither to condone them nor to condemn the poem for them, but to remove certain misunderstandings. At either extreme they are equally dangerous ; to describe *Piers Plowman* as planless is to ascribe an unlikely stupidity to a man otherwise highly intelligent ; to argue that it is well or carefully planned is to fly in the face of the poem itself. The fact is that the one quality not to be found in *Piers Plowman* is system in the modern sense of the word. This circumstance is best explained in terms of its author, whose thinking was of an exploratory rather than a theoretical character, and moved ruminatively from one problem to another, applying in every case, as his memory and his reflective powers suggested to him, the authorities of dogma with which he was familiar, and his own faculty of reasoning, pressed by his religion into the service of that dogma. The apparently capricious arrangement of much of the content of the poem is not then to be ascribed to a lack of perception in the author, but to his failure to discipline both his mind and his material.

Apparent planlessness and all, *Piers Plowman* cannot be explained without reference to these terms : the man's character, talents and experience, his particular poetic medium, and his religious theme. Nothing else but an understanding of the relations of these components to one another will account for its paradoxes, for the greatness of the poem and its apparently imperfect conception, for its sublimities and its utterly pedestrian portions, its splendidly memorable lines and passages, where thought and poetry seem perfectly matched, and the shapeless incomprehensibility of some of its explanations, the rough violence of one moment and the deep tenderness of another, the rare poetry of this passage and the boorish puritanism of that.

Moreover, such a study will afford a just appreciation of the greatness of both the poem and its author. For the man it will show that he had the quality that often goes with faults of carelessness and over-impulsiveness, namely, a generous, unselfconscious temperament ; that he was made artistically great by a poetic vision of unusual power which he took entirely for granted, with no self-important pother about the magnitude of his themes or the sanctity of his own dedication ; that strength and kindliness tempered one another in his character ; that he was utterly serious about his high purpose and could yet see the ludicrous in himself ; and that he accepted the failure which almost of necessity was his lot in life without sacrificing to it the loftiness of his principles. For the poem it will emerge that this belongs among the greatest examples of mediæval literature. Compared with Chaucer's work it will appear inferior in art but superior in high serious-ness and in its sublimity ; compared with the *Divine Comedy*, inferior in magnitude, in sustained quality, in imagination and in the taking of pains, but superior in its human kindliness and in its sympathy with mankind.

INDEX

Alliterative Alexander Fragments, 9, 57, 59–60
Alliterative long line, 9, 187–8
  effect on treatment of subject, 52–3, 57–8, 59, 188–9, 191
Alliterative Morte Arthur, 66, 69–73, 74
Altus Prosator, 180
Amadas, 19
Amis and Amiloun, 15, 28, 30
Arthur, 20
Aspice Mitissime Conditor, 147
Athelston, 10, 54
Aucassin et Nicolette, 47
Audelay, John, 169–70
Augustine, *Confessions*, 114
Aureate style, 17, 128–9, 150–2
Aurora lucis rutilat, 155
Awntyrs of Arthure at the Terne Watheleyne, 52–3

Bargain of Judas, 142
Beues of Hamptoun, 10, 27, 46, 50–1, 58
Bless the Time the Apple Was Taken, 138–9, 141
Blessed Virgin to her Son on the Cross, 148
Blessed Virgin's Appeal to the Jews, 148–9
Bodel, Jean, 7
Bowght and sold full traytorsly, 172

Candet Nudatum Pectus, 144, 145–6, 147
Candide, 50, 77
Canterbury Tales, 24, 25, 55
Canticles, 140
Carols, xi, 132, 136, 166–76
  absence of subjectivity, 168
  communal quality determining effect, 168
  compensation for their short-comings, 167
  complicated structure, 173
  criticized as poetry, 166–7
  exceptional instances, 168 ff.
  indispensability of music, 167–8
  intentions of the authors, 170–1
  literary quality, 176
  personal emotion conveyed, 171–2
  symbolism, 169–70, 174–5
Chansons de geste, 16, 40

Chaucer, Geoffrey, 8, 20, 22, 24, 25, 27, 54, 55, 56, 57, 62–5, 84, 85, 86, 87, 88, 96, 193–4, 235, 236, 248
Cheuelere Assigne, 9, 20
Chevy Chase, 90
Chrétien de Troyes, 7, 79
Christ pleads with His Sweet Lemman, 156
Christ Triumphant, 149
Christ's ' Love-Aunter ', 154
Christ's Love-Song to Man, 154
Christ's Prayer in Gethsemane, 149
Christ's Three Songs to Man, 146
Clerk's Tale, 57, 62, 63–5
Close in My Breast Thy Perfect Love, 127–8
Corpus Christi Carol, 169, 174–5, 178, 180
Courtly love, 40, 84, 88, 89
  author of *Partonope* and, 38–9
Crux fidelis, 155, 180

Daphnis and Chloe, 77
Devotional and meditative lyrics, 129–65
  kinds of, 130–1
  literary embellishment, 151–3
  solicitation of reader's emotion, 143
  sources of effects, 149–51
Devotional lyrics, 125–9
  attitude of authors to subject, 125–6
  kinds of, 125
Dialogue between Jesus and the Blessed Virgin at the Cross, 148
Dialogue between Our Lady and Jesus on the Cross, 148
Didactic poetry, 19–20, 124
Dies Iræ, 121, 180
Divine Paradox, 153
Dolours of Our Lady, 134

Ecce sto ad hostium et pulso, 155
Ecclesiastes, 118
Eger and Grime, 31–2
Emare, 10, 20, 22, 62
English Charlemagne romances, 15–16, 27, 28, 40–1
Erle of Tolous, 31, 35
Erthe upon Erthe, 122–3
Exemplum, 22, 61

Fabliaux, 61
Filius Regis Mortuus Est, 152
Floris and Blauncheflur, 8, 46, 47–8
For Thy Sake Let the World Call Me
　Fool, 141
Franklin's Tale, 66, 84–7

Gamelyn, 46, 48
Generydes, 31, 33–4
Gest Hystoriale of the Destruction of
　Troy, 10, 11, 27, 45, 56, 58
Giraldus Cambrensis, 81
Golagros and Gawane, 10, 31, 33
Grene Knight, 15
Guy of Warwick, 7, 10, 39, 40, 41–2,
　43, 89

Havelok, 27, 46, 49–50
Holy Grail, 16–17
Homo Vide quid pro Te Patior, 146–7.
Hopkins, Gerald Manley, 119
Horn Childe and Maiden Rimnild,
　15
Hours of the Cross, 133
How Christ shall Come, 157

I Have Set My Heart so High, 138–40,
　141
I Sing of One That is Matchless, 161–2
I Would Be Clad in Christis Skin,
　138–9, 141
Iam dulcis amica venito, 159
Improperia, 146
In a tabernacle of a toure, 158
In a valey of this restles minde, 158–60

Jaques de Cambrai, 163
Jeaste of Syr Gawayne, 10, 52, 53–4
Joseph of Arimathie, 26–7
Journey of the Three Kings, 142

King Horn, 15, 46, 48–9, 50
King of Tars, 19
Knight of Courtesy and the Fair Lady
　of Faguell, 20, 22–3
Knight's Tale, 34, 66, 87–9
Kyng Alisaunder, 42, 44–6
　gnomic and bucolic verses in, 45–6

Lai la Freine, 46, 47
Lamentacio Dolorosa, 148
Lamentations, Book of, 147
Lancelot of the Laik, 17, 18
Laud Troy Book, 8, 10, 26, 27
Le Bone Florence of Rome, 31, 35–6
Liber Meditationum, 145
Life of Ipomydon, 28–9
Litany, 157–8
Lollai litel child whi wepistow so sore,
　118, 119–20

Look on Me with Thy Sweet Eyes, 126,
　127
Look to Me on the Cross, 144, 145
Louelich, Henry, 10, 16–17, 20
Love Ron, 116–17
Lovely Tear from Lovely Eye, 136–7
Lullay poems, 119–20, 142–3, 152,
　175
Lybeaus Disconus, 13, 14–15
' Lyric ', various meanings of, 106–7

Maiden Makeles, 161–5, 180
Malory's Morte Arthur, 17, 67–8
Man of Law's Tale, 10, 20, 57, 62–3
Marye, mayde mylde and fre, 157–8
Matins of the Cross, 133, 134
Meditation, 129–30, 133, 134, 135,
　138
Merlin, 16–17
Mind of the Passion, 138–9, 141
Mirror for Young Ladies at Their
　Toilet, 124
Moralizing lyrics, 109–24
　attitude of authors to audience,
　114
　concessions to frivolous taste, 113
　effect, 109–10
　force derived from argument, 111
　imaginative transformation of
　moral lesson, 114, 117–20
' Mortality ' poems, 120–4

O Felix Culpa, 139
O vos omnes qui transitis per viam, 147
Octauian (Cambridge version), 29
Octauian (Cotton version), 28, 29–30,
　62
Octosyllabic couplet, 8–9, 44, 67
On God Vreisun of Vre Lefdi, 134–5,
　178

Partonope of Blois, 8, 10, 36–40, 80
Parzifal, 17, 77
Percy Folio Merlin, 20
Piers Plowman, 139, 182–248
　allegory, 238–9
　alliterative measure, 188–90
　aphorisms, 190–1, 230–1
　artistic impulse of author, 207–8
　conflicting tendencies in author,
　208–9
　cumulative effect of poem, 234
　definitions of Do Well, Do Better
　and Do Best, 240–1, 245
　digressions, 234, 243, 246, 247
　effect of author's moral impulse on
　poem, 229–33
　effect of author's religion on poem,
　199, 221–6
　fluency of author, 235–6, 238

Piers Plowman (continued)—
forces in author's temperament, 209 ff. ; as sources of artistic energy, 215 ff. ; in combination, 217–20 ; independent, 220–33
forms of author's religious impulse, 209–10
grotesque effects, 203, 231–2
indirect rebuke of abuses, 232
intellectual curiosity of author, 201–2, 211–12, 234
ironic metaphors, 205–6, 236–8
irony of author, 203–6
macaronic verses, 204, 215–16, 218
place in alliterative tradition, 188–90
plan, 243–7
poetic technique of author, 234–8
poetry of the intellect, 226–9
relation of author's personality to his poetry revealed, 191 ff.
relationship of the three versions, 185–7
religion of author, 197–8
religion unifying the poem, 198–9
response to gentle and merciful side of Christianity, 220–1
satirical elements, 183, 213–14, 234
state of preservation of poem, 187–8
sternness of author, 193–6, 197, 233
symbol of Christ the Knight, 223
symbolism, 238–43
tenderness of author, 196–7
variety of interpretations, 183–5
visual quality of writing, 236
Piers Plowman, meaning of the symbol, 220–1, 241–4
Poetic diction, differences between mediæval and subsequent, 105
Prayer by the Wounds against the Deadly Sins, 133
Prayer, four verse styles of, 126–9
Prayer of the Five Wounds, 126
Proprietates Mortis, 121

Quia amore langueo poems, 158–60
Quis est iste qui venit de Edom, 156–7

Religious lyrics, 104–81
anonymity of affecting our criticism, 105–6
attitudes of poets to material, 107–8, 111, 113, 116, 176–7
compared with Latin, 178–80
effect of subject, 108–9 ; restrictive, 178–80
limited development during Middle English period, 177–8
moral and devotional functions, 109

Religious lyrics (continued)—
obstacles to modern appreciation, 104–9
perfunctory poetic adornment, 112, 113, 116, 125–6, 128, 151–2
sameness of themes and effects, 177
validity of religious subject, 107–9
Rhyme royal stanza, 33
Richard Cœur de Lion, 42–4, 45
Roberd of Cysylle, 19
Roland and Otuel, 15
Rolle, Richard, 127, 132, 146
Romance of Partenay, 17–18
Romances, 1–103
accidental qualities, 2–3, 5, 6, 102
attraction of subject for author communicated, 26, 46–52, 58
common definable nature, 1–3
definitions modified, 101–2
didacticism in, 19–20
dilemma in, 33, 85–6
disappearance of the *genre*, 3, 100
escape from actuality afforded, 2, 99, 102
essential purpose of entertainment, 3, 9, 102
essential qualities, 2, 101–2
' excellences proper to the kind ', 6, 99, 100–2
' glamour ' not essential, 101
heroic, 35–6, 41, 71–3
ideal of chivalry the basis, 2, 29, 80, 89, 90, 99
idealization of life, 47, 48, 49, 76, 99
importance of author's intention, 84
our common humanity with, 103
physical improbability in, 51
pietistic, 19–20, 22, 62–3
place in development of European narrative fiction, 99–100
poetic elaboration in, 94, 95, 96–9
range of quality, 12, 26
' real life ' materials, 91–3, 94
sense of contact with ' other world ' conveyed, 81–4
success, conditions necessary to, 6, 65, 100–3
symbolism in, 79–80
triumph of evil as a subject, 61
types of failure, 12–13, 15, 16, 17, 18–19, 24
verisimilitude, 8, 74–5, 94, 102
virtuosity, 52–65
' willing suspension of disbelief ', 24, 85, 100–1, 102
Roman de Thèbes, 29
Ruth, Book of, 140
Ryman, James, 105

Sege of Melayne, 15, 16
Sege or Batayle of Troye, 20, 21–2, 27
Seven Sages of Rome, 57, 60–1
Siege of Jerusalem, 9, 10, 45, 56, 59
Sir Degare, 14
Sir Degrevant, 10, 66, 89, 90–4
Sir Eglamour of Artois, 13, 14, 22, 54
Sir Ferumbras (Bodley version), 15
Sir Firumbras (Fillingham version), 28, 39, 40–1, 42
Sir Gawain and the Green Knight, 9, 45, 52, 66, 70, 71, 73–6, 189, 190
Sir Gowther, 31, 32
Sir Isumbras, 13, 15
Sir Launfal, 31, 33, 34–5
Sir Orfeo, 66, 80–4
Sir Perceval, 14, 66, 76–8, 84
Sir Thopas, 4, 12, 13, 54–6
  Chaucer's purpose in writing, 56
Sir Tristrem, 15, 20, 23–4
Song of Sorrow for the Passion, 137–8
Song of the Five Joys, 134
Sowdone of Babylone, 27, 28
Spring under a Thorn, 160–1, 175, 178
Squire of Low Degree, 66, 89, 90, 96–9
Squire's Tale, 55
Stanzaic Morte Arthur, 65–9
Sunset on Calvary, 140, 178
Syre Gawene and the Carle of Carelyle, 10, 52, 53

Tail rhyme stanza, 8, 15, 67, 77

Taste, extremes of in Middle English period, 3–6
That Lord that lay in asse stalle, 169
þene latemeste dai, 121
Think, Man of my Hard Stundes, 144
Thomas de Hales, 116
Thomas of Erceldoune, 15
Three Matters, 7
Thy Blood Thou Shed for Me, 134
Titus Andronicus, 54
Titus and Vespasian, 10, 19
Torrent of Portyngale, 13, 14, 54
Troilus and Criseyde, 34
Troy, mediæval response to story of, 20–1, 27, 44, 58

Vbi Scount Qui Ante Nos Fuerount, 115–16
'Vernon Series', 111–14, 152
Vexilla Regis, 180

Wace, 81
Weddynge of Sir Gawen and Dame Ragnel, 27–8
Whan that my swete Son was thirti wynter old, 172–3
What More Could Christ Have Done, 132–3
Wife of Bath's Tale, 24–5, 27–8, 81
William of Palerne, 8, 9, 46, 51–2
Winter Song, 118, 119
With fauoure in hir face ferr passyng my reason, 173

Ywain and Gawain, 66, 78–80